The
SECRET
Behind
SECRET
SOCIETIES

Jon Rappoport

TS **TRUTH SEEKER**
BOOKS   SAN DIEGO, CALIFORNIA

Photoshop cover painting composed by Patrick Deluz
from an idea suggested by Jon Rappoport.

Backcover photo of Jon Rappoport by Erica McGrath.

Page design by David Sielaff.

Printed in the United States of America

ISBN: 0-939040-08-5

Published by
Truth Seeker Co., Inc.
P. O. Box 28550
San Diego, California 92198

Special Issue — Limited Edition — 1998
Second Printing — Limited Edition — 2003

Website: http://truthseeker.com

The SECRET Behind SECRET SOCIETIES

Liberation of the Planet in the 21st Century

Jon Rappoport

Other books by Jon Rappoport

Ownership of All Life
Notes on Scandals,
Conspiracies and Coverups

Madalyn Murray O'Hair
"Most Hated Woman in America"

Oklahoma City Bombing
The Suppressed Truth

AIDS INC.
Scandal of the Century

(with David Icke)
Lifting the Veil:
David Icke Interviewed by Jon Rappoport

to my wife, Laura,
Bonnie Lange,
and Richard Jenkins

Introduction

The way of the secret society is a way of life. At its root, it is not grinning skulls and sputtering candles in dark rooms. It is not that provincial.

The secret society reflects one invisible tradition that has existed on Earth for a hundred thousand years. It is the main Way that people have lived on this planet.

There is another way, another tradition, more invisible, more powerful.

This book is about these two avenues.

It is amazing, at this late date, that so many people think power is merely a cake of clay that six billion of us are beating at with hammers. It is astonishing that so many people think power is a mound of lumps and dust that six billion of us are fighting over.

Power has been taken by very well-run organizations. Major power.

On the other side of the coin, there is a growing crowd that thinks we must invoke fire-eating lizards or Satan to explain how power has been stolen from us.

This is a book about the organizations that have carted off something very vital in the middle of the night — and how to get it back. More than that, it is about the exact methods used to unhook us from all that we are.

I have done enough excavation to expose the central ruse, to show two invisible traditions of history.

I have gotten into the shiny stainless steel vault in the big bank, looked around, and pointed out the obvious. And then after that I have refused to budge.

I believe we are grappling, as if in a dream, with the layers of anesthetic that surround the core of our being.

1

This book is a search for ... what? A platform from which to view the place in ourselves which could revolutionize the future.

This search is not new, and we have all been over significant ground before. But we turn away, we demean ourselves, we fabricate existence and lessen its meaning. We pay allegiance to myths and gods, we accept a shrunken view of history.

But in history are veins of master substance, as it were, that can lead us back to ourselves in a new way.

The style of this book is not to set out, like file cabinets, a precise robot-march of facts which ultimately spell out a hypothesis. I rather take you along on my own adventure of discovery, because I want you to see and feel something, not merely make notes in the machine-part of the mind.

These days, the terms cult, secret society, and religion are all so loaded that their meanings are melting down.

I use cult and secret society to mean: organized groups which harbor a hidden agenda whose purpose is to dominate and control others.

This agenda doesn't rule out the existence of a merry public face. In fact, a cult may be doing good in one sphere while destroying life and limb on another front.

In this book, religion means a group which has a hierarchical power structure leading up to an invisible God. Naturally the God favors the religion which worships Him. Otherwise, why bother?

Most religions are secret societies. They have an agenda which involves controlling their devotees, all their charity-work notwithstanding.

Historically, people seek out secret societies and religions and join them to gain freedom from pain and turmoil. People also join because they are forced to. For example, the country they live in leaves no choice. Such was the case in medieval Europe, where the Roman Catholic Church held the wand of dominance.

But there is another factor. The popular term for it these days is mind control. It used to be brainwashing, hypnotism. I will discuss that aspect at length, in an unusual way.

When I use only the first name of a person, that name is fictitious. The reason is the same in all such cases: to ensure privacy. This book can offer much evidence to support its conclusions, but it cannot rest on absolute proof. Because of the nature of the subject, I have had to rely, in certain crucial situations, on the testimony of anonymous sources.

I have also, as I say, chosen to rely on my personal experience, because the story that will now unfold is empty without it.

What city is this
Whose moments tremble
Azure sky and lime lights
Walking in the intersections
Through the squares of paradise

PART ONE

1

This is a book about missing history.

I am taking core samples, drilling down into the strata of invisible events and lives and persons that have been ignored.

The first core may seem a bit fantastic. But I am clearing out a great deal of refuse, pushing off to the side some of the delirium that has been clouding our curiosity.

Curiosity about what?

About another kind of life that is closer to our desires.

2

June, 1960. The day after I graduated from Amherst College, I packed my bags, left them in the hall closet of my small empty dormitory and walked through the town.

I had lunch in the local diner and then dropped by several off-campus houses to say good-bye to friends. Late in the afternoon, I strolled to the top of the hill that looks out over the College field house and the baseball diamond. I sat down and thought about the rather amazing fact that I had just finished four years of studying philosophy. A strange trip, indeed. Most modern practitioners of this art favored a form of analysis devoted to burying, and spreading lime on, their famous predecessors, the Kants and Spinozas and Aristotles. They were killing their ancestors. An interesting ritual, except that it left the ground with nothing but old blood.

The subject of Western philosophy had really hit its Waterloo just before the turn of the century, but few people were willing to admit it. Science was then taking over as the muscle man, and its message seemed to be: Everything, including humans, consists only of atoms in motion. What may appear to be free will, love, power, joy, wonder, consciousness and the like are delusionary products of the movements of atoms in the brain and the nervous system.

Back in my room I found a few stray things on the shelf of my closet. There was a paper bag containing a small box of pastels and a pad of sketch paper. A friend of mine from Mt. Holyoke College had left them there months ago.

Without any thought, on a pure whim, I took the pastels and a sheet of paper to my desk and sat down. I began to draw a full yellow moon and clouds, which, over the next hour, turned into something more interesting. It was the first time I could remember drawing since elementary school art class.

I continued to work for several hours. Finally, I stopped and took the sheet of paper off the desk and put it on the wood floor. I stood over it and looked down. Among the gray, yellow, and white masses, I saw a threading silvery form. What was it? I kept staring at it. It reminded me of the turn of a naked shoulder, or a narrow birch tree, but really it was a suggestion of crackling energy. I was astonished that I had somehow put it there.

The last thing I learned, or thought, at College was that energy was a presence, no matter how brief, that could come out of nowhere.

A silver line on a piece of paper suddenly meant far more to me than four years at Amherst.

Why? Because it was my line.

3

In 1961 I was twenty-three and living in New York. Fresh from college, I was writing jazz reviews for *Metronome,* a well-known magazine which was on its last legs.

On a spring afternoon, I quit (for the second time) my job at a bookstore in Greenwich Village, and walked from Sullivan Street to the Third Avenue branch to tell the owner.

He had left to go to lunch, so i hung around the shop and put new deliveries on the shelves. A thin man in a loose-fitting blue suit walked up to me and asked if we carried Trevor-Roper's World War II book on Hitler. I told him we didn't. I knew that because the big distributor who handled those books had just cut us off from all deliveries for non-payment of bills. The shelves throughout the store were thinning out.

"Well," the man said, "something on healing then."

"We don't have a category for that," I said. "Unless you're interested in Wilhelm Reich."

"I have those," he said.

"They just came out. Grove Press."

"Yes," he said. "Your government finally lifted the ban. But I've got them in German and French."

"Where are you from?"

"I have dual citizenship. British and Indian."

"I don't see Indian."

"My mother was. Stepmother. You know much about Reich?" he asked.

"I'm reading the books."

His face had a very steady look. "Reich was on the inside trying to look out," he said. "He found out a lot, for some-one in his position."

"That's ridiculous," I said. "A student of Freud, who

9

breaks away from the teacher, and then is arrested by the U.S. government and dies in jail? He's an insider?"

"I know," he said. "Inside's a relative term. But compared to Reich, the healing I'm talking about is on Mars. These people don't write books."

"Then why did you ask for them?"

He shrugged. "You never know. What do you do?"

"I'm quitting my job in a few minutes."

"Good. Then you can have lunch with me. I'm between clients."

"What kind of clients?"

"Sick people."

"Doing all right in New York," I said.

The owner of the bookstore was known for long 70-proof lunches, so I didn't wait for him. I left a note saying I was quitting, and the man, whose name was Richard Jenkins, and I walked over to the Cedar Bar on University.

That's how the whole thing started.

4

Jenkins and I saw each other several times the next week. He told me his wife Rachel was living in Algiers at the moment, but she would be coming over soon. He was looking for an apartment on the upper West Side the two of them could settle into.

He alluded to some problems his mother was having "with the authorities" in Bombay, but he didn't spell the situation out.

He was thin and he was losing his light brown hair. He reminded me of a British runner, one of those men who simultaneously appears a bit anemic and very fit. I put his age at 30.

Jenkins said he had lived most of his life in London and Algiers. After several years in New York, he was ready to call it home.

He knew about Wilhelm Reich's maverick theories. The orgone, which Reich coined as the term to describe the basic particle of all energy, Jenkins said was "just one sample of a family of energies" which applied to humans and the electromagnetic fields that permeated their bodies. Jenkins claimed to have replicated a few of Reich's esoteric experiments. "They didn't turn out right for me every time," he said, "but I worked out one good variation. A very small quantity of metal and wood would, under exposure to orgones, yield a little more wood and a little less metal. Transmutation."

"What kind of exposure?" I asked.

"An orgone accumulator. Do you know what that is?"

"No."

"It's a space — a room, a closet, a cylinder, a tube — made of alternating layers of organic and inorganic material. It draws in energy."

11

I was skeptical.

After a week of conversations at the Cedar Bar and in Washington Square Park, Jenkins came over to my place on 71st Street. He examined my shelves of jazz records. "My cousin Harriet Katcher is a friend of Bill Coss," he said.

"Bill Coss publishes *Metronome*. I write reviews for them."

He smiled a little. "Auspicious events at hand ... that's what my mother's spiritualist friends used to tell me every time a coincidence of any kind popped up."

We listened to records by a piano player we both admired, Herbie Nichols, then Jenkins stood up and said, "All right, let's go over to my studio. There are a few things I want to show you."

Jenkins lived on the second floor of a building on Lexington Avenue in the 30s. The apartment was a large one-room studio with high ceilings and two big windows. The couch was a disguised bed, and a kitchenette hid behind a screen covered with a reproduction of a Tang Dynasty painting of female dancers in a faded emerald-green atmosphere.

On one wall, from floor to ceiling, were shelves holding clear bottles of herbs.

"These are for your clients?"

"Yes. Actually, not all of them are ill. In fact, many of them are quite healthy. They're trying to up the limit."

"Up it to what?"

"Beyond what people accept as normal life."

He poured us glasses of beer, we sat down near his small desk in metal chairs and he spoke about his healing practice.

"None of these herbs are given for curing disease," he said. "At least not by me. I use them only to change energy. When you do that, you're into another domain."

"What kind of energy?"

"One that integrates inside the body, that ties together physical apparatuses."

"I don't know what you're talking about."

"Look at it this way. I can fill you full of coffee and you have more energy. But there's a limit on it. It's useful for awhile, but then you develop an uncomfortable edge ... or if not, you start building up side effects you aren't aware of. Your digestion is off, your acid-alkaline balance goes to hell. On the other hand, I can figure out a way to impart energy to you that normalizes blood pressure while it also makes your thought processes slicker and easier — and there's no drawback. If I can help you to relax, and you also feel more alert and energetic at the same time, now we're talking. And this is elementary. There are subtleties about human energy that have no language. They're real. You can feel them, but we have no way to explain it in plain English."

A little while later, a middle-aged woman in a print dress walked into the studio. Richard introduced her as Grace, and he pulled out a massage table from a closet and set it up next to the couch.

"I told Grace you might be here," Jenkins said. "She said it'd be all right if you watch. But you have to be quiet."

Grace grinned and climbed up on the table and lay down on her back. She closed her eyes, and Richard placed both hands on her stomach.

He left his hands there for the next five minutes.

Then he moved his hands to the back of her neck. He didn't rub her neck, he just placed his hands there. He stayed with that for about half an hour. It seemed to me that Grace was now asleep but I wasn't sure.

Finally, Richard put one hand on Grace's knee for a few minutes. Then he walked behind the screen and washed his hands in the sink. During the whole session Richard had said nothing, and Grace hadn't spoken either. (In the totality of the future sessions I would watch Richard give, he would speak no more than once or twice.)

Grace opened her eyes and looked at me.

"I travel," she said. "Different things happen to people. I go places."

"Is it like dreaming?" I said.

"Yes. It seems more real."

Richard walked back into the room. "Grace is quite conscious the whole time. Some people fall asleep or get groggy for awhile."

Grace sat up. "I saw a train station," she said. "There was a furniture store too. A man came up to me and asked for money. He was wearing an expensive suit. I started smelling coffee. Very good rich coffee. But I couldn't see where it was coming from."

After Grace left, Richard told me she was "moving into taste and smell" in her sessions with him. Those senses had been in a vapid state, after an illness and a three-year marriage gone bad, and now they were coming alive. Not just in the sessions, but on a daily basis.

I listened to Richard talk about Grace and other clients, and of course I was puzzled. He was just placing his hands on them.

Richard said, "Where do you think this technique comes from, what I was doing with her?"

"The laying on of hands," I said. "Everybody knows. It's in the Bible, isn't it? Christ curing the crippled, raising the dead. Priests do it in last rites, don't they?"

Richard laughed. "I see," he said. "An allusion in the Bible ... and then nothing until today. Maybe not even one true mention in the Bible, if you could read the original text. Is that it? That's a tradition? Where are the books? Where is the teaching literature? Where's the whole history of it? Who were the thousand teachers? Where's the lineage, the ancestry?"

"How should I know?"

"Exactly!" he said. "You wouldn't know because there is none. I dare you to find it. Go look!"

"So?" I said.

He didn't answer. But I felt a little uncomfortable. What he was pointing out was odd. Something everybody has heard of, everybody knows about — but where is the history?

I spent the next couple of days at the library. As far as the laying on of hands was concerned — its teaching, its transmission — the stacks were mute.

5

For the next month, I watched Jenkins work on his clients. Why? Because he let me and because it was fascinating.

Old people, children, sick people, people who looked in the pink of health came into his studio. All he did was have them lie down on his massage table. Then he placed his hands on them.

In almost every case, people got up from the table feeling very refreshed. Jenkins gave some people envelopes of dried herbs for tea.

"I'm moving energy," he said. "It's not unheard of. I'm taking their old encrusted energy and moving it off, into the air. It breaks up like a little storm and becomes alive again, disperses. That's chapter one. But there's a lot more going on. You've heard of the chakras, the Asian tradition of seven or eight or nine or twelve energy centers?"

"Vaguely."

"They're like train stations. Certain kinds of energy come in and go out. It's a system, a way to think about things. Sexual energy comes in through one chakra, mental energy through another, love or heart energy has a third train station. But the truth is, there are thousands of energy centers in the body. All over the place. They're not the same from person to person."

"What kind of energy are we talking about?"

"Yes," he said. "That's what people want to know, particularly when they're used to a medical view of things. The accepted idea is, you get energy by burning fuel in the cells and that's it. Everything else is a fairy tale. But it isn't a fairy tale."

Jenkins' next client was Carl, a college student from NYU. This was the boy's second session. He couldn't lie down. He

15

said he was too paranoid to close his eyes. He had been under the care of a psychiatrist for six months, and during that time his condition had deteriorated badly. From worry about grades and alienation from his family, things had moved to depression, paranoia, and recurrent high-tension jitters. Carl had been given several powerful psychiatric drugs for three months, and then, in terror, he had cut himself off from the chemicals. He was sure they were turning his mind into spaghetti. The withdrawals were horrendous, and he had almost committed suicide. Now, three months later, he was still on quite shaky ground.

"Go ahead and lie down on the table," Jenkins said. "You don't have to close your eyes. If it becomes unbearable, then you can sit up. I'll keep working on you."

The boy stared at me. "Who's this?"

"My new assistant," Jenkins said. "He's just watching. You can trust him, don't worry."

Carl lay down on the table on his back and stared at the ceiling. Immediately his face began to perspire. Jenkins put his hands on Carl's chest. I sensed this was going to provoke a dramatic reaction. Instinctively I leaned back in my chair near the window.

Carl started to scream, and then it cut off. He raised his knees and his face contorted. He began saying "ah," "ah." It wasn't the sound of release, but of pain.

Jenkins pressed down on the boy's chest and moved his hands in circles. After ten seconds or so Carl stretched out his legs and stopped making sounds. He closed his eyes and lay there stiff as a board. Jenkins kept moving his hands around in circles.

A few minutes passed. Carl's body started to relax. Tears rolled down his cheeks.

Jenkins moved his hands to the sides of Carl's face. He held them there for five minutes or so. Carl's breathing was now deep and audible. Jenkins rubbed the boy's hands and then his feet.

He placed his hands back on Carl's chest and left them there for the next half hour. The breathing slowed down. Every few minutes different parts of Carl's body twitched.

It seemed to me he eventually fell asleep.

Finally, Jenkins rubbed the boy's scalp vigorously. This caused his client to open his eyes. Jenkins moved one hand over Carl's face, as if searching for a spot. He settled on a place at the top of a cheekbone and put one finger on it. After a minute he took his finger away and then also the hand that was still rubbing Carl's skull.

"That's all," Jenkins said. He walked behind the screen and washed his hands. Carl sat up, took out a comb and combed his hair. He stood and walked past me to the window and looked down at the street. He was quiet.

Jenkins came back in the room. "Anything you want to report?"

The boy shook his head. He walked past Jenkins to the door. "I feel better," he said. "I'll see you next week."

He left.

Over the next few weeks, I saw Carl's demeanor change dramatically. He relaxed, talked with Jenkins and me, said he had started playing basketball again. In high school, sports had been his whole life.

Basically, in several sessions, Jenkins had put Carl on the right track again.

Jenkins gave me the following assessment: "Carl hates his parents. If they say they want him to be happy, then he makes sure it doesn't happen, because he knows they'd misinterpret it. They'd refuse to accept his satisfaction, they'd stay on his ass and keep insisting he do this or that. He can't win. So he gets into a severe bind, and that bind is energy. With me, he could see I didn't care. I didn't want anything from him. So he let the bind do what it wanted to — which was unwind and disintegrate."

"That's not the whole story," I said. "What about the circles you made on his chest?"

"That vortex," Jenkins said. "I put it there. I'm not just removing, I'm introducing compatible energies. When I did that, at some level he remembered what it's like to be more powerful, and he accepted it. He bought in."

"Carl wasn't really that bad off, then," I said.

Jenkins smiled. "Yes and no. You're right. He looked worse than he was. He had a lot more resilience than you would suspect, given the way he was acting. But on the other hand, if he didn't have this experience with me, if he had just gone on thinking that things were terrible, in another year he would have been in bad shape. Maybe not in a mental ward, but definitely in a state of hardened cynicism about life on every front."

"I don't know," I said. "Is he really that stable?"

"We'll see. I'm only saying he's reached up out of the pit and seen the sun again. He can jump back in. Hopefully he'll learn a few things while he's all right, and he'll reject the idea of going back down."

Jenkins rubbed a cloth over his massage table. "You think the circles on his chest were important?" he said.

"There was a force going in, wasn't there?"

"Yes," Jenkins said. "There was. What color was it?"

"How should I know? I didn't see it. I'd say orange. That's what it felt like."

Jenkins didn't say anything.

Two days later, he gave me a client to work with.

I was galvanized. I had a strong sense that Jenkins had created energy and put it into Carl. That he invented the energy out of nothing or shaped it from ... already existing energy. From the air, so to speak.

Something outside the resolute laws of mechanical physics. Why not?

It could even be outside the closed system of energy called the physical universe — which suddenly seemed to me like a box, a not very important box.

I was immensely pleased.

I had already begun painting on large rolls of paper in my apartment on Bleecker Street. A friend of mine from high school, a painter, lived nearby, and he would drop over to my place and make encouraging comments. I was untutored and rebellious and I was launching myself and I didn't care. I painted faces and shapes and laid the colors on liberally, looking for strange and exciting combinations. Most of this would be labeled "abstract," but the feelings coming off the canvases were anything but abstract to me. They were strong and thrilling and they didn't have names.

To me, what Jenkins was doing, and what the paintings showed, were of the same family. Energy. Every time. In unique events.

I absolutely wouldn't let go of this.

I was steering without much of a rudder and that was just fine with me.

6

Carol was a fifty-year-old artist who lived in Brooklyn. She took the subway to Jenkins' studio every week. She'd been seeing him for almost a year. For her, the whole process of healing was putting her in touch with "other realms."

She was agreeable to Jenkins' suggestion that I do a few sessions on her.

Jenkins hadn't briefed me. He had only told me to concentrate on her feet and hands. So that's what I did during the first appointment — and like Jenkins, I maintained silence. I found as I held Carol's feet that they weren't quite still. If I focused well enough, I could feel small shifts and movements. Likewise, my own hands were moving too, very slightly.

After the first half hour, I began to feel as if I were steering a vessel. Carol and I were connected. An energy between her feet and my hands set up a field. In that field certain movements were "advisable." I would move and then she would move, at an almost imperceptible level. Together we were orchestrating something. I didn't know what it was. What I was doing didn't have a name, but it was definitely navigation of a kind.

By the end of the hour her feet were very warm. I stepped away from the table and sat down by the window. She lay there with her eyes closed for a few minutes and then rolled over on her side and looked at me.

"I saw a city," she said. "An aerial view. Then I was in among the buildings. Right now I can feel energy streaming from my head all the way down."

Jenkins made tea. As we sat and talked, Carol said her eyesight seemed sharper. "It'll be interesting to go back home and look at my work."

After she left, Jenkins and I took a walk over toward the East River "You're on the right track," he said. "I'm going to give you a few more people to work with. Don't worry about what to do. I'll fill you in as we go along. I won't show you methods. You just need to keep steering, as you say. You have the knack. You see, if you steer into a place where nothing is happening, you have a choice. You can stay there and wait. Eventually something will happen. Or you can just go somewhere else."

The bizarre part of it was I knew what he was talking about.

7

I worked with Jenkins' clients over the next three months.
He asked me not to talk to anyone about what I was doing,
so I didn't.

I told him I had been to a number of good libraries in the
city, and I had found no real texts on this practice we were
now both involved in.

"I learned it in Algiers from another Englishman," he said.
"His name was Joseph Linwood. He may be dead now. He
was a friend of my father."

"Did he write anything down?" I said.

"No."

Jenkins showed me books of notes he kept on clients. They
weren't case histories. They were his own thoughts on what
he was doing with them. A note might say, "More circles."
Or "Try spiral shape." "Press harder." "She's coming to the
end of her sleep phase." "Her stomach is full of shapes. Bring
them to the surface." "Behind his knees. Work there a lot."
"Put red into the chest."

I copied down some of these notes. One longer one said,
"She's working from water, not fire. Very little earth. I can
try to change the balance or go with the tendencies that are
there. For the next year or so, I should accept the situation.
She runs into obstacles, but with this water emphasis, she
survives. She outlasts everybody around her, because the
water is coming from a huge supply. The flow doesn't shut
down. Psychically she changes shape."

All of these notes, to me, were on one level nonsense. But
right next door, on another level, they were navigation-
directions. I was already seeing the effect of literally putting
colors into the bodies of the people I was working on. Sometimes I had the colors flow through my hands. Sometimes I

just bypassed the hands and introduced them directly. You may say this was a delusion on my part. Perhaps, but that was my impression. To me, there were no superior hues. They all had their moments, and the situation could shift quite quickly. I read fragments of spiritualist and metaphysical texts, but they always assigned specific values and meanings to various colors. Immediately I rebelled against this.

For example, I had a client report a significant upward shift in energy level and improved digestion the week after I moved the color black into his stomach. The next week black was completely out of the picture. I sensed it was time for silver and copper.

Likewise, I was finding out that there was no standard sequence of places on the body: You didn't place your hands on the head and then go to the neck and from there to the chest, etc. One day that might work, but on another day I felt I should start with the feet or spots above the kidneys.

One client, a middle-aged accountant, released a huge amount of stress when I placed my hand on his arm just below the shoulder. On that day, that was the place.

Jenkins was pleased that he didn't have to convince me to abandon all systems. In fact, I began to get the feeling that this was a major reason he continued to work with me.

I felt the similarity between healing and painting. Not just the colors, but the style of working. The improvisation. Creation is a slippery word, and we sometimes take it to mean a remote consciousness imposing a completely pre-worked-out plan on a blank space or "unformed matter," but the kind of creation I was experiencing was much closer to the action. Doing sessions with Richard's clients, I was reacting to what I sensed were their changing states of energy and feeling. It was all intuitive and very immediate and subjective. In the same way, working on canvas or paper I was building or moving from one brush stroke to another, from my own reaction to a mass of color I'd just put on the canvas to the next shape, the next mass.

I watched Richard, and he too seemed to be working on people in a very spontaneous way, assessing their "energy-state" in the moment and then doing something in response.

It was natural to me. I was at home. When I went to the Metropolitan Museum — three or four times a week — I had to adjust to appreciate the worlds of painting that were more contemplatively organized.

Creation, imagination. These were words that had many more meanings than they appeared to. At times, I felt that Richard was actually merging with the person on his table. He was resonating to such a degree, he was so empathic that separation between them fell away. Was that imagination? Creation? It was to me. But it was seamless, without fanfare. It was an action wedded to the moment and so immediate. I also felt at times — and this I had never seen before — that Richard became a worshipper of the person on the table. There was no sign, no ritual. He just fell into a few moments of direct felt worship — more than devotion or concern. Much more. A flash of ecstasy would appear on his face. And then he would pass on to something else.

How he moved around the table, his grace — it was a kind of understated art. A dance.

Just before Christmas, 1961, Jenkins' wife Rachel came to New York from Algiers through Mexico. He and I didn't see each other for several weeks. Then he called and told me we needed to talk. The next afternoon we met in Central Park. Rachel was with him. She was a tall woman with very fair skin, green eyes, and black hair.

"Richard's told me about you," she said right away. "I'm glad he's found somebody to work with."

The three of us walked through the Park up to 72nd Street. Rachel did most of the talking.

"What Richard's shown you so far is just the tip of the iceberg," she said. "I understand you've brought about some good energy changes in people. In a year's time you'll see a few quite spectacular things. Recoveries from debilitating conditions. Dramatic changes in personality. Withdrawn people becoming confident. All that. I've been doing research in North Africa and England. We're looking for the next link in the chain."

"What chain?" I said. She seemed to be fitting me into a scenario of her own making.

"The Linwood," Rachel said. "That's where it starts for us. You met Richard. Richard met Joseph Linwood. Linwood was his teacher. We're looking for the next connection back in time."

Richard said, "It fits together."

I said, "This is just an intuitive way of working with people. Every new client is like reading a book. The learning, if you want to call it that, has no set sequence. Things fall into place naturally."

Rachel started a new line of conversation with Richard. She mentioned names that meant nothing to me. One of them was Edward Clark.

Later on, back at the studio on Lexington Avenue, Richard explained.

Edward Terry Clark had been the vice-president of the Sterling Drug Corporation in America. For many years he ran a lobby group in Washington. This lobby promoted the interests of I.G. Farben, a consortium that eventually became the infamous Nazi chemical and pharmaceutical cartel. Clark's Farben lobby was active even during World War II.

"Clark maintained a collection of personal papers," Richard said. "After he died in 1956, his wife sold the papers to a man named Charles Kohn, who owned a collector's shop in Washington D.C. Kohn no longer owns them. They've vanished."

"What the hell does this have to do with anything?" I said.

"We're trying to build a road back into history," Rachel said. "Do you understand? We're searching for one of the people who did this healing — a friend of Linwood, a German. He was part of an effort to fight the Nazis. Maybe he was mentioned in Clark's papers, the missing papers."

Richard could see I was confused. "We're rushing things with you," he said. "It's because I don't know how long we'll be in New York."

"I thought you were going to stay here," I said.

"That was the plan," Rachel said. "But the trail is taking us back to Europe. The reason you've come up with nothing in those libraries is clear. And it's very important. We're not

dealing with a written tradition here. This healing, we believe, goes back a long, long way. If there's a literature, it's
not visible. We feel this is an oral tradition."

"Starting when?" I asked.

Rachel smiled. "Name a number. Ten thousand years
ago?"

Richard said, "As I think you're beginning to understand,
this healing isn't a system. Imagine trying to impart it down
through time. How can it be written about? You have to be
there, with somebody who does it, to see what it is. And then
if you don't have an aptitude, things go nowhere."

Rachel said again, "There is Richard, and then going back
in time there is Linwood. And then there is this other younger
man who worked with Linwood, the German, a strong anti-
Nazi in the 1940s. We think we know his name. I've been
researching him. We want to trace the line back as far as we
can."

"Why?" I said.

"Because we think the healing Richard does is only a
fragment of the original work. There's more, and it's very
wide-ranging."

"Only a fragment?" I said.

"That's right," Richard said. "Tantalizing, isn't it?"

"We don't want to lose this," Rachel said. "There are a
hundred things Richard can do with energy, and all of it is
beneficial. He can sense various energies and how they're
moving in a person at a given moment. He can feel that. His
teacher, if you want to call him that, Linwood, showed him
he had that capacity. He awoke Richard to the fact that he
had that aptitude. Linwood had previously tried to work
with three or four other people, but success was very limited.
Richard has, in London and New York, come across a few
people who seemed promising. None of them panned out.
Now he's found you. It's very early, but so far the prospects
are good. If we had the time, you and Richard would work
together for another few years. You would encounter some
amazing phenomena, and through conversation and spending time together, you'd see much more about how this healing works. But we can't. We have to go to the trail while it's

warm. You're interested in writing and research. We can continue to work together. You can help us from here ..."

I wasn't following this very well, and I thought the whole thing sounded too precious, but I didn't say anything.

Late that night, Richard gave me my first session. It lasted about half an hour. He just put his hand on my chest and left it there. I dropped off the edge of a cliff into a level below thought. My mind still chattered away, but I wasn't part of it. Instead, I lay in an energy pool, and the quality of it was quite peaceful. Long radiations of some kind moved out from me. I had very brief silent conversations with people I'd never seen before who seemed familiar. My breathing slowed down. I saw a house in a field full of stones and small trees. As I realized I was looking at the house, it grew very bright and vanished without a sound. After a moment, a sensation of peace flooded through me.

After the session, walking home, my body felt fluid, coordinated in a way I'd never experienced before.

I thought about Richard. He had shown me almost nothing. The intelligence of his approach, if it could be called an approach, was in his complete lack of interference.

But as far as an historical tradition was concerned, I didn't see how that was possible. Without a system, how could learning be passed down?

The next morning I jotted down a few quick things:

— Do you have to put energy into the body of the person?

— Not necessarily. If you want to, you do. But you can do nothing too. Just lay your hand on his head.

— Do you move energy that's already there in his body?

I was beginning to get more interested in what I was doing. I was making a leap of faith, deciding that my subjective impressions of this so-called healing process were real.

I went to the phone and called Richard. There was no answer.

Then for three days there was no answer.

On the fourth day, Saturday, I went to the studio. Nobody came to the door when I knocked.

I found the superintendent on the stairwell above the second floor.

"They're gone," he said.

"Moved out?"

"Yes."

I felt strange.

"Is there a forwarding address?"

"No," he said.

8

On Monday, two of Richard's clients showed up at my door.

They told me Richard had referred them to me. So I worked on them, on my bed. Late that afternoon I went out and bought a massage table.

In the following weeks, I worked on a dozen of Richard's clients.

Part of the time I was sure I was doing absolutely nothing to help them. At other moments I thought of myself as a masseur. Occasionally something, a connection, would stream into being, and energy would course between the client and me. Why was I even calling them clients? That seemed such an odd name. Were they patients? Were they just people who lay down on a table?

Between sessions I would take long walks in Washington Square Park. I would try to dream up systems of working, as if there were a true energy map of every body and it was the same for all people. Through a friend I obtained a chart of acupuncture points. I studied this bewildering grid and tried to make sense out of it. Of course I was completely without skill to make traditional Chinese diagnoses.

One day Evelyn, a fifty-year-old nurse, showed up at my apartment for her appointment. I had given her three or four sessions since Richard's disappearance. On this afternoon she looked a little pale and tired. She lay down on the table and immediately fell asleep. I was moving my hands in slow circles on her back, just because it seemed the right thing to do, when I began to see a very bright blue color in the space between us. Evelyn made a muffled sound, and then sat upright. She stared out the window.

"Did you see that?" she said.

"See what?"

"A man's face. It got clearer and then it faded out."

Evelyn slid off the table, and without a word she put on her jacket and walked out of the apartment. About fifteen minutes later she came back. Her face was very bright. The paleness was completely gone.

"I don't know what happened," she said, "but I feel a hell of a lot better." She sat down on the floor and did a few stretches. "My body feels flexible," she said. "This healing ... it's irrational. You can't put your finger on something and say that's it, that's what happens."

"I know," I said, "and it's driving me crazy. I don't know what to say to all these people."

"Don't worry about it," she said. "Just work on them. They came to you. Richard recommended you, obviously, before he left. So just do what comes naturally and forget everything else."

It was decent advice.

By the fall of 1962, I was feeling a bit more confident. I could rely on the fact that by placing my hands on a person a process began automatically, and one of the main features was the client's tendency to "drop off a cliff" and move into other realms of experience. It worked this way: For a brief or long period, while I had my hands on a person, he would think. The thinking, the radio stations in the head, would continue. Then the consciousness of the person would slide off the edge of that dimension into a place where thinking-thinking-thinking wasn't the defining rule. In this new space there were unusual images or sensations of energy or a sense of place:

"I was in a city. There was a turnstile at a gate. A person put a package in my hand."

"I went to a school. There was singing. It got louder, then softer."

"A woman turned around and the purple in her dress became very bright."

"There was sky, and then a piece of furniture. A cabinet. I was in a room and a man walked toward me. My face got hot."

In every case, the imagery happened fast. It just came upon the client. It was vivid. The meaning was usually unclear. But afterwards, a sense of peace moved in. Relaxation of mind and body, an easy-going clarity, and sometimes that well-oiled feeling in the body.

This wasn't the limit of what happened during these sessions, but it was a groundbase, a familiar place.

I had something to talk to Jenkins about, and he was gone.

I hadn't heard from him, and neither had any of his clients.

But I began to think that Richard and Rachel's idea about a tradition might have merit. There was something so natural about some of my sessions that I felt they must reflect a process that was part of being human. Perhaps at distant times in history, whole communities or populations worked in this way with one another. It could have been thought of as a kind of "travel," because people did have a sensation of moving or suddenly showing up in unlikely places, in scenes that were "out of a different reality."

We, of course, in this century, in the West, were married to the idea that the reality in front of us was the only one — unless we also happened to believe in a heaven you could go to when dead. I liked breaking through that, to show that there were other places, realms, dimensions. The sensation that came to mind was of walls falling down.

9

In October of 1962, Evelyn was offered a job at a hospital in Colorado. She accepted. She came to see me for her last session.

"Once I heard Richard talk about Jung," she said. "He told a few of us that Jung's true contribution was pointing out the shadow self, the part of ourselves that we shut off from the world. The self that contains our darker side. Richard said his work was an attempt to integrate the sides, dissolve the walls between energies and let them run together. The integration would let us really live ..."

I said to Evelyn, "What still gets me is this crazy idea of a tradition handed down from teacher to student, when there really isn't any teacher because there isn't any system."

Evelyn said, "Remember, you only had a short time with Richard. But over the course of four or five years — if you'd had that long — a lot would have passed between you two."

She took out a piece of paper and handed it to me.

"This is for you," she said. "Richard mailed it to me. The postmark was Greece. There was no return address."

I felt as if I was suddenly a character in a melodrama.

The handwriting was Richard's. The cryptic note said: "Sorry for the fast exit. You're part of our group now. To be able to pass into every energy and pass through it. That's the work and that's the group. It's the best kind of society. There are no blockages allowed. Nobody tries to hold on to anybody else."

"What group?" I said.

"I don't know," Evelyn said. "The one he's trying to trace?"

"Go back more than thirty years and everyone would be dead."

She shrugged and got up on the table.
I gave her a session.
That was the last time I saw her.

10

By November of 1962, I was down to two clients a week. In part this was because I had begun to paint for long hours at a stretch, and my apartment was overrun with canvas and board and tubes and cans.

Although I had no formal training in art, I was determined to jump ahead.

The riot of colors and the non-realistic shapes I was putting on canvases was like having music in my mind at all times. A recurrent theme I found or imagined in the canvases was great wars of beings in the sky. There were also nostalgic moments of streets and roads from childhood and from what I took to be other existences and other times. A white twisting painted shape in a field of blue would suddenly hit me like a revelation, but there would be no language to describe it.

After five or six hours of painting without a break, I would walk out on to the street, and the buildings would have a life of their own. They would speak. It was as if those buildings were describing their own shapes and the descriptions were their very existence. Materials at a nearby construction site were letters of some living alphabet. That its meaning was not literal made no difference to me. In fact, for that reason, the impact was all the more thrilling.

Today somebody might call that an altered state or a hallucination or ... whatever. I didn't call it anything. It seemed close to a key turning in a fantastic lock. Tantalizing. It was a bit unsettling but I tried to stay with it.

Just before Thanksgiving, I received a letter from Richard. It was postmarked Phoenix, Arizona, but the first line read, "We're not in Arizona. We're using this Post Office Box."

Richard wrote: "We've located Linwood. For five years we didn't know where he was, or whether he was alive. He's still twenty years older than I am, only now I'm forty-eight, and he's slowed down. I've been giving him sessions every day, and he's coming around, but he's pretty discouraged. There's a mental attitude of defeat. It's like a rock. He's surrounded by people who have that too, and it isn't doing him any good. They combine their small picture of themselves with a spiritualist bent. They have a group and a leader, and they talk incessantly about a Plan for Humanity. The world, of course, will be saved only by The Plan. I know people can be moved to do heroic things through their faith, but in this case it's clear these devotees are building a metaphysical structure to supply the energy they can't find in themselves. They admire Linwood and his work, but they insist on applying what they get from him to the damn Plan. It all fits in, according to them. They have a little cult going. I'm not privy to their secrets. Linwood has come to rely on them for steady income. We need to get him into a new apartment, maybe move him out of the city altogether.

"I'm sorry we had to leave so quickly, but we got the word about Linwood, where he was, and we didn't know what kind of shape he was in. The story was he was very ill. That was exaggerated, as it turned out.

"At the same time we're dealing with all this, we're carrying on the search for the other person, who'll have to remain nameless for the time being. The younger German contemporary of Linwood. We believe he's still alive. Both he and Linwood took up this healing from the same couple, I think. That's how the lineage goes back.

"The German is the anti-Nazi we spoke to you about. He may have been active in Paris during World War II. We're not sure. Our search needs to be invisible. That's why all the secrecy. There are apparently people around, ex-Nazis, who still like their old philosophy and still want to take over the world. I'm not talking about a few lunatics drinking in bars in Bolivia. As far as I can tell, these people are serious and they have resources. Whatever happens, we don't want to give away our German friend's location — if we can find it.

According to Linwood, although the man was a healer, he has extensive information on the Nazis which is still somehow relevant to current affairs. We're not sure what this is all about. All we're getting so far is that some people view the Nazis as a kind of continuing secret society. Any help you can give us on this would be appreciated.

"Don't know whether you're still working with clients. I'm sure much is happening with your life ..."

What possible help could I give Richard and Rachel?

11

In the winter of 1963 I moved to Los Angeles. I settled into a small apartment in Santa Monica three blocks from the ocean, rented a garage to convert into a studio for painting, and started teaching at a private high school in West Los Angeles.

In March, I met the father of one of my algebra students. He was a musician who had retired from symphonic work after he'd made a great deal of money in local real estate.

This man had relatives who'd survived the Nazi death camps. He spent an evening at my apartment explaining his own view of the Nazi regime:

"You have to understand that, on the surface, these men, all the way up to Hitler, were just clever and ruthless politicians. They fronted for corporate gangsters in their own country, and they had the support of scientists who were transforming their society technologically. They gave out a message of pride to the German people.

"But Hitler and some of his key people were engaged in cult-sadism. It's strange when you think about it. Here they were, talking about the Aryan personality, the youths with yellow hair and blue eyes, and they made these films that showed boys and girls doing gymnastics in the bright sun. They had a pagan belief that the sun was the source of all things, all life. But then the SS uniforms were black, and they doted on the occult, the darkness."

12

For the next ten years, I lived and worked teaching in Los Angeles.

I continued to write and paint. Nothing was more important to me. I sold paintings and drawings now and then, and had a few poems published in American magazines.

Between 1963 and 1973 I received two letters from Richard. The first, in 1965, was brief. He and Rachel were still with Linwood "in Europe," and were still looking for their German counterpart. Linwood, apparently, hadn't been very helpful in that regard.

... The second letter, eight years later, like the first, was sent through Phoenix. It was dated February 15th, 1973, and was longer. Richard said Linwood had died the year before, "peacefully."

Richard and Rachel were spending some time at her mother's, wherever that was, but they would be "moving soon." Richard's mother was coming to join them.

"I don't suppose you've done much healing work in all these years," Richard wrote, "but you still have it in you to pick it up again, even without any close compatriots around. It's a shame we couldn't have spent more time together. The whole business in New York may seem to you nothing more than a dim memory, a fantasy, and as you let us know in one of your letters you're painting now. That is its own world, and perhaps the sense of healing, as something in and of itself, doesn't penetrate anymore.

"We still haven't found our German friend. He may be dead, but I don't think so.

"I have a few clients, and it pays the rent. Rachel is teaching English two mornings a week to private students. We live modestly, and don't mind it. I still firmly believe that I have just scratched the surface, as far as my work goes. There's something else in this tradition of ours which hasn't surfaced. It is vital, and it goes back a long way. I'm determined to do whatever I can to find the answers."

Richard was right. I hadn't been doing any healing, and I wasn't thinking about it much. My last client had been Evelyn, in New York, in 1962. In Los Angeles I'd had a few situations in which there was an emergency, and I'd tried to help. That was all.

Other than that, I knew there was tremendous power in painting, and this inspired me to the hilt. For the past ten years, I'd painted almost every day.

My original experience at Amherst the night before I left for New York had since been repeated countless times. I made energy when I painted. On canvas, on board, on paper. The energy had no name, and the "abstract" shapes it took had no names. The suggestions of personages and events and non-rational places and emotions were sometimes tremendously vivid and thrilling. They were like myths placed into the everyday world. They were like waking dreams. That's all I knew, and hopefully that's all I needed to know.

13

In the fall of 1973 I met a woman named Hadidjah Lamas. She lived in a lovely house in Westwood Village, not far from my apartment. Hadidjah was a Rolfer. She practiced a system of healing which involves the re-invigoration of connective tissue. In this work, the misaligned body posture is set straight. Hidden and frozen emotions can come to the surface and release.

This brief description of Rolfing is, of course, inadequate, and doesn't give the flavor of the work itself; nor does it suggest the profundity of experience that is possible.

Hadidjah and I shared interests in painting and music. Twice she would turn her home into a gallery for me, and put on successful shows of my work.

One day I did a healing session on her, and she was excited.

After working on several large paintings in 1973–74, I found myself burning out. I wasn't accumulating an ordinary kind of stress; this was inverted, a sponginess, a slowing down of functions of thought and feeling that was increasingly irritating.

I imagined myself on vacation in Jamaica for two weeks playing golf and sipping vodka tonics on a veranda overlooking the blue, blue sea. Yes, I decided, that's exactly what I needed — despite the fact that I was a terrible golfer and lost interest in vodkas after the first round.

So instead, one afternoon, I asked Hadidjah, whom many people consider one of the best Rolfers in the world, to give me a session of my own medicine. Would she mind?

"Just put your hands on my head — and leave them for awhile. Turn off the phone, okay?"

"Sure," she said.

I lay down on her table on my back and closed my eyes.

She placed one hand under my neck and the other at the base of my spine. She held her hands there for about fifteen minutes, during which time I felt absolutely nothing. I didn't drift off to sleep, I didn't sense any relaxation creeping in. Nothing at all. Of course, I thought, this isn't going to work. I should have realized it before I even asked her for a session. What do I do now? Get up off the table and say it isn't going anywhere and thank you very much anyway? I was embarrassed.

Then out of nowhere, with my eyes closed, I saw a shape in front of my head, a foot or two away. It was dark and it was about the size of my head. It was made out of strips arranged in a cross-hatch pattern, so that the inside was hollow. I thought of a mask or protective covering for a warrior, a knight. The shape began to turn in place, rotate, gaining a little speed.

I felt absolutely nothing, except a curiosity.

The thing spun smoothly and then it moved away from me across the room and past the open door into the bathroom.

This amused me.

There was a space of, perhaps, ten seconds in which nothing happened, and then I saw colors around me — blue and yellow. And then I was lying surrounded in a very rich sea of blue and yellow and the two colors overlapped and interlapped and effervesced. It was quite gorgeous and I began to enjoy it. As seconds passed I enjoyed it more and more and broke out into a big grin. The grin kept grinning.

I just lay there and watched the beautiful color field and felt better and better.

Finally I said, "I guess we're done."

Hadidjah said, "I guess we are."

I laughed, opened my eyes and sat up. I stood, stretched, and we walked out of the room into the kitchen. "I just had a two-week vacation in Jamaica," I said.

That night I wrote a long letter to Richard and Rachel and directed it to them, as usual, through the Phoenix address.

I walked six blocks to the nearest mailbox. It was about ten o'clock. As I turned to go back home from the box, I suddenly felt sleepy and very relaxed. When I reached my apartment, I pulled a chair outside under a eucalyptus tree. I sat down, listened to the mockingbirds and fell asleep.

When I woke up, perhaps an hour later, I felt different. I stood up and stretched and walked out to the street. There was a complete quiet in me. There was no passive mind as such. No place where radio stations play on and off and fragmentary thoughts flow into one another. There were no doubts about anything, there was no substratum of guilt, there was no hint of a desire to dredge up little pieces of memories, there was no regret, no worry, no anything except ecstatic joy and peace.

I wasn't robotized. Just the opposite. My perception was extremely sharp, and the night street of small flowering trees, streetlights, and houses and apartment buildings spread out in gorgeous aliveness, as if I'd previously been seeing a dead, foreshortened and flattened-out world.

My whole life felt brand new. To choose whatever I wanted to do from this moment on, with no reference to the past.

There was no rush to decide ...

Over the next three days, the newness slowly subsided, leaving me with a sense of nostalgia, which then itself faded out. I was determined to find out how to move through that door further.

14

In June, 1974, I found a new studio to paint in.

I was doing faces in pastels. I started each one without a pre-set idea. Some faces turned out to be humanoid; some didn't. Pushing the pastel colors around on paper felt like sculpting clay. The faces suggested other times and places, and some of them came out of no time or place ...

For the next eight years I would continue to paint.

Then, in 1982, I made a big switch in my life. I started writing articles for newspapers and magazines. These pieces were mainly about politics and health.

That work in turn evolved into a book and a contract with a publisher. The book was *AIDS INC.*, and it was finally printed and released in 1988.

AIDS INC. and one of my later books, *Oklahoma City Bombing* (1995), made me seriously consider the possibility that, on the world scene, we were witnessing major staged events. This was not aimless thinking. A great deal of investigation was involved.

I began to roll key political events around in my mind, considering them as activity on a certain kind of thermometer of power. Toward the possible goal of frightening, demoralizing, and ultimately controlling populations.

Perhaps certain elites would do or say virtually anything — they would allow fraudulent medical research to stand without challenge, they would release terribly toxic "curative" drugs to the public, they would squash cheap and reliable sources of healing, and perhaps even attempt to terrorize populations by acts of sudden and tragic destruction ...

Could this really be true?

There was, by the mid-1990s, a growing underground

sentiment that secret societies were behind various planetary-control scenarios. After reading some of the available material on this, I wondered whether, out of the welter of cults, secret societies, and communities which had at one time or another appeared on our planet, there was a particular and vital stratum of hidden information. I couldn't put my finger on anything.

I was still fascinated with Richard Jenkins' search and his belief that, concealed in Earth's past, there lay an unheralded oral tradition of healing.

In July 1995, I wrote Richard a long letter, and sent him copies of *AIDS INC.*, *Oklahoma City Bombing*, and a compilation of testimony given in March of that year, before the U.S. President's Committee on Radiation Experiments, indicating that agencies of the federal government had conducted brutal mind-control experiments on children.

Three weeks later I received a note from Rachel:

> Richard died this year at 64 years old. He was traveling in the Mediterranean. He had a case of food poisoning. Someone took him to a hospital where he was given an IV. He went into shock, and before anyone could determine what happened, he was gone. Perhaps it was penicillin. He was allergic to it. Richard, Linwood, Richard's mother and my mother are all gone now. I won't burden you with the details. It's been a tough few years here.
>
> ... We had been pursuing leads from relatives and friends of this German man. I still think that if he's alive, he could be in danger. Did we ever tell you that he always considered Nazism a kind of secret society, not simply a political movement? It was on that basis, according to Linwood, that he attacked it. After reading your books, I feel confident that I can give you his name. I still fear for his life, even now, although that might be complete nonsense. The name is Paul Schuman ...

I didn't know what to do. I hadn't seen Richard in all this time, and now he was dead.

That night I lit a candle, turned out the lights in my apartment, stared at the flame for awhile, lay down on my bed and didn't sleep.

15

Richard's quest for a tradition. What could it possibly consist of? Did it have a kind of opposite which would throw some light on it?

A vague scene plays over and over again: the end of human society as a dog-eat-dog business, as a war for money and food ...

16

Now, in the summer of 1997, I've written a long, rambling letter to Rachel Jenkins. It's based on research and thinking I've been doing over the past ten years, and also on a "click" that occurred one night while I was painting in my apartment. The section I'm quoting here includes pieces of writing I'd been doing about Nazism and other secret societies. As you'll see, there is a tie-in with my feelings about painting, a very strong tie-in — which, somewhere along the line, had occurred as I was writing articles and books about politics:

"I keep thinking about what you and Richard said in New York. That Richard's work was just a fragment of a much larger tradition. I didn't see how that was possible at the time.

"But now ... In doing his healing Richard entered a space at the beginning of the session. He started, in other words, as a musician would, shifting into a slightly different 'realm' and then playing.

"Then he sensed the energies and colors and shapes and feelings coming off the other person on the table. He answered that with his own energies and shapes — which he invented, in a way.

"A dialogue went back and forth.

"There are so many ways he could respond to the emanation of the other person. His choice involved the invention of forms and energies which he put into that person.

"This is art, art on the wing. It reminds me of jazz, improvised.

"Suppose the larger tradition Richard mentioned is just that? A kind of art.

"And suppose that when we look back into history, we find places and times where some kind of creation was taking place but was misunderstood or ignored, because there was

47

nothing to hook it on to. I know that's vague. Let me just put it this way: Suppose we are ignoring something major about the past because we are seeing it in the wrong way?

"Some reading I've done on several secret societies fits in here. Take Nazi Germany, the Soviet Union, the Holy Roman Catholic Church. I believe these are three of the major cults of our time. But think of their real leaders as artists who work in a sabotaging way, in order to control populations. This artist metaphor is not trivial. I don't mean it as a convenience for thinking about 'the bad guys.' I mean this literally.

"The whole business of cults and secret societies has made an impression on me, because they are worlds of their own, and you can see how human beings are duped into living lives within highly artificial boundaries. That piece of trickery applies to the whole human race, but the means of conjuring the boundaries are clearer in the setting of the cult.

"I don't know if you're familiar with Jackson Pollock, the famous American painter of the 1930s and 40s. He dripped and spilled paint on large canvases he tacked down to the floor of his studio in Long Island. His whole activity was a kind of dance, as he circled the canvas, stepped on it at times, and dripped paint from sticks. He talked about 'being in the painting' as opposed to standing on the outside and calculating each move. He worked quickly. Most painters of that breed who became famous as so-called Abstract Expressionists talked about space. The space of the painting. The space you made. The space you found.

"Healing to me is very much like this. Richard gets into the space of the painting, except in this case the canvas is the person lying on the table, who talks back through his energies.

"Well, in a secret society, there is already a space. One space. And the trick is to get you to believe in it, to take it on, to put on the coat and leave it on, to think it is the only coat there is and the best coat and the highest coat. Do you see? This really is art, and to ignore that is to miss the whole point of how the deception works.

"Goose steps. Blonde soldiers. Black leather coats. SS chiefs overseeing torture in the death camps. Hunting down Jews and Gypsies behind closed doors ... Nazi party members, a long line of nothings, each nothing ready to follow the Fuhrer's orders to the letter forever. Without question. All based on art.

"More art. The recommendation for destruction of all private property and all ideas of private property. Paradise. Utopia. Pink and purple of a new day above the beautiful green trees. People loving each other. Nothing private.

"That was out of the 18th-century Illuminists (Illuminati). Of course, when you eliminate all private property, you invoke an impossible ideal. Humans can't pull it off and like it. You pave the way for a few human beings who — espousing generous this and that — will actually take ownership of ALL land. The essential inheritor of this particular utopian art is the Soviet Union of the twentieth century.

"Lenin and Stalin stood for the universal giving of resources, but as leaders they had the hearts of concentration camp commandants. Equality doled out in a huge gray emptiness.

"Or another cult-art mural starts with the announcement that the gate is finally open to every citizen to live out his true destiny — which involves the full exercise of power based on a prior elite history all true-blooded citizens share.

"Hitler was the king of that painting. Build them up before you let them down. Before you homogenize and flatten human power.

"I believe Nazi Germany was the watershed moment. After that, we had thrust on us an almost psychiatric equation of power and insanity, as if the entire modern world could only become mature by realizing that mediocre and adjusted people were its best products.

"... For the Germans, it took a grandiose vision — a grandiose painting — to stir them from the destruction of World War I. They grabbed on to an ancient past of the so-called Aryan race, a people from whom 'the pure German' was supposed to have descended. The fact that no one has ever proved the existence of an Aryan race is entirely beside the point. But it is a painting. See it that way. Conjure images of ancient Teutons, Aryans, and gods of Valhalla, and the German soul goes ping. At least it did in 1920.

"The image-making was compelling. It involved the work of more than a hundred German scholars who explored a myth of a past in which Pure Aryan Blood was King.

"These scholars, aided by well-off citizens and dedicated drawing-room clubs — and by Hitler and Himmler and Hess — brought home the bacon.

"The overall conclusion was Yes.

"Yes, this German race once existed in a sublime state of blood purity, untainted by lower forms of life. Once it controlled much of the planet, actually, by virtue of simple inherent body-strength, superhuman mental powers, and psychic/mystic third-eye omniscience!

"What?

"Yes. This was the painting.

"Then the painting showed that these fantastic German powers were diluted and polluted by incautious sexual joining of Aryans with lesser races — mainly the Jews.

"Otherwise, the 'research' concluded, Germans would still be physically huge and Viking-like, would still rule seas and continents, would still be taking what was rightfully theirs (basically everything in sight), would be residing in your standard colossal castles above winding mountain roads, would be emanating for the throngs a superb glow signifying at the very least an elevated and pure state of health at all times.

"The amount of 'scholarship' which, following World War One, went into establishing a special German past was staggering. The painting was definitely a group effort.

"'O citizen. Don't worry if today it takes a wheelbarrow full of paper currency to buy a loaf of bread. That is the devious doing of the Jews and their financial chicanery. Don't worry if the machinery of the country lies in ruins and you can't find a job and are teetering on the brink of abject poverty. We are the true rulers and we will rise again. We will mangle those who have infiltrated us and compromised our blood. We will force the issue. The boundaries of Germany are arbitrary and deluded. We will build a juggernaut and take Earth for our own. That is truth. That is history finally put in its proper perspective. That is our destiny reborn.'

"Hitler came on board with that.

"Elite scenes in the huge German painting — the mural — abounded. See Northern caves of ice. The Arctic. See ancient

Germanic giants there rising out of their slumber, thousands of years ago to take on the whole Earth. See the radiating lines of force coming from the third eye of these ancestors. 'The Sun is our source, our god. It has our color, the gold, and we flourish in its presence.'

"One night, it clicked. At least I felt a first click. This was a kind of literal painting I hadn't deeply considered. It was accomplished by a group with a leader, and it invented a landscape it hoped would last forever and be worshipped as ... what? The Real World of the Human Soul.

"On one level, of course, I already knew about this kind of strategy. But for some reason, the point now was coming home with extreme lucidity. It was as if I were visiting a museum of human manipulation, and all I could find were groups of artists. They were in a trance and they were trying out different ways to take over the human mind.

"... Lots of disparate material on the palette of the Nazi artists as they painted a new world for the German people.

"Start with a little cultural atmosphere and backdrop — an ongoing national pagan/occult revival: the popular Madame Blavatsky's *Secret Doctrine*, the Valhalla gods, an ancient and secret Arctic homeland of original German giants, a rune-fad, Masonic initiatory rites, Knights Templar, peasant solstice fertility practices, the Tarot, Masters of the Himalayas, Hermetic Order of the Golden Dawn, the Bhagavad-Gita, astrology, Tao. And more.

"Such a mystic/occult stew of influences was edited and reshaped to show that psychic and physical giants — the old pure Aryan ones, the German ancestors — once dominated in Tibet, the Arctic, America, India, and other incredible key spots around the planet. Never mind that no historical research could establish that!

"Nazi artists dredged up a hodgepodge of heraldic and mysterious symbols and used them to stitch together a legend of a glorious bygone era. The blonde, blue-eyed Teutonic people — instead of confronting their washed-out defeated Germany floundering on all fronts after World War I — could look back on mighty mythical ancestors, who scholars and researchers said had once emerged from a strange uncharted land called Thule, somewhere in the Arctic. From underground caves, as actual physical giants, these hyper-Teutons took to the seas, and eventually ruled in foreign lands.

"Many men in Germany wanted to enter that painting and live in it, take up residence, abandon their former ideals.

"This is a way to understand the actions of a cult. Flesh out the painting they are creating. See the whole landscape, and most importantly, realize that they are claiming there is only one painting, one universe — which is as they imagine it. And so the devotee signs on to the narrowing of his own imagination.

"Jorge Lanz von Liebenfels, who served in the early days as an intellectual inspiration to Hitler, invented an anti-Semitic secret society called the Order of the New Templars. This group searched for a Holy Grail it ultimately defined as German Aryan blood itself, purified of "lower-order" (Jewish) content. Von Liebenfels said that the original Aryan race had, among other powers, telepathy and all-knowingness. His Order of the Templars would restore these powers to Germans and, at the same time, eliminate from the face of the Earth or enslave all inferior races.

"Peter Levenda, who's written an excellent book, *Unholy Alliance*, remarks that Hitler legitimized the New Templars and completely accepted their specific proposal for incineration of lower-order life. Hence, the World War II ovens in the concentration camps.

"Nazism was a cult fed by other cults. In addition to the Templars, there was the *Germanenorden* (German Order), another exotic invented secret society. You may know about these groups from trying to find that German healer. Anyway, if not, *Germanenorden* was begun in 1912. The leaders, including industrialist Theodor Fritsch and Baron Rudolf von Sebottendorff, organized a series of initiatory levels and rituals, 'replete with [mythic past glories of] knights in shining armor, wise kings, mystical bards, and forest nymphs ... patterned after Masonic ceremony ... its Theosophical-style philosophy encompass[ed] everything from eastern mysticism to runic lore to a rabid, pseudoscientific racism.'

"More aspects of the Nazi painting.

"*Germanenorden*'s explicit targets were Jews and also Free-masons. *Germanenorden* lamely used the Thule Society as a cover name. The Thule Society was the known title of a German mystical-literary group, whose symbol was a dagger over a swastika. *Germanenorden*'s members included Franz Gurtner, who would become the Justice Minister under Hitler, and Munich police chief Ernst Pohner. The group occasion-ally took on the work of carrying out assassinations.

"Thulists did manage to create a worker's group within *Germanenorden*, and in 1919 this German Worker's Party was renamed — to sound appealing to the German Communists — the National Socialist German Worker's Party. This was to become Hitler's political organization.

"Fast forward ... the famous Nazi-artist Leni Riefenstahl's 1934 film documentary, *The Triumph of the Will*, shows Hitler's mass rally at Nuremberg. I'm sure you know it. It's very clear: The power being built by the Fuhrer was one to be created by millions of nameless ciphers organized in regiments of workers and soldiers and children awaiting orders from the top. The idea of free individual expression is completely missing. What you see is a sea of standing thousands, in perfectly squared-up regiments, plugged into their messiah. Proud nobodies ready to do anything.

"'You are a potential god. To realize your capacities, join the club. Pick up a spear and march. If that doesn't sound like ancient Aryan godhood, ignore the discrepancies and keep your mouth shut.'

"The cult. All order, no individual imagination.

"The cult. A painting of a Secret Elite Past joined with the present — designed to inspire — which sucks in Germans yearning to embody a higher power, to escape humiliation, etc. The payoff? A membership card in a fascist ant-colony.

"Occult connections all the way across the big Nazi board.

"One of Hitler's advisors, Thulist Dr. Wilhelm Gutberlet, owned a device called a sidereal pendulum, and stated to Hitler that by use of this instrument he could silently pick out Jews in any gathering. Hitler consulted Dr. Gutberlet in this arena.

"Part of the Nazi cult 'mural' of the universe includes a science laboratory/factory. The Teutonic gods pass judgment on the sperm and ova of various racial types. Will they be permitted to breed? The gods — and their favorite Aryan descendants, the Nazi Party devotees — have the power of life and death over the future. So the myth is extended from the far past of the ice caves to the far-ahead centuries of gene manipulation on a grandiose scale.

"This is what now occurs to me very forcefully: it is the duty of every cult to deny the possibility that multiple universes can be created. Why? Because they are painting their universe and calling it All That Is. Even if they start off with multiple realms, they ultimately weld them together and coalesce them into the Final Single Painting.

"That leaves us with a workable definition of freedom. The latitude and the capacity to create many universes. Many worlds. Many spaces. Many paintings. Many dimensions.

"I'm not completely clear on how far 'many universes' goes — but all this connects to Richard's healing work, I believe. Because in that healing people travel and see things. They find various scenes or worlds, if you will, and they bring back memories of those places. Multiple realities, multiple realms, multiple energies. If that assumption is denied, and every cult or religion I know denies it, it would inhibit healing, it would lock people in.

"It does lock people in.

"Richard's kind of healing, as I witnessed it, said, Look, there are many dimensions and places of energy, but in this everyday world we deny that. We try to convince ourselves there is only one dimension and we are living in it. But when people lie down on the table they experience a whiff of the truth — the multiplicity of reality. They may not be able to articulate it, but they experience it. And then things go one step further. The rigid separating walls of energy between dimensions or planes or realms or worlds or universes or 'paintings' begin to dissolve, and that brings healing.

In other words, healing starts out by admitting that there are multiple dimensions and then it dissolves the walls between them which were put there, in fear.

"The feared German SS, under Himmler, was a huge cult of its own (50,000 men by 1933). Headquarters in the ominous

Wewelsburg Castle. The dining room was perpetually set for the Inner Twelve, Himmler's closest men.

"'... the most dreaded police force and secret society in modern history,' Himmler's SS — also called *Schwarze Orden* (Cult of the Black order) — specializes in arrest, interrogation, medical and mind control experiments, torture, and murder on a grand scale. Seen from the correct angle, these acts are more than political. They're a ceremonial carrying out of duties based on prior secret SS cult-initiations and oaths — which in turn are based on an invented mythic Teutonic history of godhood, power, blood-purity and world rule.

"Although the precise oaths of the SS are still secret, it's said that periodically they would pick out one of their own, a true Aryan type, and chop his head off — and then use the head as an intermediary communication device between themselves and various 'disembodied Masters of the East.'

"What many Americans would now call a Satanic cult resembles the SS, except that when you throw in SS-run concentration camps like Dachau and Auschwitz, you stretch the mind's ability to hold on to the word 'cult.' It appears that you must be talking only about a government or a nation, a strictly political entity. But that's not so. Nazism spilled blood as a cult-rite of passage.

"Everybody now realizes that, armed with supplies of cash, gold, and art treasures, thousands of SS members survived World War II and fled to other lands. It's preposterous to imagine that, having been initiated into the Black Order of the SS, and later in possession of wealth, most of these men would simply lie down and renounce their blood-ties. The agenda would go on. It did.

"It's significant that Auschwitz, run by the SS, not only involved itself in heinous medical experiments and mass murder, but in the hiring out of labor. The notorious and gigantic German chemical cartel, I.G. Farben, built a rubber plant at Auschwitz. It paid the SS a pittance to send over inmates to work at the factory every day. Those selected who were too weak to work, or who couldn't last the day on their feet, were killed.

"So the SS cult had very close links, not only to Hitler, but to Germany's highest-ranking corporate elite. These connections would have continued after the War, because, for example, one of the longest sentences handed down at Nuremberg to a Farben executive — on charges of slavery and mass murder — was only seven years. It was doled out to Dr. Fritz Ter Meer, who, after his release, was made chairman of the supervisory board of the Bayer Corporation, now the largest chemical company in the world. Can you believe it?

"... The created art of the cult, the secret society, is used to get from the promise of power to the reality of slavery. This is done on a fast arc.

"This is a kind of art that is not studied per se in colleges and universities. And with good reason. Once you look at certain groups as artists seeking to invent and impose a mural of a universe, all sorts of revelations about the way power operates, on many levels, become clear.

"Again, I am not using this description of Nazism as a metaphor. I am saying that secret societies really are artists inventing their worlds. They really do this. Whether they know it completely or not.

"I am also saying that if the guises of power on Earth were seen and well-analyzed from this point of view, they would start to crumble.

"In Nazi Germany, as well as other such cults and societies, 'power' for the devotee is obtained by proxy, by kneeling before the already-created painting of a myth, by swearing eternal allegiance to the image of the messiah who, sooner or later, strolls on to the mural to embody all that the painting stands for.

"In the case of the secret society called the Illuminists (*aka* Illuminati), their ideas about destroying all private property which they put forward in 1780 took over a century to percolate, until Lenin seized the reins of Russia. Worship of that cult messiah, which was supposed to produce a renaissance in the millions of citizens of the nation, ended up, at best, making everyone a functionary in a bleak, slow-motion bureaucracy that stretched from East Germany to China.

"This says something about the kind of power you obtain from ideas and images that are frozen into an absolutist painting, even if the painting promises Christmas on Earth.

"The cult, the secret society, creates the painting. The devotee, unaware that he can invent his own paintings, his own worlds, worships the well-done ready-made version.

"In late-eighteenth-century France, revival occult Pythagorean groups settled on 'mystic' geometric figures to explain and enhance the legitimacy of their ideas. The two principal shapes used were the circle and the triangle.

"And in that same period, there was the Illuminist conspiracy-cell of nine men. It was conceived as a circle. The Rosicrucians used the circle in the same way. In fact, Adam Weishaupt's Illuminist symbol for human progress within his secret society was a circle.

"These geometric shapes were considered 'inner universal reality' of a sort, and therefore gave a metaphysical certitude to the activity of the secret society that employed them.

"The triangle, of course, was a basic symbol for the Masons. It signified harmony, and on seals of Masonic orders the triangle was often inscribed. Pythagoreans used this shape to surround some other vital signifier. A 'point of sunrise,' which was said metaphysically to animate the elements of nature, would be placed, as a dot, in the center of a triangle.

"Here's the 64-dollar question. Was the flavor of all this off-the-cuff symbolism and myth, in eighteenth-century France and twentieth-century Germany, one of discovery — or creation? Most certainly discovery. The leaders of these groups didn't let on, or know, that they were inventing artful emblems and myths; oh no. For them the whole business was constructed to mean they were penetrating to the core of the universe to find out what the inner truths and intrinsic symbols actually were — and once having done that, they would return with the spoils.

"And these cultists subsequently found many followers who would deeply believe in the reality of the spoils. So the method worked.

"People took invention for discovery.

"Are you likely to believe in your friend's God if he tells you he just invented Him?

"Obviously not.

"This is cult-painting at its most obvious. Give them the triangle and the circle and tell them that these shapes mean certain profound truths, and that'll help them sign on to live in the painting, to make their home in its universe.

"But there is no root meaning to a universe, any universe — except the one it may have been arbitrarily imbued with by its creator(s). I admire Cezanne and Van Gogh, and I sense the underlying feeling that they transferred to their worlds, but that doesn't make me want to join up as a slave to their inventions.

"The solution to secret societies and the tyranny of groups is art, creation in the widest sense. The artist can create many worlds. Many artists can create a profusion of worlds.

"A cult, a hierarchical religion, a secret society is one world. Only. It is the equivalent of a painter asserting that he has made the quintessential canvas-space and has filled it with the quintessential energies and shapes of all time.

"So here is what we have. We have the existence of a profound creative impulse in all people.

"Then we have the art of the secret society used to repress that creativity by trying to mesmerize people into living as slaves inside the already-made Single Exclusive World of the cult painting. This applies to our planet and the way, in general, institutions have established control over populations.

"Then we have the existence — which is something of a mystery — of many different worlds, dimensions of experience and intuition, realms, which you do not simply travel to in powered vehicles made out of steel and plastic. You get to these places interiorly. If this alternate-realms idea seems too bizarre, then just think of it all as interior spaces of the imagination.

"But I'll say this: you won't get to those mysterious worlds and scenes if you are fundamentally transfixed by a single painting perpetrated by a secret society or cult or religion or government or institution. They are all secret societies because they have private agendas away from the light of day which are designed to limit and narrow and control and harm people ..."

17

In the days that followed my sending this letter to Rachel, other thoughts occurred to me:

Here is the beginning of the perverse formula for control:
Describe all human energy and power and creativity as bounded by a single space.
Convince people that this space is the highest reality possible.
Tell them the space was put there by a particular invisible being.
Now dress up the space with fancy and fascinating and esoteric details, to keep everyone occupied.
The Formula of the Secret Society.

Of course there are other tricks too, and we could embark on a treatise that covers the ways of manipulators, from the bait and switch to the rolling hypnotic voice of the salesman, to the sudden doling out of "love" to the new adherent, to the imposition of malnutrition and ill-health, and so on. But the Formula stated above is the big picture, or a major chunk of it.

18

The Communist Party, obviously taking up ideas from the late-18th-century cult called the Illuminati — ideas about destroying all private property — corrupted the entire meaning of Christmas on Earth in favor of gulags and coercion at every level of work and thought in the Soviet Union for 70 years. Yes, there were honorable people who truly believed in the abolition of private property and the universal sharing of material resources. Many of them were awakened to these ideas coming down in time from teachings of the Illuminist secret society. Yes, there were people in Russia who deeply wanted to create a national commune of equality. But what happened was the opposite.

We could rail forever at the betrayal of noble ideals, but in fact a principle is at work: the erecting, like a heaven, of a Pattern of Truth within the fabric of the cult mural.

"Natural law" or "inner principles of the universe" or "hidden history." Those are some general patterns.

And of course, in a modern nation like the Soviet Union, the pattern of society WAS the ultimate good and the ultimate god.

Once faith has been cast in favor of a pattern of truth, in favor of that aspect of the cult painting, the best-laid plans will circle around and devour their own tails. Why? Because the pattern is revered above all, and allegiance to it cuts off the human being from his fluid core. The result will be sacrifice and martyrdom to the pattern and then deep disillusion at every level. Finally, the whole horrible structure will come down in rotten pieces.

And of course, what is The Pattern? It is just a clever, complex aspect of the painting "they made for you."

19

By art, by a mural, make a single space and convince humans that power exists only within that pre-defined space, which is run by Someone Else.

Convince them that within the pre-defined space, the best life is to (1) uncover a hidden pattern which "illuminates" the space — and then (2) study and meditate on and understand and swear allegiance to the pattern. Then you're all set.

If they follow your advice, you'll be their slavemaster. That's how insane worlds are made.

20

I'll now describe two clients I watched Richard Jenkins work on, at close range, in New York, in 1961. To an important degree they illustrate these statements about Pattern.

In the winter of 1961, in New York, Richard gave sessions to Ralph, a man who fit perfectly the mold of a bureaucrat. He worked for the County as a record-keeper in the court system. He was fifty years old. His fingers were always ink-stained, and his pallor, slouched posture, and drab suits begged for a green eye-shade.

He had high blood pressure. He heard ringing in his ears. He wanted the ringing to stop.

He was only five pounds overweight, by his calculation, so it didn't seem to him that simple dieting was going to do the job.

In Richard's first session, all he did was put his hands on Ralph's chest and leave them there for an hour.

Ralph fell asleep after ten minutes and stayed that way for the rest of the time. After he woke up and walked around the room a little he said the ringing had stopped.

The next day he called and told Richard the ringing was back, but it had vanished for several hours at a time the day before, so he knew something was happening. He scheduled a session for the following week.

In the second session, Richard put his hands on Ralph's chest for half an hour, and then moved them to his shoulders for the rest of the appointment. Ralph was asleep most of the time. Afterwards, he said the ringing was very faint.

On his way out, he told Richard he had been a socialist when he was younger. "I was very active in several labor

62

groups," he said. "I'm still committed to it, but I wish the people would act differently. They don't have the same fire anymore."

In the third session, Ralph fell asleep, and then periodically his body shuddered. The shudder seemed to go from his shoulders downward each time, in exactly the same tempo. Twice he opened his eyes and looked at the ceiling, then went back to sleep. I got the impression he had been in an operating room.

Several days after the third session, Ralph called Richard. He had developed a head cold. What did Richard think? Should he come for his next session or wait until he was better? Richard told him to show up unless he didn't feel well. The day before his appointment Ralph called to say the cold was gone. It had dried up overnight. He was surprised.

This time, during the hour, he didn't fall asleep. He told Richard he saw images of books and places and buildings he had never seen before.

He was the last client of the day. We all went out to supper together. Ralph said he had devoted thirty years of his life "to the system." It was his considered opinion that bureaucracy was the only way to join together great numbers of people trying to do service for one another.

"A society has to survive collectively," he said.

In Ralph's fifth session, he started to cry, stopped himself, then fell asleep. He woke up near the end of the time, and a few more tears rolled down his cheeks.

Afterwards, he told Richard he remembered his college days. He had gone to school at a "progressive university." During the session he had gotten very clear flashes of that time. The weather, the trees with spring leaves in the quadrangle, political meetings in teaching rooms.

"Very boyish stuff," he said, "but the clarity of it, it came back to me like a rocket. It was alive."

He said that words like revolution and socialism had really meant something to him in those days, and now he had come all the way down the line living out a pale reflection of that, in a bureaucracy that was hopelessly bogged down in procedure.

During the next few sessions, Ralph had flashes from

much earlier times in his life, fragments of conversations in rooms, scenes of streetcorners in Brooklyn where he'd grown up, lakes and ponds in upstate New York.

His eyes seemed more alive to me, and his conversation was a bit more emphatic, less flat.

Ralph took two weeks of vacation time and went to visit his son in Oregon. His ex-wife lived in Vancouver, so he saw her as well, for the first time in four years.

When he came back, there was some color in his face. He'd gone hiking with his son. He seemed much more animated. He talked about the restaurants in Portland. The food, he said, was marvelous. He'd thought a great deal about his "revolutionary youth," his early years in college. He'd once read works by the "real revolutionaries," men and women who believed in true equality in life. Their form of sharing was community, not a political leadership taken over by a few people to direct millions of featureless proletarians ...

Ralph began making inquiries about communities in the Northwest. It turned out there were several of these, and they welcomed visitors. Each community was structured differently. The one common denominator, at least on paper, was that everyone participated in decision-making.

Ralph had a new lease on life.

In his next three sessions, while Richard had his hands on Ralph's stomach, Ralph began breathing spontaneously and deeply. Several times his face flushed bright red.

"Layers of crap are falling away," he said. "I don't even know what it is."

He commented it seemed a gray smoky substance — that had been infiltrating his body — flew away.

By the fifteenth session, Ralph lost interest in communities. He decided he would take his savings and move up to Oregon near his son. He considered various small businesses he could start.

In session, Ralph was experiencing a "waking up" of his arms, legs, and lower back. "It's as if they've been encased in wood," he said. "I thought I was feeling them, and I'm sure I was, but nothing like this. I think I can start hiking long distances."

At the end of the seventeenth session, Ralph said he had traveled to "a place that was like a dream. There were five or ten people standing around. They were all talking at once. It was as if I knew them. As soon as I saw them clearly they blew up. Just disintegrated."

Two days later Ralph called Richard to say he was walking around during the day feeling "an effervescing in my body. It's very pleasurable. It's an energy. I'm seeing things more clearly. My vision is better ..."

Ralph quit his job with the County two months later. After placing ads in Oregon newspapers, he was getting inquiries from people who wanted to sell their businesses. Ralph was looking for a company with not more than ten employees.

"Gradually I want to make it worker-owned," he told Richard. "Do it right, so we all feel excited. Never get back to that procedural stuff that's nothing but paper ..."

Somewhere around his 20th session, Ralph said a jumble of shapes and symbols flashed by his head. Afterwards, he felt a huge relief of pressure he didn't know he had, and dozed for a few minutes on the table. The next day he was full of energy, and walked five miles in the city.

Ralph was now enthusiastic about life. It was written on his face. Richard said they could take things a lot further, but he also knew Ralph was itching to leave town and move up to Oregon. He was very motivated.

(After the fourth session, neither Richard nor Ralph had ever mentioned the ringing ears again.)

The last night I saw him, Ralph said, "This healing unglued me from what was filling up my mind."

"What do you mean?" I said.

"This may sound crazy, but it was as if my whole mind had become a series of shapes of the life I felt obligated to lead. I had committed myself to support an ideal world in the form of an organization, really. An organization I imagined could run humanity. I ended up working for a part of that organization, but long after I realized it wasn't the answer, I couldn't get out. My mind was filled up with old shapes. I used them to dominate myself. They hemmed me in. In the sessions, they began cracking piece by piece. Came apart like real buildings and offices. The feelings connected to the whole thing came apart too. They blew up or just dissolved. I still have that original idea of sharing with other people. That's got happiness in it again. Now I can really do it, for the first time ..."

It was driven home to me. There are all kinds of patterns that become woven into the mind, as energy, and we become devotees to those patterns. When they crumble, we feel: freedom.

If you want a literary parallel to this, simply read *Age of Reason* by Thomas Paine. It is an effort by an exceedingly brilliant mind to subtract what he considered was dross (pattern) from the myth of Christianity, in order to leave in its place freedom.

21

In early 1961, I saw Richard Jenkins work on a client, Allen, in New York. Richard gave Allen approximately fifty sessions. I was there four times, and Richard and I spoke about what was happening to Allen on several occasions.

Allen worked for the U.S. State Department. At the outset, he made it clear that he couldn't speak about his work. Richard told him that didn't matter at all.

Allen was forty years old. He appeared to be quite confident and easy-going. He had come to Richard because he was experiencing fatigue, and because he was having headaches on a regular basis. Richard said he didn't treat symptoms, he just worked on energy. Allen accepted that without question. Richard told Allen to stop drinking so much coffee. He gave Allen two bags of herbs with orders to make tea and sip it on and off during the day, every day.

In the first session, Richard worked on Allen's feet. He held particular spots and massaged the insteps. Then, sitting in a chair at the end of the table, Richard just held his hands on the bottoms of Allen's feet for half an hour or so.

Allen started talking at that point. Sometimes Richard would tell clients to be quiet, but he let Allen ramble.

Allen said he was in a business deal that involved commercial property in North Carolina. He said he had recently started going to church again. He was doing a few things in his private life he wasn't proud of. He said life in general had once been so easy for him, but now the problems he was having were closing in. He started laughing. Then he stopped, became quiet and fell asleep.

After the session he said he wasn't usually talkative "in that way. I don't skip around and gab about things. Just discount it."

Richard said there was nothing to discount.

The next time I saw Allen was after his tenth session. He told Richard his headaches had gone away for awhile, but now they were back. The fatigue was a little better. Richard said nothing. I noticed that Allen's complexion had become more pasty. He seemed to be in the middle of a crisis. After he left, Richard told me the healing work was driving Allen toward a confrontation.

During the fifteenth session, Allen fell asleep for a few minutes. When he opened his eyes, color rushed into his face. "I feel better," he said. "Something lifted. A cloud."

At the end of the session Allen talked. "I thought I was going crazy," he said. "My marriage has been falling apart. I have a very responsible position at work, but in the last year I've become privy to some information. I'm king of the hill in my area, and I control what's going on. I can't give you details. They all like me. They put things in front of me, on my plate, that would benefit me to accept. I accepted these things. I went along. My future was looking very good. Unlimited, really. I was a fair-haired boy. I guess other people just live with that."

"Live with what?" Richard asked.

"With having more and more authority," Allen said. "In one way you love it, but then I began feeling hollow. I should have felt just the opposite, you know? I should have been overjoyed. I was on a road straight to the top. Other people take that in stride. I thought I was built like them, but I'm not. In these sessions, I'm starting to feel another part of myself. It's been very uncomfortable, like crawling through a tunnel. But now I think I'm getting somewhere ..."

Later, over lunch, Richard told me he believed Allen had been "one of those power people who was ready to live his whole life off the sensation of control. It was as if he had been born to do that, and then he found out, much to his horror, that it made him feel like nothing."

The next time I saw Allen he had had forty sessions from Richard. He looked much healthier. During his appointment, he dozed for a few minutes on the table.

Afterwards, he said he had "visited" an incredible sector

of a city under construction. The materials and the machines were totally unfamiliar to him. Like Ralph, he used the word "relief."

"It was such a relief to see this place," he said. "I have no idea why. It's as if something was keeping me away from there. Maybe I was keeping myself walled in. I'm traveling a lot more in these last few sessions. You know, it gives me a sense of freedom, when I come back from these quick little excursions, as if I've taken off a rope."

When Allen left, Richard got out a pad and jotted down a few notes. "Allen has been talking to me about power," he said. "Very interesting. He says he had been groomed, almost from birth, to accept a position of authority. He came from an upper-crust family around Boston. The idea was, he would accept all the good fortune that flowed to him graciously. It would be smooth sailing. Everything was geared to the idea of taking success with grace, because that would make other people around him feel less jealous or upset when he passed them by. Then, when he grew up and started working, the payoffs to all that preparation began to arrive. He liked it for awhile. Who wouldn't? But to his horror, the whole thing began to turn him sour. I guess there are some slippery activities going on at the State Department, and he's been playing the game, turning his eyes away from it. He found out he had a conscience, and also he just didn't get a charge out of his destiny. I think it bores him. He has power of a kind, but it isn't really exciting. He's finally getting through that shell of nothing that surrounds him, and real energy is definitely showing up. So he's beginning to get the idea that he can replace one type of energy with another one that's much more real. So real he can taste it. He told me that if he'd known, at the beginning of our sessions, that this was going to be the direction things would take, he probably wouldn't have shown up. You don't come across too many people like him. Most of them just glide through life and become sipping alcoholics. They're sophisticated. They're a bottle with a vacuum in it, instead of a bottle with blue lightning. But Allen is in transition. He's finding life in himself he never knew he had. It's very vital. It never goes away, it's just covered up. When you think about the fact that whole nations are run by people like him, you can see why we're in the mess we're in. Part of their power, a major part, is to really feel nothing. That means they can commit crimes at a distance, and think, so what? With a little practice, Allen might have gone the whole distance and become a sadist. Some of them do. It's good that he's out of that. He's getting a real taste of freedom ..."

Several weeks later, Allen, Richard and I had supper together in a little restaurant near the UN building. Afterwards, we walked over to Grand Central Station. Allen told us he had "been on the scene" at the end of the War when numbers of Nazi scientists started coming into the United States.

"They were dispersed into different projects and agencies," he said. "But there was no animosity on the part of our government at all. Everything was chummy. A few of us were amazed at the parade. We knew it was all strategic, and we were trying to get better Nazi researchers than the Russians, but still, I thought it was insane. The feeling of it was insane.

"The Nazis got out of Europe with a tremendous amount of money. Gold, jewels. We felt the Vatican paved the way for their escape. These are lots of murderers I'm talking about, mass murderers, SS people ..."

Allen looked around at the street. "This sounds so stupid," he said, "but I can feel the air tonight. I'm not made of concrete anymore. At first that scared me, but not now ... I was raised in a cult of indifference. We thought of ourselves as natural aristocracy. People who were a certain type. Descended from kings, I guess. It was never entirely spelled out, but the sense of it was there. We had the lineage. Other people didn't. After all, if I didn't believe that, then other people would have become a problem to me. Who were they? Why were they upset more often, and so on."

"Suppose everybody gets energy," Richard said. "Real power."

"Everybody?"

"Yes."

Allen began to smile. "Why not?" he said.

22

In painting you begin with the idea or feeling of space.
You put masses of color and energy into the space.

The way to take life away from people is to convince them that all life exists in a single space, never outside it. That what they should do is study the space and discover its core pattern — which may be physical or metaphysical or both. They should, more and more, rely on the pattern they are discovering and give their loyalty to it. In this way, you tell them, they'll become illumined to the degree illumination is possible.

Now, when you have done this to people, and when they have bought it, what do they have?

They have a Someone Else who supposedly made the space and they have a Pattern. They can argue among themselves, if they wish, about which of these is superior, but the argument is not going to lead to an open door.

No open door.

This is part of the Formula of the Secret Society, and it has dominated the planet from time immemorial.

23

Near the end of August, 1997, I received a startling phone call from England. The woman on the other end of the line hit the ground running. She said, "This is Carol Schuman. I got your number from Rachel Jenkins. She doesn't want to be part of this. Her life isn't the same since Richard died ... if it's all right with you, I'll tell you some things about Paul."

"Paul Schuman?"

"He was my father."

"Was?"

"He died in 1978, in Jerusalem. He was researching the Dead Sea Scrolls."

"I'm very glad to speak with you," I said. "How old was your father?"

"When he died? Eighty-two."

"I got the idea he was young during the Second World War."

"He was over fifty when the War ended."

I told Carol I didn't know where to start. My mind was racing.

"Well," she said, "I'm sure I only have a part of what you want. My father tried to protect me from certain things. But there's something you need to know about me. When Rachel found me, and we talked, I didn't want to speak with you, or even her. It's not that I don't think my father's work was important. Not at all. But it brought him a great deal of uncertainty. I've been subjected to the effects of that all my life. I'm in the theater. I'm an artist. That's what's important to me. I'll tell you what I know, and then that's it. Then we won't talk anymore."

"Whatever you want to do."

"Good. Let me tell you about the Nazi part first. Then we can get on to the other side of it ..."

I took a breath.

She really wanted to get this out of the way. No preamble, no embroidery. Just one time through and move the hell out.

"My father," she said quickly, "started working against the Nazis in 1934, in Germany. He knew some of the theoreticians, as he liked to call them. These were people who were trying to design the future of the country. They wanted to eliminate the Jews and lots of other people too. It was either enslave or kill. That was their plan. Africa would be put into complete slavery.

"Paul watched Hitler arrest astrologers and psychics and people who worked in the occult. Hitler put them in camps, because he wanted to corner the market on all that. He didn't want to be known by the world as a crazy man who dabbled in black magic.

"Paul wrote letters to people he knew in America and Canada. He told them about Hitler's reliance on the occult. Paul believed Hitler was going to send people to war again. He felt that Hitler viewed his own ongoing leadership of Germany as emerging from an occult base."

Her voice was very smooth, as if she had been over this ground in her mind many times, to prepare a presentation for someone ... and whoever it would be, the torch would be passed and then it would be over for her. I imagined Paul had dragged her to a number of cities and countries over the years, so he could continue his work. Or else he had left the family, and her mother had brought her up. I didn't think she'd delve into that ground.

I asked, "Was your father chased by the Nazis because he was a healer? As you say, Hitler and his people looked into all sorts of occult, esoteric activities, and also psychics, healers. Then he closed the whole area down and had the people arrested."

"From what he told me the answer to that is yes," she said. "At one point early on I think they were trying to find out about him, his work. Then there was a time when everything changed. I believe they wanted to arrest him and we escaped. That may have been why we went to England ... But he was involved in other activities that got the Nazis mad at him.

"In 1934 my father told people that Hitler saw himself as a messiah. In that role he would put the whole world right, genetically, by excluding or destroying a significant percentage of the human race. Paul wrote articles about Hitler being an occult student and tried to have them published, to discredit him in the eyes of other governments, but no one would touch them. Paul went underground in France for awhile. This was just prior to Germany's invasion of Poland. I don't know what he was doing then. We spent most of the war in England. By this time, he said, no one was interested in Hitler's background or his motivation. They just wanted to beat him and end the killing."

I thought about the fact that both the Nazis and the CIA were famous for exploring the areas of occult, psychic, "New Age" activity ...

Carol continued. "My father knew that thousands of war criminals were escaping in 1945 to America and South America. He went to Nuremberg and spoke with several of the American officials who were trying cases, the war criminal cases. He felt that if the prosecutors understood the depths of the SS psyche, for example, their efforts might be more profound. Especially when it came to the German business executives, the top echelon who built the whole war machine for Hitler.

"Between 1945 and 1978, when he died, Paul spent a lot of time accumulating and mailing out information on the activities of Nazi war criminals. He got into conflict with several governments who were employing those people as spies or researchers. He told me that the American people would be horrified if they had a thumb-nail biography of each Nazi their government was employing.

"I can tell you that, during the War, Paul put together a phony cell of psychics. This was in England. I don't know whether he did this under the auspices of the British government, or on his own. The word got out — I believe it was in 1943 — that Mussolini had been kidnapped by an opposition element in Italy. Paul told me he and his friends posed as a Hitler-friendly group, and they began sending messages across the English Channel into a contact in Germany. Hitler needed to find Mussolini to keep the Axis alliance intact, and nobody knew where he was. Paul and his friends pretended to look psychically for Mussolini, and they sent the message over that he was a prisoner in Greece. I don't remember the exact area. They hoped this would cause the Germans to waste time looking in the wrong place. It could have saved lives in Italy. I think they actually got an encouraging word back from Himmler. And then all communication stopped."

"Was Paul interested in the activities of Himmler and his SS people?" I asked.

"Very. The occult goings-on there in the castle were very revealing. Once every year, as you probably know, Himmler and his Inner Circle spent a period of time conjuring — doing occult techniques. They were in total seclusion."

I said, "I've read that the SS periodically sacrificed one of their own. They chopped off his head, and then the head was used to communicate with various disembodied spirits in the East. They tore out cats' eyes too."

"Paul mentioned something like that," she said. "The SS did all sorts of grisly things supposedly on behalf of 'Spirit.' This has been written about. The whole emphasis of their training was to make them immune to violence and horror. The SS was a society separate from the world. They gave up their family names and adopted names from the past. You know, mythical Aryan titles. They took mystical oaths. If they betrayed their Order, or even broke an important rule, they and their family could be murdered. They were the glue that held the whole Nazi Party together. The lunatic monks."

"Except," I said, "they were ordered to procreate liberally with Aryan-type women. At the special breeding farms Hitler set up."

"Throughout the 1930s," Carol said, "all the way up to the time he died, Paul was in touch with an American soldier. I don't know the man's name. One of their topics of discussion was the possibility that some group or several groups had an agenda that involved destroying the United States.

"Paul was convinced that this group was essentially Nazi

in character, and that it was operating on the idea that the best way to take over a country was to reduce it to chaos first, and then move in.

"As far as my father's healing work was concerned, he managed to do that for the last fifty years of his life, but rarely in an organized way. He didn't have an office. Linwood learned a great deal from my father — but the words 'teaching' and 'learning,' as I'm sure Richard has told you, don't have much meaning here. There isn't any system. My father said this to me over and over. He looked at a treatment, or a session, as a kind of theater. The result depended only on your capacity to grasp the essentials of what was going on in yourself. It wasn't so much a matter of discerning the state of the patient. I say patient — I don't believe Americans use the medical terms. Paul knew the problem was in energy or feeling, and he knew he would get to it by expressing what was in him.

"It's a funny thing," Carol continued, "but people close to someone who is gifted in this way often don't respond at all. I mean family in this case. Neither my mother nor I wanted treatments from Paul. Once in a great while, when we agreed to let him work on us, we didn't feel very much happened afterwards. I think resentment was part of the reason we held ourselves back. We thought, well, if he isn't going to act like a regular father and husband, then we'll be damned if we'll reflect anything back to him. A competition set in. We didn't want to be put in the same boat, in his mind, as his other patients. We were supposed to be different, special.

"But I saw people come out of treatments with him totally changed. Not that they were always happy, because he sometimes tapped into very deep things in them, things they wanted to forget. But he didn't care. He went for liberation, as he said. He wanted people to be masters of the universe. That was one of his joking phrases, but he wasn't joking. He said that anybody ought to be able to lift up a house with his mind and move it out into the country and set it down in a nice spot by a stream, and move in.

"He had a mentor, actually two people, a husband and a wife. I never met them. He started with them when he was very young, still in his teens, and I don't think he saw them after he was twenty-five. They were from North Africa. I don't know what city or town. Paul spent several years living with this couple. They all moved to Paris together. He said they never told him what to do with a patient. Of course, many things would come up between the three of them in conversation, and this was very helpful up to a point. At first Paul wanted to meet the mentor of this couple. They told him that wasn't possible, because the man, an ex-Tibetan monk of some kind, from the Kargyupa sect, was traveling in Indonesia. Eventually word came back that he had been in Bali. That's apparently where he died. This man was involved with some Tibetan practice of visualization. His version of it was supposedly a modification of the original. That's all I know about it.

"Paul believed that, in the very distant past, there had been communities where, in various ways, higher consciousness was pursued completely apart from any religion or doctrine of metaphysics. Spontaneous healing was an aspect of an entire spectrum of advancing human powers."

"What do you mean, advancing powers?" I asked.

"Paul used that phrase. He meant projecting a thought to another person, being able to move matter with the mind alone, the creation of matter, the ability to travel in many spaces without a physical body, but instead an energy body. All of that and more."

"And," I said, "he believed there was a continuous historical tradition of advancing powers, a tradition that had nothing to do with religion?"

"It's hard to say, about the tradition part. Sometimes he thought that way."

"It's not in the history books," I said.

"No."

"Perhaps there's a thread of inspiration that would tie all these people and communities together, down through time."

"You mean an idea like a messiah?" she said sarcastically.

"I mean a principle of some kind that doesn't bind people."

"That liberates them."

"Yes."

"The idea has occurred to me," she said.

"Did your father ever suggest something like that?"

"No. But he said there had to have been communities of creators."

"That was the exact phrase?"

"Yes. He gave an example. He mentioned the original Taoists, whoever they might have been, and then he said something even more curious. A community of people who put on the Greek tragedies. The original community."

"He had been researching this himself?"

"I suppose so. I don't really know."

"You said he was looking into the Dead Sea Scrolls."

"Yes, when he died. He never told me much about that. I remember he was involved with what he called Cave 4 documents. That's a designation the scholars use to distinguish various sets of materials. Of course, Paul was also researching other things in those years, not just the Scrolls. He read works by Giordano Bruno, for example."

"Was he specific about the Scrolls?"

"He said he was interested in the problem of the messiah. Don't ask me what he meant."

"You know, " I said, "you may be the last person I ever talk to who can give me clues to the tradition, if there is one."

"Well," she said, "my father did some amazing things as far as healing was concerned. I want you to understand that. I know a woman who was able to move an object with her mind for a few minutes after he treated her. Looking at a bracelet on a table, and it slides all the way across and falls off the edge."

"Did your father have any of those abilities?"

"Not that I'm aware of, except his ability to trigger the healing process. Although he wasn't aiming at cures, people who had been treated by him were known to have lost diseases. One patient of my father, a medical doctor, a psychiatrist, had an interesting experience after a healing treatment. He went to see a schizophrenic man at a local asylum. On the way over to the hospital, on a whim, he went into a shop and bought a clear glass marble, a large one. At the hospital, he sat down and held up the marble and told the patient to look at it. Call it force of will, or whatever you want, but the patient looked at that marble and in a few minutes he became functional. Not sane, but able to function. There was no logic to it. A month later the patient left the hospital. The psychiatrist kept telling my father about it. My father said the psychiatrist had just taken his first step toward becoming a healer, but it was obvious he would never go any further, because of his fear of jumping into unfamiliar territory. 'But you see,' my father said, 'this is how the relationship starts. If this were to progress any further, I would see this psychiatrist once a week and we would talk. He'd tell me about his own healing work with others, and I would tell him a little about my own. Gradually this would develop into a friendship, and we would feed each other. We wouldn't recommend technique, we would just talk. Things would come up, a kind of learning would take place, but not in a step one step two fashion. Not at all.'"

"Yes," I said. "I know what you mean."

"It sounds like Zen," Carol said, "but historically Zen became codified."

"Did your father work with many medical doctors?"

"No," she said. "He saw a great many artists. Poor ones, unfortunately."

"Did he ever talk about his own tradition versus the tradition of groups like the Nazis?"

"Yes, of course. It was hard to ignore. There is a history of trying to take from people what is innate to them, and there is the unknown tradition of trying to restore to people what they have forgotten is theirs."

"Is that your father's thought or your own?"

"We share it."

"You two probably share a great deal."

I kept her on the line for another minute or so, and then she said she had to go.

"Nothing else you can tell me? There's so much more. I want to hear about some of his other patients."

"No," she said. "All I can do is wish you luck ..."

24

The conversation with Carol Schuman, daughter and somewhat reluctant messenger of Paul Schuman, left me with a great many ideas.

I made a list of potential avenues I could explore.

1. Paul's two mentors — North Africa, Paris.
2. The Tibetan monk — Bali.
3. Communities of evolving consciousness.
4. Communities of creators.
5. Original Taoists.
6. Greek tragedians.
7. Dead Sea Scrolls — Cave 4 documents.

The first two items would take me on a straight line back into the past beyond Paul Schuman, but since all three people involved had to be dead, that was no road.

Communities of evolving consciousness and communities of creators ... In an initial search of various library sources I found nothing that impressed me. In fact, anytime I verged on thinking I'd discovered a past group of artists who had a bent for healing or "consciousness," they turned out to be organized around some mystical sect or cosmology that was drastically limited — full of magic symbols which might inject rich allusions into poetry, but bereft of real direction.

I had a feeling I wasn't looking at some of these groups in the right way. Maybe I was missing something.

The "founding fathers" of Taoism was a myth that was impenetrable. That was because the essence of Taoism was no-system. Philosophic structures, Taoists would say, came long after people had lost the instinct for following the natural Way of Living. That Way had no code of behavior. It was just the Tao.

Perhaps Paul Schuman simply saw an affinity between Taoism and his own inclinations about healing.

The idea of a community of Greek tragedians — say, 5th century BC — did not show up from my research. The original performances of Sophocles, Euripides, and Aeschylus were done by local amateurs. I attempted to discover whether the language of those plays was sufficiently different from common speech of the day to be considered esoteric. In that case, perhaps a community of people had grown up around that. I discovered that although the language of tragedy was elevated and artificial, and although the chorus sang and danced their lines in a kind of meter, the uneducated audience had no trouble understanding what was presented.

That left Carol's reference to the Cave 4 documents of the Dead Sea Scrolls.

I then added several more items out of Carol's conversation to my notes: Giordano Bruno; Tibetan Buddhism; and advanced powers. Next to the last item I wrote "paranormal," a more modern term.

Of course, there were hundreds of ways to connect these subjects.

Bruno was himself an ex-monk — sixteenth-century — who defied the Catholic Church and its rigid views. He wandered about Europe, preaching a sometimes-lucid form of mysticism, and a surprisingly modern astrophysics.

Tibetan Buddhism was, in several ways, a spiritual philosophy different from all others on the planet. I made a note to read a long out-of-print book on the subject by John Blofeld, a book I had browsed in the early 1960s in Los Angeles.

The paranormal was a subject as broad as the sky. And Paul Schuman's interest in it was not hard to infer, if he had seen it demonstrated in his patients from time to time.

I decided on an open approach: accumulate information on Bruno, Tibetan Buddhism, the Dead Sea Scrolls' Cave 4 documents, and "the paranormal," without going overboard. I would hopefully see a way of narrowing down things.

25

At this point, as I launch into research on Paul Schuman's "clues," I want to assure the reader that I will try to tie them together. There is an unknown amount of work to follow down each possible trail left by Schuman, and at least several chapters will take them up. This is all for trying to understand what may be a hidden tradition in human history. A tradition which includes, but is larger than, the kind of healing I have been discussing.

If such a tradition exists, is it concealed inside an ancient civilization, in caves, or is it invisible because past events which seem to us unrelated would, if properly seen, suddenly join and produce a new awareness?

If such a tradition exists, how does it contrast to the modus operandi of secret societies?

These are the questions I'm going after.

I won't try to give a blow-by-blow, book-by-book account of my trip through each Schuman topic. I'll more or less bring forward the sets of results en masse.

26

The Dead Sea Scrolls

Between 150 BCE and 70 CE, a sect called the Essenes lived "in the wilderness" at the western shore of the Dead Sea, eight miles from Jericho.

This community thought of its numbers as representatives, students, and preservers of true Judaism, as opposed to the "heretical" reigning priests in the Jerusalem temple.

Consisting of no more than 200 members at any one time, the Essenes had, as their overt goal, the seeking of God. Members "... were to love one another and to share with one another their 'knowledge, powers, and possessions' ... They were to be scrupulous in their observances of the times appointed for prayer, and for every other event of a liturgical existence ..."

In 1947, a Bedouin boy happened upon Aramaic and Hebrew manuscripts hidden in a cave by the Essenes, possibly shortly before the community's destruction by Roman soldiers in the summer of 68 CE.

Several scandals have come to light concerning modern scholars' handling of, and access to, these voluminous Dead Sea Scrolls, which, as it turned out, have been found in eleven caves.

Reading the English translation of the Scrolls, you are struck by the fact that the Essenes were a sect dedicated to obedience to law. Scroll documents allude to behaviors as necessary — or unacceptable. The sect's membership standards, its daily life and practices, its handling of transgressions and expulsion were all to be broken down into regulations and followed to the letter. The rules were of great specific concern to members.

In fact, one could say that the mural created by the Essenes was a detailed moral universe, and only in that context would they allow members to seek God on a long-term basis.

God's central and exclusive (and swaggering) position in the firmament-mural is clearly indicated in a Cave 4 document, *The Song of Michael and the Just:*

> ... a throne of strength in the congregation of 'gods' so that not a single king of old shall sit on it, neither shall their noble men ... my glory is incomparable, and apart from me none is exalted. None shall come to me for I dwell ... in heaven ... who is comparable to me in my glory? ... And who can deal with the issue [statements] of my lips?

Another Cave 4 document, called *The Wicked and the Holy,* goes further in delineating the boundaries of the Essenes' universe:

> In accordance with the mercies of God, according to His goodness and wonderful glory, He caused some of the sons of the world to draw near (Him) ... to be counted with Him in the com[munity of the 'g]ods' as a congregation of holiness in service for eternal life and (sharing) the lot of His holy ones ... each man according to his lot which He has cast ... for eternal life ...

Of course there are those who are inspired by such words. I readily admit that to me, beyond their poetry, they sound like a prescription for bondage carried out over a never-ending period. Would one necessarily want a God to "cause" or magnetize him, like an iron filing, to come near and serve Him forever? I gauchely prefer a document called *The Declaration of Independence* — because it has a little line in it about the right to the pursuit of happiness, an individual choice which is, by implication, changeable — without the fear of ostracism or rejection. The Essenes demanded a severe group-shunning of members who overtly turned away from the path of the group's God.

The Cave 4 document designated 4Q286-7, titled *Curses of Satan And His Lot,* sculpts the to-be-avoided evil wrinkle in the moral space invented by this community: "[... Be cursed, Ang]el of Perdition and Spir[it of Dest]ruction ... [and] may you be [da]mned ... Amen, am[en].

"[Cursed be a]ll those who practi[se] their [wicked designs] and establish [in their heart] your (evil) devices, [plotting against Go]d'[s Covenant] ..."

Metaphysical light vs. dark. Superstructure good vs. evil. Consider the authors of these Scrolls as artists and see what they are inventing — in which invention sect-members will dedicatedly live their lives. Consider that. Although good vs. evil of course has its counterparts in real life, the creative polarizing, to an extreme, of these concepts is an invitation to tyranny, to elitism, to internal spying and paranoia, to mountains of rules.

What a community like the Essenes does — regardless of how much good it performs — is define a painting for people to inhabit. Then it states that Someone Else runs the painting. Then it implies that the painting contains a pattern to be plumbed and understood — which takes a great deal of effort. In this case the pattern is a moral good-and-evil fabric which is inextricably woven into the "canvas" — and prescribes rigid behaviors, as well as suppression of deviation from the rules of the group.

Again, regardless of how much good the group does, it does no business with individual power and freedom. Those are foreign notions.

The Cave 4 document designated 4Q521, titled *A Messianic Apocalypse,* begins to flesh out the traditional deeds of a messiah, after it asserts with aggrandizing force that "..... [the hea]vens and the earth will listen to His Messiah, and none therein will stray from the commandments of the holy ones."

What are some of the traditional acts of the messiah? He "restores sight to the blind, straightens the b[ent] ... will heal the wounded, and revive the dead ...."

In another age, would Paul Schuman call these, with more than superficial intent, "advanced powers?"

Internationally respected Biblical scholar Dr. James Tabor, in a 1991 video lecture on the Dead Sea Scrolls, explored the notion of the messiah and the actions which signaled that he "was the One the world was waiting for."

Without necessarily concluding that the Essenes gave birth to the person now known as Jesus, Tabor discusses three secret scrolls from Cave 4 which were assigned to the Catholic scholar Abbe Jean Starcky for translation. These scrolls, Tabor states, have, in certain respects, very close resemblance to Biblical texts — namely Isaiah 35 and 61 and Luke 4.

The subject? The coming of the messiah. There are clearly tests which must be passed if a man is to be elevated to this supreme status. When Jesus is questioned by disciples sent to him by John the Baptist — when he is asked, "Are you the One?" — Jesus summarizes what he has done. He says the blind have received sight, the dead are raised, the lame walk, the lepers are cleansed, and the deaf hear. As Tabor points out, this reply is "coded" language, which will be well understood by John, and which will indicate that Jesus — or in the Scrolls, an Essene Teacher — has passed the test to become a messiah.

The fact that such tests are mentioned in both the Bible and the Dead Sea Scrolls naturally brings up the question of "the Essene Jesus." That issue has been debated on several grounds by scholars and religionists. My reading of this debate reveals no clear-cut answer to the question of whether Jesus was an Essene. However, it does raise fascinating points. Were there at least two different men, historically, who would be assessed as potential messiahs on the same standards? Was there, in fact, a tradition of messiahship in which the production of miracles was the keystone?

Was this what Paul Schuman was interested in? Is this why he had studied the issue of the messiah in the Cave 4 documents? Because "paranormal miracles" were key factors?

Given what his daughter said, it makes good sense to me.

27

The Paranormal: Advanced Powers

Several thousand books have been written about it. It covers wide, wide spectra of human action and experience. People make claims for it on television magazine shows. Print magazines devote themselves to a monthly exploration of it.

What about a scientific analysis of the paranormal field? How much has really been done?

Margins of Reality is an enormously important book by Robert Jahn and Brenda Dunne. Jahn is Professor of Aerospace Science and Dean Emeritus of the School of Engineering and Applied Science at Princeton University. Brenda Dunne is manager of the Princeton Engineering Anomalies Research laboratory.

The book discusses their controlled studies which examine the direct influence of consciousness on matter.

"Some of these experiments," the authors state, "study the interaction of human operators with various technical devices and systems. Others concern the acquisition of information about remote geographical targets inaccessible by known sensory channels."

Jahn and Dunne's trials show that, beyond any possible random variation, the mechanical operation of a machine can be influenced by the intent of the operator. A kind of "Dalton's desk," as it is called, was employed in one series of experiments. This device allows 9000 small plastic balls to cascade down from an entrance funnel into bins formed by a tight display of 330 nylon pegs.

Operators sat eight feet from this device, and attempted "to distort [the random range of] the distribution of balls in the bins toward the right ... or to the left [of center] ..."

The conclusion? The authors state, "At this writing, 22 operators have completed a total of 76 experimental series ... Of these, 8 operators, or 36%, have generated significant overall data bases ..." A significant overall data base would mean the distribution of the falling plastic balls distorted the known random range, and also matched the stated intention (*e.g.,* overload left of center or right of center) of the operator.

This is, as Dunne and Jahn would say, anomalous. Beyond random results. It indicates the direct effect of consciousness on matter.

More extraordinary than this result is the outcome of attempting to measure "operator signatures." Using three very different types of random-generating devices — cascading balls, a flow of electrons, and digital generation — two operators revealed that their graphs of performance maintained a pattern of similarity from one device to another. The degree and tempo, so to speak, of their ability to distort the random physical world showed a consistency over the range of these very different kinds of equipment.

Jahn and Dunne state that operators used various approaches.

Some operators self-impose preliminary meditation exercises, employ visualization techniques, or attempt to identify with the device or process in some transpersonal context. Others invoke competitive strategies, attempting to outperform other operators, their own earlier results, or simply the laws of chance ...

If there is any unity in this diversity of strategy, it would be that most effective operators seem to associate successful performance with the attainment of some sense of 'resonance' with the device.

For example, one operator states,

I don't feel any direct control over the device, more like a marginal influence when I'm in resonance with the machine. It's like being in a canoe; when it goes where I want, I flow with it. When it doesn't, I try to break the flow and give it a chance to get back in resonance with me.

The feeling of resonance was very familiar to me. It happened every time a person had been on my table and I had done a healing session. Richard has said that, for him, there was a potentially infinite number of "melodies" in that respect. The two most obvious were: He could simply resonate with the overall energy of the person; or he could introduce a new energy which would result in the person expanding his energy-reach. In either case, a kind of integration (healing) would occur.

28

Further experiments undertaken by Dunne and Jahn involved what they call RPR: Remote Precognitive Perception. This tests the ability of a person to identify a geographical target at a distance before another pre-selected person shows up at that scene. Of course, the geo-target is adequately concealed from the "remote perceiver."

To avoid obtaining only anecdotal results, Jahn and Dunne constructed a rather complex mathematical model, so that they could determine performance above and below a set norm. Acknowledging that this type of experiment offers challenges to scientists seeking quantitative certainty, Dunne and Jahn nevertheless conclude, from their work:

> Using ... [our] experimental protocols and analytical scoring methods ... individual percipients [remote perceivers] can acquire statistically significant information about spatially and temporally remote target locations by means currently inexplicable by known physical mechanisms.

In fact, some of the most convincing results Dunne and Jahn obtained were in cases where the perceiver misread an element of the remote target in a startling way.

For example, parts of a Saturn rocket at NASA, in Houston, were chosen as a remote target. The pre-selected person, or agent, went to that location in Houston. (In all experiments an agent was used, because he might provide a "beacon" the perceiver could lock onto.) The perceiver totally missed the chosen target. Instead of remotely perceiving the Saturn rocket from his location in Princeton, New Jersey, he saw a scene in which the agent was playing on the floor with a group of puppies.

It turned out that "Later that evening," write Jahn and Dunne, "before learning any details of the [perceiver's incorrect remote] perception, the agent visited a friend's home where he played at length with a litter of newborn pups, one of which he was prompted to purchase."

Again, the remote perceiver "saw" this before the agent met the puppies.

To my surprise, I've discovered that supplies of reliable experiments in paranormal areas are large, the results are clear, and the extent of confirmation and replication of the research is formidable. Unfortunately, no ongoing currents of "news" have been fashioned out of these results. The experiments are generally treated by the press as quirky, unverifiable happenings, at best suitable for program-filler on slow days.

Who knows what would happen if even 5% of the cumulative evidence of paranormal occurrences were alive and well out in the minds of the general populace? By a kind of contagion based on acceptance and a growing confidence, we might see, before our eyes, a large upsurge in paranormal achievements — an evolutionary step. Of course, in that case, a great deal of nonsensical "knowledge" about humanity would have to go on the junk-heap of history — especially if the range of paranormal occurrences were not just percolating in a small elite — but at every level of society.

29

With a background at Princeton and the Stanford Research Institute, Dean Radin has also been Director of the Consciousness Research Laboratory at the University of Nevada, Las Vegas. He has worked for Bell Labs and Contel. His recent book, *The Conscious Universe: The Scientific Truth of Psychic Phenomena*, provides a truly remarkable overview of accomplished results reported in paranormal research.

Radin leaves no doubt that the paranormal has already been proven to exist by the most conservative experimental methods, and that the delay in public acceptance is largely due to a skewing of facts in the press and in certain halls of academia.

The "ganzfeld" technique is a method to test telepathy. The so-called sender is absolutely isolated, by experimental design, from the receiver. What is sent telepathically is usually an image. The image may be selected, for example, by the sender from a pack of photos.

After the sending period is over the receiver is shown the pack of photos. The receiver then ranks the photos in degree of resemblance to his impressions during the sending phase. If the receiver ranks the actual telepathically sent photo "number 1," the session is scored a hit. Any other outcome is considered a miss.

Details of experimental design have been modified over the years by various researchers. Attempts have been made to upgrade the ganzfeld approach through better scoring methods, more certain isolation of sender from receiver, and blinding of any intermediaries who might unconsciously (or intentionally) tip off the receiver about what was sent to him.

Radin offers a number of examples of hits. For instance, from the work of well-known researcher Charles Honorton, a 1990 experiment — in which video footage of a suspension bridge collapsing into water was telepathically sent to the receiver — yielded the receiver's following impression, recorded during the sending period:

> "... Something, some vertical object bending or sway-ing ... Almost like a ladder-like bridge over some kind of chasm ... it's coming down ..."

Honorton, in 1982, presented a paper at a national Para-psychological Association meeting "summarizing the results of all known ganzfeld experiments to that date." Honorton concluded that the weight of the evidence was clearly on the side of accepting telepathy as a real occurrence.

Psychologist and confirmed skeptic Ray Hyman[1] took issue with Honorton, and both men agreed to do meta-analyses of the history of the scientific ganzfeld literature.

Their opposing views were published in 1985.

Subsequently, Hyman admitted that, on 28 studies which showed hit rates at all, the percentage of hits, collectively, was remarkable. But Hyman wasn't ready to concede that the explanation was actual telepathy.

What ensued was a professional debate between Honorton and Hyman. It spanned the next six years. During this time, upgrades were made in the experimental ganzfeld design: Computers were introduced to automate procedures; video players recorded the pools of image-messages which the sender would choose from; and electromagnetic shielding was introduced to further isolate the receiver from accidental or deliberate "message-leaks."

By 1991, new computerized "autoganzfeld" studies had been run. The research literature showed 354 sessions, using

---

[1] I'm told Hyman has subsequently given both grudging acknowl-edgments and outright denials of "anomalous" (paranormal) results on studies of psychic phenomena. If this is so, I myself can't discern a pattern of logic in Hyman's reactions.

240 men and women, in eleven separate studies. The overall hit rate for the eleven studies was 34%. This remarkable outcome was about the same as the total hit-rate calculated by Honorton and Hyman in their 1985 meta-analyses of the entire ganzfeld literature up to that time.

Hyman published a statement in which he called these new results "intriguing." He then asked for further work from "independent laboratories."

Dean Radin summarizes just such ganzfeld research from 1991 to 1997, carried out by seven separate researchers. He concludes that "each of the six replication studies ... resulted in point estimates [significantly] greater than chance [could account for]."

Looking at the history of the ganzfeld research literature from 1974 to 1997, which encompasses 2,549 experimental sending-sessions, reported in over forty journals, Radin concludes that initial positive results have been replicated over and over.

"Psi [telepathic] effects do occur in the ganzfeld," Radin writes.

Radin proceeds to examine the complete allied research field of perception at a distance.

From the 1889 "ESP cards" of French Nobel laureate Charles Richet, to the huge body of work of researcher J.B. Rhine, and beyond, Radin reports on experiments in "guessing" concealed cards.

By the 1940s, Radin writes, "142 published articles described 3.6 million individual trials [at guessing the faces of carefully concealed cards] generated by some 4,600 percipients in 185 separate experiments."

Radin states that in the most tightly controlled of these experiments, the hit-rate of accurate guesses was significantly above chance. He quotes a statement reacting to these and related studies from the chairman of the Department of Psychology at the University of London, H.J. Eysenck (1957):

Unless there is a gigantic conspiracy involving some thirty University departments all over the world, and several hundred highly respected scientists in various fields, many of them originally hostile to the claims of the psychical researchers, the only conclusion the unbiased observer can come to must be that there does exist a small number of people who obtain knowledge existing either in other people's minds, or in the outer world, by means as yet unknown to science.

Radin reviews what have popularly been called remote-viewing experiments, carried out with $20 million from agencies of the U.S. government, between 1972 and 1994 at Stanford Research Institute and at SAIC (Science Applications International Corporation).

Radin confirms that results in psychically locating and describing secretly selected geographical targets have been successful. He cites a government report issued on SAIC remote viewing studies done between 1989 and 1993. An oversight committee, which included statistics experts, a Nobel prize-winning physicist, and an Army major general, concluded that remote viewing ability is quite real.

Even Ray Hyman, the dyed-in-the-wool skeptic on ganzfeld experiments for six years, stated, "I agree ... that the effect sizes reported in the SAIC experiments probably cannot be dismissed as due to chance ... So, I accept Professor Utt's assertion that the statistical results of the SAIC and other para-psychologists' experiments 'are far beyond what is expected by chance.'"

Radin goes on to examine the history of mind-matter interaction research, concluding that "After sixty years of experiments using tossed dice and their modern progeny, electronic RNGs [random number generators], researchers have produced persuasive, consistent replicated evidence that mental intention is associated with the behavior of these physical systems."

What about "mental interactions with living organisms?" Radin recounts three separate studies done between 1962 and 1972, in which researchers in New Jersey, France, and the Netherlands "all observed significant changes in receivers' finger blood volume when a sender, located sometimes thousands of miles away, directed [stimulating or calming] emotional thoughts toward them."

Psychologist William Braud is credited with having accumulated the "largest systematic body of experiments" in this area. His work of seventeen years at the Mind Science Foundation in San Antonio, Texas, consisted of 37 experiments (655 sessions) using 602 people and animals, run by 13 researchers. "The thirty-seven experiments combined," Radin summarizes, "resulted in odds against chance of more than a hundred trillion to one. Fifty-seven percent of the experiments were independently significant ... where 5 percent would be expected by chance."

These experiments involved separated senders and receivers, with the receiver hooked up to a monitor that continuously measured skin conductivity — "electrodermal activity." Such activity is associated with unconscious changes in emotion. The sender, at randomly chosen moments, was told to think about the receiver with one of two motives: to emotionally arouse or calm him. The results of such attempts are measured by electrodermal fluctuations.

Clearly, the positive statistical results of these studies show that contact, through thought, is being made between human beings at a distance.

Radin concludes, "The [positive] implications for distant healing are clear."

Although Paul Schuman was obviously not alive during the period of much of this research, he might have been aware of some earlier forerunners of it. Regardless, I felt certain that the sorts of results which I have been discussing were part of what was on his mind as he considered "advanced powers."

Suppose, when he read Cave 4 documents of the Dead Sea Scrolls, he was in fact seeing the so-called miracle tests for a messiah in conjunction with this arena of paranormal activity.

That was reasonable. Of course, such a crossover similarity has been pointed out before. But for a man immersed in healing, it can pique the interest in a compelling way. For example, Paul may have begun to conclude that many different manifestations of the paranormal — of which healing is one — were connected by common threads. Threads of awareness, of attuning to events and people, of imagination, of desire to surmount ordinary experience.

In that case, he could have thought that new universes were just over the horizon for him. After all, if he had already found one zone, healing, why wouldn't other zones become accessible to him?

And if he could expand in that way, perhaps many, many other people could, too.

30

Giordano Bruno

I continued my exploration of the clues Carol Schuman had left me about her father Paul.

I was, of course, aware that I was operating on supposition. But ... why not? When that's the door that is presented, walk through it.

Carol mentioned that Paul had an interest in Giordano Bruno, the 16th-century ex-monk who had left his position with the Catholic Church and taken to the road, so to speak. Teacher, philosopher, poet, dramatist, and outspoken critic of "limitations of thought," Bruno traveled all over Europe fearlessly spreading his ideas, in various venues, until his arrest by the Church for heresy.

Bruno's works are not easy to tackle. But you always feel you are on the edge of discovery, and gems are planted along the way.

He is a revolutionary thinker who straddles several realms. One of his masterworks, *On the Infinite Universe and Worlds* (1584), stretches the imagination as God, the individual, the infinite, the universe, planets, space and time are all thrown into a cosmic soup — just as they are, almost at the same time, subjected to close analysis to determine their exact meanings and relationships.

Bruno's simultaneous approaches tend to make the mind of the student ricochet like a ball bearing in a pinball machine.

What would Paul Schuman have seen, or reacted to, in this?

I was very taken by Carol's reference to her father's healing sessions as a kind of improvisational theater.

Such reliance on one's own resources as a healer — or as an artist — would have enormous personal consequences. In such a state of mind, rigid concepts tend to melt down and flow as usable energy. There is a sense of that in Bruno's writing. A capacity to gather in energy-strips of the cosmos and sift them, make large sudden leaps of vision, turn set-pieces of traditional Church metaphysics on their heads.

In *Giordano Bruno: His Life and Thought*, author Dorothea Waley Singer traces a line of influence through Bruno back to "the philosophers of Islamic Spain." The effect of this unheralded tradition was the revolutionizing of European thought on the basic image of the cosmos.

Singer: "... the earth no longer formed the summit of a hierarchy. The universe itself came to be regarded as a continuum rather than as a hierarchy."

This staggeringly modern idea, which through Bruno began to take hold in Europe at the end of the 16th century, implied that energy could transfer or broadcast its essence through space in any direction without impedance, without coming across ideological check-points or central ruling barriers that were set up by Divinity.

If healing is a transference of energy — and one kind of it certainly can be that — Bruno would be illustrating that the medium of space is extremely cordial to its progression.

In his seminal work, *De magia*, Bruno enunciates what could be taken to be a maxim of paranormal ability:

> Thus it is that [the individual soul] doth apprehend most distant species, in an instant and without motion ... The power of each soul is itself somehow present afar in the universe ... Therefore certain impediments being removed, suddenly and at once it [the individual soul] hath present to it the most remote species which are not joined to it by motion.

Whether one takes healing and the sending of energy as events in wave-physics or as "instantaneous arrivals" at distant points, Bruno has described the phenomenon and affirmed it. Not only that, he also depicts the "traveling" aspect of healing in which a person instantly connects to places/images/happenings from another mysterious place.

Bruno bypasses the pre-defined universe of Catholicism, with its hierarchy of priests and saints and divine, judging entities. The Church of Rome hated him for it. Bruno was called an atheist by the Inquisition at Rome, which insisted on taking over his case from the Inquisition at Venice, where he had originally been arrested.

Bruno's writing is saturated with references to spiritual essence cloaked in various names. To call him an atheist is like labeling Einstein nothing but a hard-headed mathematician.

But the Church was reeling from the unexpected exposure to a mind — Bruno's — that suddenly cast off limits like petty housekeeping duties. Such duties of the Church consisted of relentlessly creating a universe replete with rules, named entities in full dress, and human sin that must beg for redemption.

Like any good cult, the Church had painted a space, had said it was run by Someone Else, and had conjured an intrinsic pattern embedded in the space. In a lifetime, with a great deal of work, one might understand and appease this complex pattern by relying on its link to the divine — called a priest.

The alternative to this devotion was an eternity in fire and lakes of feces.

Bruno, again in *De magia*, beautifully, and with great generosity, depicts the idea of resonance, which I've alluded to above as a feature of healing and paranormal sensing:

> Thus since the soul of the individual is continuous with the soul of the universe, it is not impossible that it may be carried to bodies which do not interpenetate with it ... as if innumerable lamps are lit and together give the effect of one light, nor doth the one light impede or weaken or exclude the other.
>
> Similarly when many voices are diffused throughout the same space, even as with light rays. Or as we say popularly, the rays are spread out to receive the same visible whole, where all penetrate the same

medium, some in straight lines and some obliquely, yet they do not on that account interfere one with another; so the innumerable spirits and souls diffused through the same space interfere not at all with one another, nor doth the diffusion of one impede the diffusion of the infinity of others.

The imagery of this joyous, if slightly vague, piece of ontology caused a huge reaction in the Church — for its omissions. Bruno's animated universe is not about guilt. He makes no pronouncement of authority, as in Who runs cosmic space? He places no one in hierarchical relation to another. Bruno in fact clears the decks for the non-denominational triumph of the human spirit. At once mystical and lucid, Bruno applauds Reality as he finds it. He refuses to build into the universe an absolute need for human redemption sought through the channel of a single sacrificial lamb.

Though Bruno could have become bogged down and vague in a metaphysic of interconnected souls, he also shocks us as he springs out in Whitmanesque glorification of the individual — long before it was physically safe to be moved by such feelings and visions:

"Henceforth I spread confident wings to space; I fear no barrier of crystal or of glass; I cleave the heavens and soar to the infinite. And while I rise from my own globe to others/ And penetrate ever further through the eternal field, That which others saw from afar, I leave far behind me."

At the end of *The Five Dialogues Concerning the Infinite Universe and Worlds*, Bruno has Albertino ask for a fresh reinterpretation of the cosmos. If we understand that he is uttering these words at a time when the Earth-Heaven space authored by the Church of Rome was a closed issue, when individual freedom and power were potential clues to heresy, we can perhaps begin to taste Bruno's courage:

Open wide to us the gate through which we may perceive the likeness of our own and of all other stars. Demonstrate to us that the substance of the other worlds throughout the ether is even as that of our own world. Make us clearly perceive that the motion of all of them proceedeth from [the impulse of] the inward soul: to the end that illumined by such contemplation we may proceed with surer steps toward a knowledge of nature.

Bruno seems to verge on saying that each one of us, as a soul, animates the universe.

That would not only clear the deck of so-called rulers and gods and various invented watchdogs who claim to dominate the infinite (for our own good), it would suggest the potential for retraction, as it were, of the whole physical universe into the individual soul.

Bruno comes close to turning upside down the entire formula of the secret society and exposing it for what it generically is: self-appointed insiders who define a universe, manufacture its ultimate content and administer it.

In this exposé , Bruno is an unlikely ally with a tradition which was walled off from Europe in the 16th century, the mysticism of Tibetan Buddhism.

For his trouble, his wisdom, his great spirit and his poetry, Bruno was stripped naked, tied to a stake, and taken to the Square of Flowers in Rome on Saturday, February 19, 1600, where the Church burned him alive.

31

Mystical Tibetan Buddhism

Is there a clue to "a hidden tradition" in the environment of Bruno's time?

Forces on the planet which, sooner or later, are seen to be repressive follow a pattern.

It is one thing to celebrate a felt God with inspired art, with frescoes on the walls of churches throughout Italy.

The artists themselves come to be recognized as creative forces. But when their work, their adornments, are used as mesmerizing emblems within the universe of the Holy Catholic Church, which Church has set itself up as the Earthly arbiter of all matters spiritual and moral ...

Of course, no period of civilization presents this dual aspect of human life more sharply than the Italian Renaissance. Da Vinci, Michelangelo, Piero, Raphael — their use by Holy Rome to "televise" images of the Church's spiritual world to the people was brilliant. At least from the point of view of men who wanted to control the minds of human beings all over the world. At the same time, secular patrons were so anxious to commission works by the great artists of the time that, gradually, the personal stature of these painters and sculptors grew into a form of demi-godhood.

The human being as creator.

The human being as designer of worlds of his own making.

Were various historical messiahs in this same crux? Did they in fact create "miracles" which were paranormal occurrences, and were they then used by religious cults to symbolize universes whose ultimate purpose was the tyrannical rule of humans?

In 1961, when I began to paint every day in my apartment in New York — results or execution or skill were not my goals, to be sure — when I threw caution to the winds and untied my imagination, I found that I was looking at my own abstract paintings piling up all around me as worlds, as events in spaces that were beyond the everyday. To me, these paintings were not decoration, they were even more than windows. Looking at them for long periods of time, I found meanings. These weren't describable with exactness, but they were flying, battling, triumphant, energy-loaded happenings ... and the consequence was, oddly enough, that my life was changed forever.

I moved into another echelon. By the action of creation I arrived in spaces where aesthetics and emotion were intensified, were infused into line and energy and object on the canvas, were the currency of reality itself. And when I turned away from the paintings and walked outside on the streets, this transformation held. The essence of my paintings walked with me. The world of the street was not any longer unchangeable, irreducible Reality; it was a space another "painter" had made ... as if a moment ago. It was fascinating, it had curves and hidden corners I had never noticed before, and like the shapes in my paintings the buildings on the street spoke of themselves and, in a non-ordinary language, spilled out emotion. And how fantastic that was! But I knew for all time that the street was another painting — miraculous, yes, because paintings were miraculous — but no more than that. Not a final reality. Not a final oppressive reality. And somehow, that became a very great comfort for the soul.

If Giordano Bruno came close to saying that the individual being somehow animates the physical universe, then the mysticism of Tibetan Buddhism appears to take it the rest of the way.

It is not my intent to summarize all the spiritual practices of this ancient (and current) group, particularly since practitioners and teachers have a variety of interpretations, but a few of its basic concepts are vital to understand:

The physical universe is not the work of God or gods. It is

actually a delusion, in the sense that we mistakenly take it to be objective reality. The physical universe is a manifestation of mind.

With that concept in tow, certain sub-groups within Tibetan Buddhism move to a practice that challenges the primary human delusion head-on. In his book, *The Tantric Mysticism of Tibet*, John Blofeld spells out this visualization practice, after warning his readers not to leap into it. The Tibetans spend years preparing themselves for it.

> Visualization is normally performed in a meditation cell ... However, some adepts, especially those of the Kargyupa sect, prefer solitude while they are mastering it. Walled up in a room or cave for a specified time — say, three or seven years — the adept hears no human voice but his own ... his days are devoted to a chosen sadhana (visualization practice). By the time he emerges, he has become so skilled in creating mental constructions that he clearly perceives the exterior world in its real character as a manifestation of mind.

Blofeld goes on: "[Tibetan-style visualization utilizes] forces familiar to man only at the deeper levels of consciousness, of which ordinary people rarely become aware except in dreams. These are the forces wherewith mind creates and animates the whole universe ..."

One of the vital visualizations consists of a "deity or personified mind-force."

> A minute description [of the deity] has to be memorized [such description given by a teacher and/or mandala-painting or scripture]: posture, clothes, ornaments, hair, body-color, eyes, expression, arms, hands, fingers, legs, feet and sometimes environment. Beginners have to create the parts separately and, as more and more are envisioned, those created first vanish. It is as though a sculptor's statue were to begin melting while he was still at work on it. With practice, however, the adept learns to evoke instantaneously a figure complete in

all its parts ... the deity ... enters the adept's skull and alights in his heart. Mastering the art of visualizing a colored figure that is perfect in every detail is only the first step, for the figure will be static — a mere picture. With further practice, it comes alive as a being seen in a dream. Even that is not enough. As higher states of consciousness supervene, it will be seen to exist in a much more real sense than a person, let alone a dream; moreover, persons, like other external objects of perception, are of little consequence to the practice, whereas this shining being has power to confer unspeakable bliss [to the visualizer] and, after union, to remain one with the [visualizer] adept and purify his thoughts and actions. In time, the sense of [this deity's] reality may become too strong and endanger the adept's concept of everything (the mind-created deity included) as being intrinsically void. The Lama will now order him to banish the deity — a task more difficult than its creation.

Much could be said about this remarkable description, perhaps the single most amazing statement in all of Western spiritual commentary. For me, entering into the metaphysic behind it introduces a slippery slope. But in general, for Tibetans, the void is a term which is meant to show that all is created, and that behind creations — including an invention as wonderful as a deity — is really a state prior even to potential form. Blofeld is indicating that awareness of the void is a central lesson for all adepts, and immersion at too deep a level in any creation is a mistake that has to be corrected. In this case, the adept is told to get rid of his invented companion-deity.

There is a large number of introductory lessons and practices which the student must engage in before getting down to the kind of creation described by Blofeld. I feel that, as a non-Tibetan, such preludes of mantra-sounds, symbols of concentration and evoking, culturally-based entities which are used to signify various human traits ... all of this makes studentship hard. I don't feel a kinship with the forms of the Tibetan culture at a deep enough level to take them on as the substance of the most profound kind of education.

That being said, the Tibetan statement of the role of creation in all realities may be the clearest and the most important ever enunciated on Earth.

As we've seen, on an elementary but quite interesting level, the scientific results of large numbers of paranormal studies show that the physical universe can be affected directly by mind. Why not extrapolate, take this much farther? That, in a sense, is what the Tibetans have done.

Given Paul Schuman's interest in Giordano Bruno and the paranormal, it seemed to me that the visualization practice of his mentors' teacher, the Tibetan ex-monk, had to be close to the one I've just described. A practice which goes far beyond simply invoking a spirit. A practice which, in fact, creates reality.

Indeed, much could be written that extends out from the above quotation by John Blofeld, from the visualization practices of the Tibetans.

Start with the stark idea that gods can be made by us. And that we should be celebrating this fact to the extreme, not using it to minimize the possibilities of life. Look at the specific practice of the Tibetans, in which the deity created by the student actually assumes traits. It can "confer bliss" to the student. It can "purify his actions." This deity is not merely a cardboard photo. The student, it is claimed, has the capacity to invent a creature which is, in its own way, alive.

Alive.

32

If you can see the mechanisms by which cults and secret societies plentifully create limitations for humans ... if you can see this done over and over throughout history, isn't it reasonable to ask why this is necessary, if, as many "experts" are fond of saying, humans are intrinsically quite limited?

Why insist that a human concentrate his vision on one fabricated world he didn't make — unless he has the potential to make worlds, and to drastically affect the composition of this world ... with his mind?

33

If Paul's interest in the paranormal was as I imagined, that definitely fit in with the other clues I was putting together.

Research in the paranormal shows that, beyond doubt, people can directly modify the universe-as-we-know-it with their minds. They can reach out into remote space and "read" the landscape. They can communicate meanings without words — with energy or thought — over a distance. They can change the random flow of matter in space.

Is it eminently rational to think that we, as human beings, are defined by being able to do only A LITTLE BIT of that?

Shall we blindly accept that?

34

"If individual reality becomes fluid," perverse elitists say, "then how can we control huge numbers of people? The world itself, on every level, will stop being singular, and the obedience we require will disappear. We won't be able to wield, forever, authoritative patterns and their unchanging symbols."

Absolutely correct.

35

The Formula of the Secret Society

Let us return to one of Paul Schuman's interests: The Essenes.

The Cave 4 documents of the Dead Sea Scrolls feature a test for messiahship, as I explained earlier. The elements are these: A messiah has given the blind sight; he has raised the dead; he has made the lame walk; he has cleansed the lepers; and he has given the deaf hearing.

These are remarkable feats.

But for a moment consider the following:

In an experiment called "Human Consciousness Influence on Water Structure" (*Journal of Scientific Exploration*, v.9, no.1, pp. 89–105, 1995, Pyatnitsky and Fonkin), the study-authors report, "The ability of human consciousness to change the structure of water is indicated by experiments utilizing light-scattering ... recordings. Alterations of scattered light intensity, correlated with an operator's intention, can exceed by factors of 10 to 1000 the statistical variances observed before or after operator interaction. Such effects have been demonstrated by several operators, and appear to be operator-specific, although enhanceable by training."

The results of this and many other studies do, of course, make a link to the kind of miracles discussed in the case of a messiah.

Now, if you take the Bible and the Cave 4 documents, and many other religious accounts of messiahs, you see that the stories are all cut from the same cloth, as is the background religious myth that is built up to pigeonhole these messiahs.

No one can prove that the messiah miracles were really

performed by any of the men I'll discuss now. In fact, there is scholarly doubt that some of these men ever existed. But what can't be overlooked is the juxtaposition of the miracle-account and the subsequent casting of the man who DID the wondrous things into a sticky bind that tries to envelop the human race.

Historically, this is the cult of cults.

Consider the following:

1.   The savior called Mithras was born 600 years before Jesus, in Persia. He was "born of a virgin with only a number of shepherds present."

2.   Mithras was called The Way, The Truth, The Light, just as Jesus was.

3.   In Mithraic times, on December 25th, "there were magnificent celebrations with bells, candles, gifts, hymns ..."

4.   At death, Mithras' body was put in a tomb which was made of rocks and called Petra. (Peter was the rock on which Jesus would found his church.)

5.   "The followers of Mithras believed that there would be a 'day of judgment' when non-believers would perish and believers would live in a heaven or 'paradise' (a Persian word) forever and ever."

6.   Horus, the Egyptian God who is said to have existed 3,000 years before Jesus, was called the way, the truth, and the life — just as Jesus was.

7.   Horus received a water baptism from Anup. Jesus was similarly baptized by John.

8.   Horus was born in Annu, called the house of bread. Bethlehem, Jesus' birthplace, was also called the house of bread.

9.   Horus and Jesus were both depicted as "The Good Shepherd."

10. There were seven in a boat with Horus. Seven fishermen shared a boat with Jesus.

11. Horus was called both the lamb and the lion. So was Jesus.

12. Both Horus and Jesus are identified with a cross.

13. Horus was said to be the son of a virgin and of a God.

14. Both Horus and Jesus had 12 followers, disciples.

15. Kersey Graves, author of *The World's Sixteen Crucified Saviors* (NY: Truth Seeker Co., 1875), cites the case of a "heathen Savior" Virishna, who was born at least as long ago as 1200 BCE. Virishna was issued from a virgin. As with Jesus (and Herod), Virishna was also "threatened in early infancy with death by the ruling tyrant, Cansa."

16. The birth of Virishna was attended by shepherds and angels.

17. Virishna brought about miracles. He cured the sick, made the blind see, cast out devils, and brought the dead back to life.

18. Virishna was killed on a cross between two thieves. Then he rose up from the dead and went to heaven.

19. Graves also mentions "an ancient Chinese God, known as Beddou." Born in 1027 BCE to a virgin, his life was threatened at an early age by a king. He "cast ... out devils ... performed a multitude of the most astonishing miracles, spent his life fasting, and in the severest mortifications ..."

20. Quetzalcoatl of Mexico, born about 300 BCE, to a virgin named Chimalman, "... led a life of the deepest humility and piety; retired to a wilderness, fasted forty days, was worshipped as a God, and was finally crucified between two thieves; after which he was buried and descended into hell, but rose again the third day."

21. The Egyptian God Osiris was born on the 25th of December.

22. Killed, Osiris eventually rose into a second life. Resurrected in the spring, he lived as a God on Earth. His ritual "consisted primarily in the celebration of a Eucharist meal, in which the communicants ate the flesh of the god in the form of wheat-cakes and drank his blood in the form of barley-ale. By so doing, his divinity became their own ... [and they became] heirs with him in his eternal kingdom."

23. Versions of Osiris appeared in subsequent cults: the Adonis-Aphrodite cult; the cult of Cybele; Orphism; the Pythagorean cult. Exactly what form the gods of these groups took and who they were is difficult to say. What they had in common was a link to the savior who, by his own sacrificial death, could confer a piece of immortality on believers. All these and many other similar cults predated the birth of Jesus.

24. Persian Zoroastrianism contained the doctrine of prophecy concerning "a great virgin-born savior." The scheduled times of arrival for this messiah were/are 341 CE, 1341, and 2341.

   This list does not constitute the full number of cults and religions which have stated a messiah story. And about those mentioned here, there is debate. Did all these messiahs actually exist? Were they men who, as in the case of a Jesus reshaped by the Apostle Paul, were mythologized into roles of supernatural saviors?

   Much has been written and argued about these questions, though not many scholars fully expose the number and similarity of messiah stories. Obviously, the Catholic Church and Christianity come up the main losers in the extraordinary history of saviors in various cultures and times.

   My points are these:

   A number of cults, which came to play major roles in the

lives of several billion people, took over the theater-art of
The Messiah Story. It plays very well. These cults have
painted and defined a space in which a man is born without
sex, of a virgin. The man is a humble teacher who lives a
righteous life, who loves God (or who is a God during his
life). This man performs miracles — raising the dead, giving
the blind sight, and so on. This man is eventually killed and,
in that death, atones somehow for the weakness and the evil
of all humankind — or at least for all his faithful believers.
This man, in a true miracle, rises from the dead and lives
again, and this proves his status and the legitimacy of what
he has done. His atonement is real, it works, and others may
seek salvation through faith and proper ritual.

The solidity which has come to characterize these messiah tales can be seen, at its best, in the Catholic portrayal.

The Messiah Story is no small thing, no mere fairy tale for
a rainy day. It is shaped and built to last the ages and paint/
define a universe in which righteous people have but a single
choice for their eternal futures.

Regardless of whether such messiahs actually lived or did
the miracles attributed to them, regardless of the amount of
retroactive reshaping of "saviors' lives" to create a restricted
universe of guilt and atonement for the masses ... there is a
hidden effect for the people of Earth. By repetition of this
Story, over thousands of years, it becomes clear, through
implication, that a man who can make "miracles" (paranormal
events, to use the terminology of today's researchers) must
be a savior. Therefore, there can only be a few "paranormals,"
since there can't be thousands or millions of saviors running
around the planet.

No, we must only have a few great ones, so that the rest
of us can take solace in their transcendent lives, and bring
our own minor existences into line by prayer, devotion,
confession, hope for redemption, by following rules laid
down for us and by struggling up the ladder of faith.

Is this a cultic pre-defining of space or what?

To go further with the repressive implications, any person
who can perform miracles must be sent by a deity, and owes
his/her entire allegiance to such divinity. In fact, paranormal

abilities come into being only through the grace of some higher Somesuch. These abilities are not part of us. The last thing the cultic mind wants to admit is that these extraordinary capacities are intrinsically part of us.

And here is another historical propaganda-implication: To do miracles is to die on the cross. Messiahs are the sacrificial lambs. They come to their day of pain, and they die.

Beyond this, never, never, never do the saviors try to show us how to do what they can do. Their miracle-making is not a gift to be imparted.

So, according to the cultic architects, we shouldn't think of paranormal healings and the direct effect of mind on matter and rising from the dead as things that can be done by us. Think of them instead as fabled miracles that bring with them grave and somber responsibilities for a few men.

This is the cult-myth of myths.

This is history as subliminal mind control.

This is the ceiling that has been placed on the human race through sheer trickery and appeal to our desire to resonate emotionally with tragedy.

What do you think will happen if the exercise of all sorts of tremendous paranormal abilities spreads and seeps further and further into the planetary culture? When more and more people can do it? When doing it is not a science or a religion but an expression of something deep within us?

That will be a dawning, yes?

36

Perhaps Paul Schuman was trying to piece together the plus and minus of a very long planetary tale.

What is the tradition that Paul and Richard and Rachel Jenkins were looking for? That I now find myself looking for?

I wrote down words and phrases, trying to get a feel for it: The Tradition ... healing, multiple dimensions, fluidity, the removal of walls which are not truly walls, the removal of delusionary repressive art, such as the messiah stories, the joining of separated energies, the deep soaking-in of art, the taking away of reality which has been propped up for us, the restoration of individual creation of realities, the paranormal, the reduction of cultish Earth-control to dust, the taking down of cosmological systems from austere pulpits and podiums of authority. Spontaneity, improvisation.

Is this a tradition?

All this?

Yes.

Shall we call this tradition a process? Is there a word that describes it? One word?

I spent time searching for terms. I temporarily settled on one because it would enable me to discuss the tradition at greater length.

Imagination.

Creation by imagination. The bringing into being of multiple realities.

At the same time I didn't want to imply that the whole tradition was only the sort of imagining in which things and scenes and realms were projected from nothing onto a vacuum.

No, this tradition also involves creation in an expanded unfrozen free spectrum of *merging, becoming one with, worship, empathy, traveling in an interior way to places that mysteriously already exist*. This form of imagination is so fluid that the mergings and the worshippings don't stick up like glue, don't eventually give rise to clans and cults and institutions of doctrine and coercion.

What ties together the healer, the person who can bring about all the paranormal events, the visualizer of deities who can create a personage that is in a real sense alive, the capacity of a being to reach out across the universe, the artist?

Fluidity yes, but not only that. Empathy but not only that. It is what would be liberated within a person when he is liberated, so in that sense freedom is a correct word, but it is too wide.

The tradition is the opposite of the formula of a secret society, a cult, a religion, an institution that creates art in order to imprison the mind. The opposite.

I think back on many sessions I have watched Richard Jenkins give, on days and years of painting in studios, on days of going into museums and looking at wonders all around.

Liberation, un-hypnotism.

A tradition that, in one aspect, asserts that a human being, a being, a soul, can potentially make and vanish any part of the universe and make novel realities out of nothing.

I can find no single term that absolutely covers this tradition, so I shall call it imagination, knowing that we will need a wider interpretation for this word, a sense that involves more than creating what wasn't there before, but also takes in moving through realities that are already there ... that takes in everything that I have mentioned in this chapter.

Of course there is a great deal to be done to flesh in connections and show that this Tradition of Imagination is coherent. For the meantime: The act of imagining or creating needs to be seen as intimately involved with what we could call "enchantment" in a physical, mental, emotional, artistic and theatrical sense.

This refers, in part, to the moment when a painter looks

at his canvas and puts the first brushstroke of paint on it, the moment when the dreamer takes his first step across the threshold of a room into the dream, the moment the healer places his hands on the person who is seeking transformation, the moment the actor walks out onto the stage to deliver his first line as a different personage, the moment a person moves through interior space to a location that is not the physical world but is unaccountably familiar, the moment a receiver is ready to feel the transmission of a telepathic message, the moment a poet cracks down walls surrounding his being and moves into new territory, the moment a singer begins ...

37

When I say that imagination or creation takes in such actions or states as empathy, fluidity, merging with, and worship, I know that I am stretching the conventional definition. But think about it. Worship, for example, is the assumption of a role, an attitude in which the object of attention reached out to is made to increase magnificently in stature, in beauty, in soulship. If that isn't an achievement in the realm of art, what is?

It is just that we have learned to freeze that attitude, to play that role as the highest of all postures in a picture-frame of gilded religion. Who legislated that?

Worship the frog, the blade of grass, the concrete sidewalk, the gossip gab-sheet, the night of stars, the ocean smashing on rocks, the funnel of a tornado, an ant. Some of the great poets — Whitman comes to mind as perhaps America's greatest — did that.

It is a shining aspect of the Tradition of Imagination. But frozen, warped, forced to maintain its humility, worship is a part of the opposite Formula of the Secret Society.

38

Now that we have made this beginning, this stating of the Tradition of Imagination, the examples stream in.

The closest historic parallels, in the West, to the aspect of Tibetan teachings I'm telescoping may be Henri Bergson, the 19th-20th century philosopher, and William Blake (1757–1827). Blake, while immersing himself by poem and etching in a world of religious-spiritual entities, also placed the creative act at the center of life in a ferocious way.

In the didactic poem, "There is No Natural Religion," Blake establishes a startling position vis-à-vis creation. "The bounded is loathed by its possessor. The same dull round, even of a universe, would soon become a mill with complicated wheels."

Spoken like an artist who has visited many shores and abhors boredom.

In "All Religions Are One," Blake enunciates this principle: "That the Poetic Genius is the True Man, and that the body or outward form of man is derived from the Poetic Genius." Rarely, on this planet, has such a startling alternative to by-the-book creation myths been offered.

In the same poem, Blake writes a variant on that theme: "As all men are alike (tho' infinitely various), So all Religions ... have one source. The True Man is the source, he being the Poetic Genius."

Blake thus stands the Formula of the Secret Society on its head. This is one reason academics have given his philosophy a wide berth. He is simply too inspiring on the potential creative power of humans.

As to his stance on art and its core role in the life of the individual, Blake makes this remark in "The Laocoon

Group:" "You must leave Fathers and Mothers and Homes and Lands if they stand in the way of Art. Prayer is the Study of Art. Praise is the Practise of Art. Fasting, etc., all relate to Art."

Two brief comments within The Laocoon Group reveal extensions of Blake's uncompromising view: "Art Degraded, Imagination Denied, War Governed the Nations." "... Israel Deliver'd from Egypt, is Art deliver'd from Nature and Imitation."

Aristotle made the first great and binding definition of art as "the imitation of nature." With his last statement above, Blake establishes one of the earliest and clearest positions in the West on art that surmounts the Aristotelian prison. Blake places the artist at the center of creation.

If we, as a society, could elevate the values of art and imagination to the foremost pinnacle, he is saying, war itself would wither away.

Blake's genius was as a poet. That he also saw so well the meaning and place of creation is unique among artists of the West.

39

Buddhism was brought into Tibet about 1300 years ago. The original Lamas (adepts) were Tibetans and Indians who had attended the Universities of Nalanda and Vikramashila in north India. The student body at Nalanda numbered 30,000.

Tibetan Buddhism contains a number of sects and subsects. The Vajrayana tradition, for example, which utilizes major visualization practices such as the one described in an earlier chapter, consults a "special section" of the Tibetan Buddhist canon ignored by other sects. This section apparently describes these deity-visualization practices, and was itself originally translated from Sanskrit. Therefore, the tradition, as an import, seems to have arrived from India.

Tantric practices in North India 1300 years ago were quite popular. They included what were probably less refined versions of the later Tibetan visualizations.

I have no doubt that, depending on who is teaching the subject, and who is learning it, Tibetan visualization could function to deepen one's dependence on an already invented Pattern of inner truth. That would, of course, be a losing proposition. There is that danger in any philosophy that purports to bring about individual liberation while spelling out "the nature of the universe."

The student is taught that reality has an intrinsic anatomy, and then in the next breath he learns that reality is his own invention. Various explanations are given to show that these two views can be reconciled: It is all a matter of levels, aspects, higher and lower, of the truth.

Is it? Often the student opts for the Pattern, and freedom and the whiff of adventure are slowly drowned in a stagnant pool.

It is not my intention to pull apart the body of the subject called Tibetan Buddhism. I have no interest in making a judgment about its position relative to human freedom. From what I can discover, Tibet has maintained a remarkable equanimity, even in current exile, about the existence of a practice — deity visualization — which obviously could carry the practitioner beyond rote obedience to religious ceremonies and authority. Historically, it is, in fact, clear that the states of consciousness attainable through deity-visualization — as far as the Tibetan theocracy is concerned — would take the practitioner to places beyond any ruling Tibetan government/religious hierarchy.

The Tibetan theocracy seems to tolerate this idea.

40

Tantra is a word that means "thread," and implies a time-continuum. As Geoffrey Samuel points out in his excellent book, *Civilized Shamans*, the Vajrayana deity-visualizations derive from an earlier tantric tradition in India. Shamanic and magical in practice, it intensely sought higher states of consciousness.

It appears that the root, in India, of this form of tantrism dates back to 400 CE, and perhaps earlier. Samuel estimates that in India single isolated gurus would have attracted small groups of disciples.

Beyond this — so far — I haven't been able to trace the history of Tibetan deity visualization.

41

Here is another account, by author and world traveler Alexandra David-Neel, of Tibetan tantric deity visualization:

A deity is imagined; it is first contemplated alone, then from its body spring out other forms sometimes like its own, sometimes different. There are often four of them, but in some meditations they become hundreds or even innumerable.

When all these personages have appeared quite clearly around the central figure, they are one after another absorbed in it. Now the original deity remains again alone and gradually begins to disappear. The feet vanish first and then slowly the whole body and finally the head ...

One may also imagine a lotus. It opens slowly and on each of its petals stands a Bodhisattva, one of them being enthroned in the heart of the flower ...

Many novices do not proceed farther. Thus dryly described, such visions cannot but appear absurd ...

They provide the recluse with spectacles which rival the most beautiful fairy-plays that can be seen on the stage. Even those who are well aware of their illusive nature may enjoy them, and as for those who believe in the reality of the divine players, it is not surprising that they are bewitched.

However, it is not to amuse the hermits that these exercises have been invented. Their true aim is to lead the disciple to understand that the worlds and all phenomena which we perceive are but mirages born out of our imagination.

"They emanate from the mind / And into the mind they sink."

In fact this is the fundamental teaching of Tibetan mystics.

This assessment is extraordinary because, again, it places us, as beings, in a central place of creation.

Misinterpretations have arisen, based on attitudes which some people have taken toward the idea of the physical universe as delusion or mirage. As in, "A delusion just hit a man in the street going sixty miles an hour and he is now in another delusion called the hospital."

Obviously, we have already made our definition, and it does not fit the Tibetan view. For us, a mirage is thin, it has no weight, it is not lasting, it is translucent and distorted, it causes a person to act irrationally, and so on.

Therefore, we say, the universe is not a delusion, and all those people on the other side of the world must be crazy. They are trying to deny the reality of their own painful, poverty-stricken lives, and this is their strategy. That is all there is to it. QED.

Not so.

The Tibetans simply have a different definition. It is based on their being convinced they have had the experience of creating something at least as real as the physical universe.

Let me relate a personal experience. Over a period of sixteen weeks, I have tried out a simple version of the Tibetan visualization technique John Blofeld described. I picked a rather jolly image of a genie from a film I had seen some years ago, and I "brought him up."

This was not a sacred enterprise. It was an experiment.

With my eyes open, I placed this genie around in my room, on the couch, on the bed, standing next to the bureau, sitting on the toilet, suspended in mid-air — wherever I wanted him. I made him very tall so I could see only his legs, and I made him three inches tall sitting on the lip of an ashtray.

I did this every day, for a few minutes, for sixteen weeks. I did it on the street and at home and in the middle of conversations.

I liked this genie.

Sometimes he was just there laughing, and sometimes he walked around a bit.

One night, I was lying in bed, and I imagined the genie in a small size on my windowsill. At that point, a question suddenly occurred to me out of the blue. It evaded all the million "rational thoughts" I'd previously collected on the issue.

"I've been creating this genie, and I've been doing it every day ... did anybody create me?"

At that instant, I felt and heard an explosion at the back of my head.

When my surprise died down, after about twenty seconds, I realized I felt different. Very different. I had just shed a skin. I felt very relaxed and contented.

The world, such as it was, I realized quickly, was in fact my oyster.

If I wanted to generate knowledge, wisdom, I could do that, much as one might unfold a little toy out of his pocket. I was in an exceptional state of good humor. Things might be out of whack in the world itself — and of course they were — but I was not immersed in the bubbling morass. People were running around in their own peculiar directions. If they wanted to straighten themselves out, all they needed to do was ... what? Well, just realize which synchronizations they needed to tune. Yes. For example, a friend of mine couldn't sleep at night. She was always up at 2 am for three or four hours. Now I saw that this was simply and only a matter of her sense of time. It was faster than other people's. The acceleration factor had made their 6 p.m. her 11 p.m. This wasn't a neurosis or a deficiency, it was a fact. She could accept it, in which case everything would be all right, or she could make a few internal adjustments in skull-land and change the time-rate.

The clarity of this little cameo was on the order of a mountain peak in December under a full-lit moon.

I mentally sauntered through various modest situations in the lives of people and I saw, like a tinkerer in his workshop, how their problems could be dispensed with in mere moments, either by accepting them as "slightly different gear and cog settings" or by using their innate fix-it faculty (which I had just found for the first time) to reset the relevant screws.

Without congratulating myself too heartily, I dropped my cogitations and just cruised into feeling like Cary Grant in *His Girl Friday*.

Amused, inwardly thrilled (as in very few moments of my life) by second-to-second existence, ready to trip the light fantastic, argue, gab, win the prize, whatever it might be, and generally take on things and events and people coming down the pipeline.

I got out of bed, made a few calls, put on some clothes, and went out on the town.

If my visualization practice for those few months had brought me to the brink of an extraordinary experience as the payoff — and it had — then I knew there was something to this.

Without drugs, without precedent, realities don't just change like that. But they did.

42

More on the Tradition of Imagination.

Author Alexandra David-Neel describes Tibetan exercises of becoming:

> For instance, the disciple has chosen a tree, as an object of meditation, and has identified himself with it. That is to say that he has [temporarily] lost the consciousness of his own personality and experiences the peculiar sensations that one may ascribe to a tree. He feels himself to be composed of a stiff trunk with branches, he perceives the sensation of the wind moving the leaves. He notes the activity of the roots feeding under the ground, the ascension of the sap which spreads all over the tree, and so on.
>
> Then, having mentally become a tree (which has now become the subject), he must look at the man (who has now become the object) seated in front of him and must examine this man in detail.

David-Neel goes own to describe another such exercise, in which the student, using his imagination, has his consciousness "leave its habitual abode [in the head]" and go to his hand. "... he must feel himself to have the shape of five fingers and a palm, situated at the extremity of a long attachment (the arm) ..."

Then the student, as the hand, has to view the rest of the body.

"One attains," David-Neel writes, "by the means of these strange drills, psychic states entirely different from those habitual to us. They cause us to pass beyond the fictitious limits which we assign to the self."

Consider this statement by Walt Whitman:

"There was a child went forth every day,
And the first object he looked upon, that object he became,
And that object became part of him for the day or a certain
part of the day,
Or for many years or stretching cycles of years."

Resonance. Fluidity. The extension of realities. Creation.
The Tradition of Imagination.

We visualize something.
We merge with something.
We become something.
We dream of something.
We project.
We invoke.
We worship.
We conjure.

We can move smoothly from one of these aspects or ways
of the Tradition of Imagination to another, like the sun's
shadow moving on a sundial, without even knowing it.

When, for example, we create an image of someone we
desire we may swoop into a state of worship. Then after a few
moments or a few hours or a few days, we may merge with
(become) that person. Or move into a non-rational dream.

Those who have fashioned religions have, with few exceptions, frozen down this many-sided process into worship, as
I said in an earlier chapter.

They have, consciously or unconsciously, played on the
natural human capacity to "move" through the spectrum of
imagination, and they have made a counter-universe in
which worship is the primary or only accepted form when
push comes to shove. This is an effort to narrow the mind
and being of humans, and it has worked.

When you take away the trappings and the clever scripture
of most religions and secret societies, you are face to face
with a very workable form of mind control. By engaging the
human process in one gear only, (and by pre-defining the
only single universe which exists, run by Someone Else), you
set the stage for long-term tyranny. That is what it comes
down to.

Two vastly divergent existences:

The Formula of the Secret Society, and the Tradition of Imagination.

43

Although they administer it, those who run the most powerful elites on the planet do not fully understand the depth and nature of repression. They couldn't. Because, at the root, they are suffering from the same disease as their pawns. They, too, unknowingly have sacrificed their wide-ranging imaginations — and their fluidity — and they are living in half-light.

The future of this overall repression for the human race is violence which produces something worse than chaos. It eventually makes robots all around. A world as a machine, from top to bottom. That is a place where all beings go to live when they have forgotten the real joy of their fluidity. When they have never learned about a different Tradition. The Imagination.

PART TWO

44

The Formula of the Secret Society: A Case History

Here is an account that shows how a combination of cult-art and coercion can hold a person inside a secret society, particularly when the art, the pre-defined space, is manipulated in a hide-and-seek way, replete with contradictions and progressive "revelations" and far-out vignettes. A pattern is created which is very complex, and the idea is to make the member want to understand that pattern.

This report is not as bloody or sensational as many.

I was told by a man who perhaps once worked for the CIA that he could introduce me to a woman who had been in a secret society. He thought I would be interested in her story. This man said he had worked in El Salvador, and his sketch of his mission there generally and vaguely conformed to published reports about American activities carried out against the Salvadoran people.

The man told me he had taken part in surveillance against Salvadoran university students in the 1980s. Some of these students were working with revolutionary groups. Several teachers were murdered at that time. I had interviewed Miguel Parada in Los Angeles in the early '80s. Parada was a brave and temporary president of the University of El Salvador who was in the U.S. on a fund-raising trip. The military had already partially taken over the University, burned books and disappeared several student leaders. Some years later, I was told Parada had been murdered too.

The American (possible) ex-CIA employee told me he had been a minor advisor to death squads within the Salvadoran military. The job of these squads was to carry out torture and murder of peasants and revolutionaries — to terrorize the part of the Salvadoran population which might go over to the side of the revolution.

I asked this man how he had come to know the woman who had been part of a secret society. He wouldn't tell me. I asked him if the CIA had any connections to this group. He said no, and told me the group no longer existed. Several days later, he introduced me to Karen, who was in her early 30s. I found her to be extremely well-read in mystical literature.

When Karen was nine, her mother moved from Ohio to Texas and married a man who was involved in a cult, a secret society. This group at first appeared to be informal, consisting of ten or twenty friends who studied Rosicrucian philosophy.

Karen's mother discovered, after doing a little research, that there was no single central Rosicrucian doctrine. As with the Masons (after 1717), and other mystical groups, many people had taken a popular group-name for their own to gain a following, and to inject doctrine and symbols from outside sources — alchemy, hermetic philosophy, Christian mysticism, Tantra, to name just a few.

Karen's mother Jane had come across a central fact about secret societies. They are often fractured into various sub-sects with different ideas — but still maintain the central name. This confuses everyone.

The Masons are a perfect example. The best-researched version of Masonic history I have found shows that, prior to 1717, the secret degrees of initiation were only three. The society went public, in England, in 1717 and announced its existence. After that point, every ambitious cult-organizer with a program and a platform in Europe jumped on the bandwagon and started his own Masonic Lodge with his own unique degrees of initiation. From three, the number of degrees swelled to 33, and in some cases, to 65. Some Lodges became political and conspiratorial, others piled on imagery and tales of ancient mythical masters of the East, of legendary spirit-hierarchies connected to Egypt, of so-called ascended masters whose company of names became more bloated with time.

Understand, each divergent Masonic lodge did not announce itself as independent. Quite the opposite. These spin-off groups claimed more profound "historical authenticity" or "higher truth" as their reasons for being Very Masonic, More Masonic, Most Masonic.

Jane's new husband in Texas, Carl, and his friends had invented a Rosicrucian group that was a cover story for sexual rites. According to Karen, in the three months she was in Texas, before her mother fled with her to another state, she herself was fondled on an altar during ceremonies in a dark room in the back of a store. She watched a boy being "baptized" in a tub full of "blood-colored water," and saw her mother in chains being led off into a car by Carl and a friend of his on a Sunday morning.

Jane was raped by Carl several times; she reported this to local police. The police arrested Carl. The District Attorney's office declined to prosecute the case because there was no reliable physical evidence.

When Karen graduated high school, in California, she joined a mystical society which was an entirely independent and bizarre impostor of the old German group, Brotherhood of Saturn. Saturn may have had its own beginnings as early as 1700, in Scandinavia. Karen was promised 33 degrees of attainment and initiation. She subsequently discovered that the 19th degree, called Magus Sigilli Solomonis (Magician of the Seal of Solomon) by the German Brotherhood of Saturn, was named The Hexagram by her own group. Karen found out that the hexagram — a familiar figure formed by the meshing of two triangles into a six-pointed star — is often called the Shield of David or the Star of Israel. It is displayed on the flag of the State of Israel, and is the key symbol of the nation. Known also as the Seal of Solomon, after King Solomon, it was a prominent symbol of the old Catholic secret society called the Knights Templar.

In fact, Karen discovered that this hexagram/star, through time, has done quadruple and quintuple duty. It is the primary mystical symbol for "the integration of opposites," and for the merging of the four elements, Earth, Air, Fire and Water.

For the European alchemists, it summed up the capacity of what was called Quintessence, or life-force, to keep a state of order among the four elements, which otherwise would fly apart into chaos.

"I studied the symbol," she said,

because they wanted me to have it tattooed on my wrist. I thought I should at least understand what it meant before I went ahead. The more I read in libraries, the more meanings I found. In the Kabbala, the Seal shows a merging of the God of Light and the God of Reflections. I found scholarly books that claimed Solomon, the name itself, means 'highest light' in three languages, if you break it up into its syllables.

In purely Jewish terms, the star stands for the six days of creation by God (six points of the star), and the blank center is the day of rest, the Sabbath.

Also in the Jewish tradition, the star — whose upward pointed triangle stands for fire and whose downward triangle signifies water — became the sign for alcohol. As in "burnt water" or "fire water." This star, hexagram, shield of David is translated *magen David*, which of course is a spelling very close to the name of a popular Jewish wine.

"The mystical group I belonged to," Karen said, "had many meanings for the Seal of Solomon. It confused me a great deal. They had it decorating their meeting room in a dozen different places. They had robes for advanced members which showed the star on the right sleeve and a swastika on the left. A gold-painted six-pointed wooden star hung from the ceiling above the podium they used for meetings. At first they told me the star was an object of meditation. Then they said it was an inner form on the 'plane of divination,' as if by meditating on it I would be able to tell the future. Then they said it was the sign of a knight, a warrior, whose job is to bring knowledge to the world. Then they said the star connected us to the past, and they showed me research from several scholarly dictionaries. The star had been found on a Roman silver plate at Coleraine, in Ireland, fourth century, and on a Jewish grave marker at Tarentum, third century. We were impressed by the longevity of the symbol. They took it back much further. There are several books written about the legendary continent of Mu, by James Churchward, in which he shows a version of the star and dates it at 25,000 years ago. I never did find any evidence for the existence of Mu.

"Finally, one night at a meeting, they told the new members that the star was the merging of light and reflection, and all humans, in their current state, were mere reflections of a higher possibility, a higher realm. The light-and-reflection idea is actually in the Kabbala. A Kabbalistic or alchemical meaning of the two triangles is male and female. The male principle is the upward pointing triangle, and the female is the downward triangle. My group got around to the merging of male and female reflections to produce a more powerful state of being. I could see they were going to pair me off with a man in the group I thought was very unattractive. He was one of the nineteenth-degree people.

"I asked if this was a regular ceremony of the group. I was told it was, 'when the time was right.' Jim, a fifteenth degree, told me I should visit a special site outside of town.

"He drove me to a farmhouse. I don't know who the owner was. It looked abandoned, but one room was very fancy. There were wall hangings of gold-painted figures dressed in warrior and angel costumes. A few of the male figures had scorpion tails. The ceiling was painted with blue clouds and black flying disks and spheres. In the corners of the room were silver-colored throne chairs made out of wood. The floor was covered in detail with all kinds of strange symbols in a flowing script. I have no idea what the symbols meant. Jim told me this was a meditation hall. He also said it was used for sex between assigned members. I thought this was a fantastic place. I had never seen anything like it. It made me feel special. I wasn't scared. I wanted to be in the room. It was like a theater, but it really meant something. I was sure every symbol in the room had a special meaning. I'm a scholarly person some of the time, so to me, at eighteen, this was a banquet. I saw myself going to libraries and finding out where the symbols came from. I was in love with it right away. It really sold me on the group. I even considered making a room like that for myself at home, but I didn't.

"Jim assured me that no harm would come to me if I went along with the group's rituals. I asked him why I should cooperate. He then went into a long story about the Seal of Solomon and how it actually predicts the future. My future, he said, was already written. It was inscribed in the center of the Seal. Where, I wanted to know. In the Great Records, a library that existed in a different dimension that was available to our members, psychically, if they were above the seventeenth degree. He had read my record, and I was supposed to be matched up with this man I didn't like.

"Jim said he could intercede for me. This would involve another connection with Great Records to search for alternative possibilities. He took my hand. I was frightened. He led me out of the room and through the barn again. We walked to his car. He drove to a place I won't mention. It was out in the country. A man was waiting for us in his car. He wore a suit and I could see he had a walkie-talkie on the front seat. He said he was from the County, and he wanted to talk to me about my little brother, who had been truant from school quite a bit. He said the County could take him from my mother and put him into a foster home. That was all he said.

"That's how Jim and I started our relationship. It was basically extortion. But I wasn't sure about that. Maybe Jim was trying to protect my little brother. That's what he said. I was confused. I tried to get my mother to leave town, but she wouldn't. The relationship with Jim lasted almost a year. During that time I saw people in the group sacrifice animals in another room in a different place. I only went there twice. I hated it. I had to kill a fish while it was in a tank of water and pass the parts around after it was cut up. I don't even eat fish. This was done to get me to cross a line, to get me to do something I wouldn't ordinarily do. Guilt was the thing. We were all bound together by our sin, if you take the Christian point of view. I don't, but the principle is the same.

"They put up some drawings of mystical figures for the

group on the walls of the room in the barn. Colonel Henry S. Olcott, who was the main follower of Helena Petrovena Blavatsky, who founded Theosophy. Also drawings of Madame Blavatsky. Jim and the others had stories about these people, how they were in contact with our group through afterlife realms. I finally met Peter, the leader of our group. He had been on a trip to Europe. He told me Madame Blavatsky and Colonel Olcott were now ascended masters who could give the group special instructions and insights.

"The thing was, I read Madame Blavatsky's works, and I finally figured out that she had done the same thing. She had claimed that she was in contact with different masters, the Brotherhood of Luxor, from ancient Egypt, and the Great White Brotherhood, from Tibet. She made them up. I'm sure of it. But back then I wasn't sure of it.

"They had Madame Blavatsky in the fold, they said they had Tuitit Bey, the head of the Brotherhood of Luxor, they said they had the ghost of Carl Jung occasionally visit them and give sage advice. They had Seals of Solomon everywhere and crosses too. The cross, they said, stood for the union of the sexes. It was a universal meeting point.

"A man named Mr. Franks showed up at a few of the meetings. He was an outsider, but I felt he had business with the group. I didn't know what it was. Drugs, maybe. I couldn't tell. They didn't trust me enough to say.

"When I had been in the group for six months, they gave me a book to read. It was done on a computer, and there were illustrations. The book gave the so-called ancient lineage of our group. The book said our group owed its existence to a Girtablullu, which I've since looked up. It does exist in mythology. It's from early Mesopotamia, two thousand years before Christ. The Girtablullu is a super-being. He has the head of a human being, with horns, a human body, the claws of a bird, the back end of a bird, a scorpion's tail and a penis with a snake's head. He's supposed to be a very strong helper against demons.

"The book then goes off in a completely different direction. The Girtablullu is the husband of an Egyptian goddess, and they have children who are outcasts from Egyptian society, because of their appearance. These outcasts roam the world for many centuries and settle in desert regions, interbreed and have families. They leave a scripture.

"The Girtablullu scripture, strangely enough, talks about the Indian yantra, which is a form of the Seal of Solomon. At least Peter — the head of the group — tells me this is what the Girt manuscript refers to. The yantra has possibly been tracked back four thousand years in India. That's when the mythological Girtablullu supposedly existed.

"Meanwhile, this book they gave me to read says that the triangle is the formation-pattern of the cosmos, that the universe was made while a God or Spirit-Energy was contemplating the triangle. The three equal sides stand for a balance of forces. The male force, the female, and the Other Principle, the Quintessence.

"Quintessence is a term from alchemy, and it means the life-force. The book says that to develop this Quintessence, you have to extract it from objects and living things. This is taken to mean that animals have to be sacrificed. This is not the meaning from alchemy.

"I was amazed that the system of this group was so complex. The higher I went in degrees, the more I saw that politics was one obvious aim of the group. How to get and keep members. What to tell them so that they joined and stayed, how to get donations from members and their families. Secret prayers and incantations were handed out, and there were long explanations that went with them, tracking them back to ancient Egypt and the Mayan civilizations. I found nothing in any book in libraries that matched this. I mean, Egypt was never like this. The super-mystical societies of Egypt and the mystery schools there had names I had never heard of and couldn't locate.

"Getting new members and keeping them was equated with spiritual ability. If you were strong, you could bring in people to the meetings. We were told this was our group, and then on the other hand all the teachings and the doctrine came from somewhere else. So it was a contradiction, one of many.

"We were told that all our envisioning was necessary to make the group grow larger and have its thought influence the world. In the higher degrees there were long ceremonies in which we were taught about the secrets of collective group-will, through concentration exercises, and we were used to focus on certain geographic areas of the planet, in many cases for the purpose of preparing the ground for the arrival there of missionaries from our headquarters.

"These concentration secrets were said to come from ancient Egypt and Sumer, and we were given a history to go with them. There was a story about a fallen god of Egypt who crashed some sort of advanced vehicle in the desert ten or twelve thousand years ago, and healed himself and drew followers from nomad tribes. He showed them how to find water under the Earth.

"As far as I could tell, this group I belonged to had collected lore from all over the place. I never met anyone in the group who seemed intelligent enough to have written the materials. I was told by Jim that Peter really wasn't the head of the group, he was only the local person in charge, but that there were others from out of town, out of the country, out of the galaxy who were always there and could help us.

"The Seal of Solomon kept coming up time and time again. They used it as a device for focus — but they also tied it into Egypt. Egypt had six periods of greatness, they said, and this corresponded with the six points on the star. Egypt was composed of alternative dynasties of male and female power, even though the outward rulers were mostly men. This balance or integration was symbolized by the meshing triangles of the Seal. Egypt was the land where sexual union was first given its complete due, twenty thousand years ago. In other words, ceremonies and rituals which brought out the greatest intense energy in sex were stressed in secret Egyptian teachings. Twenty thousand years ago, aspirants learned that to achieve the amount of necessary energy for carrying out materializations, you had to multiply it in the body and the aura through sex. So sex wasn't looked at as a romantic thing with marriage as the goal or the expression. Sex was a tantric avenue. A materialization was said to be possible once a person reached the heights of sexual expression. A materialization meant the bringing into being of objects and energies.

"I was told that above the twentieth degree you learned the most advanced sexual ceremonies and began the visualization of materializations."

Karen met members of this group who were "almost rednecks with a taste for violence," and people who were much more scholarly in their interests. Meetings were semi-public and attended by between thirty and forty people. Secret meetings, ten to fifteen. The core membership was perhaps forty.

Karen was once told that when the world was created, the Spirit-Energy which did it had really contemplated the Seal of Solomon. This was the catalyst that allowed the creation to progress and succeed.

"We were led in many group meditations on the Seal. The idea, I suppose, was that it would prepare us for the act of our own creating. Of course we were told that only by the concentration of force and power within our group could we hope to achieve more than simple focus on a sign or symbol. In other words, manifestation or materialization was a property of the group mind.

"I used to do simple candle exercises. They were recommended by Jim and others in the group. We had candles with the Seal of Solomon on them. I would sit in a dark room and focus on a single burning candle. After doing this for a few months almost every day, I felt stronger. My concentration was better. I was quite excited. I told another woman in the group and she warned me to be quiet about it.

"I began to look at the meditations and the ceremonies in a different light. They were there to give us a feeling of solidarity and not individual strength.

"There were rumors in the group that we had a connection to fascists or Nazis. It wasn't said that way. It was framed in terms of wealth. We had connections to a few wealthy men who had an agenda that involved Nazi objectives. The rumors always contained a disclaimer. We weren't in with the Nazis, but if they had money to throw our way, well, why not? Perhaps they thought we were on their side. That was all right.

"Jim said he had been to Illinois and had spoken with a few of these people, these Nazis. He said they weren't bad at all, they just didn't have the metaphysical background we did.

"People would keep referring me back to the Seal of Solomon. I couldn't see how that tied in. The more I studied the symbol, the less clear things became. Peter said I had to have faith, and I would learn about the ultimates, as he called them.

"Peter would take me to cemeteries. We would walk around between the grave markers and he would point to some of them and say they had been drained of life by the Spirit-Energy and the Girtablullu because they no longer had anything to contribute to life. I asked him if he meant they had been killed. He said of course not. The group had nothing to do with that.

"I kept studying the Seal of Solomon and found out that the Knights Templar, a medieval European secret society of Catholic knights, had used the Seal as their symbol. They supposedly started the Masons, and broke the symbol into two pieces which formed the open triangles — the compass and the square — that are the signs of the Masons. The Masons, like us, had thirty-three degrees of initiation. This convinced me again that these groups took ideas from each other. There aren't any copyrights in cults.

"In the group, Peter was placing a lot more emphasis on the Bey, as he called him, the mythical head of the Brotherhood of Luxor. We were supposed to ask for things from Bey and pray to him to give us light and allow us to see the Vision. The Vision was the meaning of the Seal of Solomon. We were supposed to look for that and find it, seek and find, seek and find.

"Peter showed us new drawings and posters of the Seal. I don't know where they were coming from. He said we should study the little symbols around the edges of the Seal and try to intuit what they meant. Then a few days later he brought in a whole glossary of these little strange signs and letters. I think they really were alchemical notations, but Peter said they stood for the deaths of great men and women throughout history who had found the truth of the Vision, who had penetrated to the core of the Vision.

"Finally, one Friday night at a private meeting, Peter told

us that the Vision was sacrifice. This was the meaning of the Seal, the surrendering of self into harmony with its opposite. He went on for some time about the ordeals of Jesus and said that was what we all were being groomed for. The days of Sacrifice ahead. We were going to find a new land for our group in the desert or the mountains close by, and we were going to build a paradise for ourselves, which would serve as an example for the world of how people should live and work together. This would be a community of the Spirit-Energy, and we would learn much more about Him in the years ahead. Our community would be dedicated to Him, in fact, and His glory would be reflected in us for all the world to see. Building this paradise would be very hard work, and we would have to dedicate ourselves to it every day for the rest of our lives.

"I didn't want any part of it. That was going too far.

"My mother and I made plans without telling anyone. We shipped out our belongings to a friend quite some distance away. She just walked out of her job one afternoon, and she and my brother and I drove out of town about a hundred miles. We stayed at a motel overnight, and then we got up early and went on toward our new life. I never looked back. I don't know what happened to all those people. It was very hard to say how serious they were about various things."

For some time after I read over Karen's account, I was impressed with how flippant the whole mythology, the whole cult-mural of the group seemed. But then I decided that the great religions of the world were not much different. Perhaps they had just had more time to percolate, to sort out the ritual and the symbols and the meanings and make their "paths" more elegant. Because, on reflection, what could be more bizarre than dying for the sins of others? Let's see: I have sinned; you die for me because there is no way I can by myself undo that sin; sure. Forget Napoleon Hill and Dale Carnegie. The people who sold that one were miles ahead of the competition.

45

The Formula of the Secret Society

Karen told me that her group gained a great deal of strength because of its rituals and initiation ceremonies. Of course, people wanted to belong, and have "friends," but the ritual itself was a paramount factor in attracting and keeping members.

"When I joined," she said, "I was blindfolded and led through some kind of tunnel in a cellar in a house we used sometimes. At least it felt like a tunnel. Maybe it was just a hallway, but I heard water dripping and echoes.

"I came to a door. They told me when I turned the key I would be out of the world I had known and into a new world. I would leave the concerns of the old world behind and find a new life. As suspicious as I was, this made an impression on me. I wanted to escape, to find something. I think everybody does. I turned the key in the lock and the door creaked open. I could see light through my blindfold. I was led inside a space. Different people spoke to me. They asked whether I was pure in my heart, whether I really wanted to belong. One man had me kneel in front of a bowl or a fountain. Water was running. He told me a story about ancient Egypt and the struggles of the gods to bring a new message to the world, a message of miraculous transformations. It wasn't only his words, it was the sensation that I was in another realm. I was part of a play, and all the focus was on me. The same with the rituals later on after I was in. We would have members dressed in costumes of different periods, Puritans and

Egyptian priests and slaves. The room we used, with all the wall decorations and ceiling painting — we had lights and some eerie drum music. Once I got used to these ceremonies I liked them. I looked forward to them. They took me out of the humdrum. They were better than plays because it seemed that everybody meant what they were saying. They meant what they were doing. Your friends were suddenly other people and they meant it. It was serious. You don't get that anywhere else. Even after I doubted the whole purpose of the group and things started frightening me, I still got a charge out of the initiations and the ceremonies. I hated the animal sacrifice part, but that was done in another place, and the mood was different. I didn't go there more than twice. The costume ceremonies were different. Interesting things happened. It wasn't the usual boring everyday nonsense.

"I was cast into a role of a goddess. At first it was Isis, and then Diana. They would dress me in white and have me stand in front of a doorway. I would move around the room then and look people in the eyes and sometimes touch them, as if to reassure them everything was all right ultimately, in the higher planes. I enjoyed this. People thought of me as a goddess and when I wasn't too embarrassed I started giving advice. It sounds silly now, but then I felt recognized. I was praised. In some of the ceremonies I was given messages to read from ascended masters. I was a connection. Do you see? I had wisdom. And at times I really felt I did. I was being given a chance to get into that role. Life doesn't give you that. Life is too straight. But here there was a part for a person who had wisdom, knowledge of higher planes, and I could step into that role if I wanted it, if I had the courage."

I asked Karen the first thing she remembered about the group that attracted her.

"A red satin robe," she said, "with a yellow stripe along the sleeves. It was gorgeous. It was hanging in a closet in one of the meeting rooms. A girl I knew took it out and showed it to me. I was thrilled at the time. It looked so beautiful, and I thought whoever wore it was lucky. Just over the heart was the Seal of Solomon. That was the first time I saw it. It was so perfect. The two triangles. The sleeves of the robe were very wide. I thought of them as Chinese. I asked the girl who owned the robe, and she said it belonged to the initiators, the people who brought you into the group. I felt that if this costume was used for that ritual, it must be worthwhile to join the group. There was a red satin hood that went with it. It had a black diagonal across the front. Even now, after all those years, I still like thinking about it. It's so exciting, the idea that somebody actually wore this. As if, what they're thinking and doing must be important if they have the robe on. See, there was a promise. That's what I felt. I felt that something would be revealed to me, after all those years of growing up and knowing nothing that meant much. The symbols on the floor of the room in the barn, those painted disks on the ceiling. People seemed to care about the mysterious things."

46

Karen introduced me to a man named Avi, a former member of the group "at another level." He helped me see how far a little secret society, with its "curtain of enticing art," could go up the line toward really nasty consequences.

Avi told me that the group definitely had Nazi connections, that beyond the mystical symbols, the stories, the Seal of Solomon, the ceremonies, the costumes, the ascended masters, there was another compartment.

I asked Avi what the group's Nazi connections had been.

"Drugs," he said. "Cocaine."

He shrugged. "Karen didn't know."

I spent a little time reviewing several old radio shows I had done on KPFK in Los Angeles on Nazi "influences." According to one line of scholarly thought, it was the German psychiatrists who really influenced Hitler to set up the extermination camps and begin the elimination of "inferior genetic types." Earlier, the psychiatrists had been sterilizing German inmates at mental hospitals, and had been murdering some of those inmates under the heading of euthanasia.

The Nazis credited their eugenics laws to American pioneers like Paul Popenoe. America had a considerable tradition of sterilization of mental patients in California, and before the Second World War there were very reputable medical doctors in the U.S. who wrote articles upholding eugenics as a tool to weed out "compromised" people whose genes were "obviously defective."

The Nazi Party, in its fervor to elevate the pure Aryan and dispose of so-called lower genetic influences, spurred on research fanatics who wanted nothing more than to experiment on human bodies and brains.

In general, business connections between American and
German corporations and major players, before, during, and
after World War II are legendary.

Leading up to the War, a number of industrial and banking
leaders in the U.S. and Britain and Germany — as well as
government officials in those countries — supported both
the U.S. and Germany.

These agreements held during the War. The banks which
represented all these men were National City Bank and Chase
National Bank in the U.S. The Nazi lawyers who handled
matters among these elite "double-agents" were Gerhardt
Westrick and Heinrich Albert. Emil Puhl, a Nazi economist,
functioned as a kind of go-between. Puhl worked for the Nazi
Reichsbank and the Bank for International Settlements (BIS).

BIS had originally been set up to receive German repara-
tions from World War I. It however became a conduit for
money to Germany out of the U.S., England, and, eventually,
from conquered European nations. Again, this money flowed
to Germany. To Hitler. In gold alone, we are talking about
$378 million. U.S. government officials were aware of this
and condoned it, even though they were both contributors
to, and administrative officials of, BIS.

In December 1941, Standard Oil of New Jersey, General
Motors, ITT, and Ford had a total of $200 million invested in
Germany. It stayed there during the War.

This is only the beginning of a much longer story, in which
many of the names are known.

Avi told me that the cult in California he and Karen had
belonged to sent cash to a Nazi cult out of the country.

"Cash?" I said. "Why does a Nazi group need money if
the big shots got out of Germany with millions?"

"Rich church, poor church," he said. "Ever hear of it? The
Vatican owns huge tracts of land but their private schools
can't buy new books. Same with the Nazis. The nest egg is
held back and the groups have to hustle."

"So that's it? This California cult sent cash out of the
country? That's the connection?"

"They sent it to Chile."

"Who to?"

"The Colonia Dignidad. In the south."

"I've heard about it."

"Well," he said, "then you know they helped overthrow President Allende. It's a Nazi torture center. For real Nazis who got out of Germany after the War, and their protégés. They set up a sophisticated communications link there, so they can talk to other Nazis in different countries. They're allied with the worst right-wing lunatics in Chile."

"I've read about it," I said. "They have 30,000 acres. Sound-proofed torture rooms. They hook people up to shock machines and sit in other rooms. It's remote control. Amnesty International finally got in and inspected the place."

"Insane."

The Colonia, an estate outside the town of Parral, is notorious among Nazi hunters and human rights groups like Amnesty. People have disappeared there and have never been seen again.

I said, "I understand they do cultish rituals too."

"I think so," Avi said. "The ancient Teutonic stuff. The California cult group has sent a few people there. A few of their members."

"For what?"

"I don't know what they told them, but the result may have been torture. I guess you could say they supplied victims for the Nazis."

"What the hell for?"

"How should I know?" he said. "Torture is for the torturers."

In another conversation with Avi, I was told that Karen's group in California also helped distribute cocaine from Colombia and Bolivia into the U.S.

"Ever hear of Carlos Lehder Rivas?" Avi said.

"The head of the Medellin cartel."

"Once."

"He testified against Noriega in Miami."

"That's right," Avi said. "Carlos was a Nazi. He set up a political party in Colombia, the MCLN, in the early '80s. A Nazi party. He was always talking about Hitler as the greatest man who ever lived — and how he was going to use cocaine as the weapon to destroy the United States."

"He was a cokehead, right?"

"Yes, but I think he meant what he said."

"You mean, cocaine would poison people's brains on a large scale?"

"Something like that," Avi said. "Addict people, and Carlos would make a hell of a lot of money, too, and use it in various ways against the U.S."

"So the group? You handled cocaine?"

"A select number of us. We dealt with cutouts, a few levels down from the Cartel, from the big people in Colombia. We never met the chiefs. But Nazism was the connection. The agenda was to destroy the United States."

"Did you run guns, too?" I asked.

"No. That was Klaus Barbie's thing, in Bolivia."

"You were a committed Nazi?" I asked.

"I was committed to money. I was on board as a semi-pro, you might say."

"So what happened?"

"We lost our connection to Medellin. Also, I began to see that Carlos was right. If we got enough drugs into the U.S. we could change history — for the worse. I guess I have a little bit of conscience. Not much, but it's there. I don't like Nazis."

"Did many of the people who joined this cult, this secret society in California, know what was going on?"

"No. It worked in layers. Some people came in because there was a big chunk of mysticism. Other people liked the blood. The animal sacrifices. Not many. And then there were those who operated in the drug area."

"What about the people who disappeared into Chile?"

"The Colonia probably killed them. They were innocents, I guess. I wasn't involved with that. I only heard about it later. Probably a few eager beavers in the group here thought they liked Nazism and went down there. They thought they'd get some kind of advanced training. Instead they became guinea pigs. See, to some people, the Colonia looks like a community. A farm, a free medical clinic, a bakery. They have their own power source there. I think the generators are there for a time of chaos. That's just my guess. A potential retreat for Nazis from all over the world. There was an American there. Michael Townley. He designed the remote-controlled torture rooms. An electronics guy."

"Are you sure," I asked, "that the California group sent down a few people to Colonia, and that they were tortured? Killed?"

"That's what I heard," Avi said. "I can't guarantee it. I wasn't there. Maybe this was made up to scare people. How should I know?"

Of course it was not only the Nazis in Chile who had a hand in overthrowing President Allende. The American CIA was involved up to its hips.

There is much speculation about the number and names of German scientists who were imported directly into what became the CIA after World War II. The human experimentation in the concentration camps has a similar foul ring to the 149 MKULTRA mind-control projects of the Agency. We do know that top Nazis Reinhard Gehlen and Otto Skorzeny folded directly into CIA efforts to gain intelligence on the Soviet Union after World War II. Gehlen's own German spy network on the Eastern Front was lifted nearly intact into the CIA.

John Marks, author of *The Search for the Manchurian Candidate*, states that SS doctors Kurt Plotner and Walter Neff did mind-control research on prisoners using mescaline and hypnosis at Dachau, and that records of their lunatic experiments were taken at the close of the War by the Americans and hidden in CIA and Pentagon files. Classified. They have never been released. Why not release them? To save Americans the horror of learning what humans will do to one another? I don't think that is the reason. The obvious reason is to protect what is considered "usable technology."

In *Blowback*, his book on American recruitment of Nazis into government positions, Christopher Simpson states,

> Between 1945 and 1955, 765 scientists, engineers, and technicians were brought to the United States under Overcast, Paperclip, and two other similar programs.

At least half, and perhaps as many as 80 percent, of the imported specialists were former Nazi party members or SS men, according to Professor Clarence Lasby, who has authored a book-length study of [U.S. government Operation] Paperclip ... [for example] Major General Walter Schreiber, who had once been instrumental in medical experiments on concentration camp inmates by the Luftwaffe ... Overcast and Paperclip were just the beginning ...

Consider this possible scenario: Certain elements within the CIA, protected by secrecy and a vast unquestioned budget, and elements of the SS who escaped Europe in 1945, or who were baldly promoted into the upper levels of the new German society with the help of Konrad Adenauer, joined forces. And that resultant group, which has spread discreetly into other elements of U.S. intelligence, are a most powerful secret society of the day.

For those who are utterly baffled or enraged by the suggestion that groups of apparently opposing ideologies could secretly join together, let me offer a quote from Hitler's own architect and master designer, Albert Speer. It is a glance into the creation of pre-defined spaces for the masses:

I recall, incidentally, that the footage taken during one of the solemn sessions of the 1935 [Nazi] Party Congress was spoiled. At [Nazi filmmaker] Leni Riefenstahl's suggestion Hitler gave orders for the shots to be refilmed in the studio. I was called in to do a backdrop simulating a section of the *Kongresshalle*, as well as a realistic model of the platform and lectern. I had spotlights aimed at it; the production staff scurried around — while Streicher, Rosenberg, and Frank could be seen walking up and down with their manuscripts, determinedly memorizing their parts. Hess arrived and was asked to pose for the first shot. Exactly as he had done before an audience of 30,000 at the Party Congress, he solemnly raised his hand. With his special brand of ardor, he turned precisely to the spot where Hitler would have been sitting, snapped to attention and cried: "My Leader, I welcome you in the name of the Party Congress! The Congress will now continue. The Führer speaks!"

He did it all so convincingly that from that point on I was no longer so sure of the genuineness of his feelings. The three others also gave excellent performances in the emptiness of the studio, proving themselves gifted actors. I was rather disturbed; Frau Riefenstahl, on the other hand, thought the acted scenes better than the original presentation.

By this time I thoroughly admired the art with which Hitler would feel his way during his rallies until he had found the point to unleash the first great storm of applause. I was by no means unaware of the demagogic element; indeed I contributed to it myself by my scenic arrangements. Nevertheless, up to this time I had believed that the feelings of the speakers were genuine. It was therefore an upsetting discovery, that day in the studio, when I saw that all this emotion could be represented "authentically" even without an audience.

I asked Avi if he had ever seen any CIA people around the California group.

"There were rumors," he said. "I can't be sure. See, with the Colombians, with Carlos, there were always stories about the CIA cooperating in the cocaine trade. Not the whole goddamn CIA, but certain people. There was one guy who came to a few meetings of the group in California. He was interested in promoting a little hypnosis project."

"What kind of project?"

"To increase group loyalty."

"How did it work?"

"I think he would put people in a light trance and then play tapes about the group and its mission. Maybe flash some symbols on a screen."

"Did it ever get off the ground?" I asked.

"I think the people in the group, the leaders, were opposed to it. This guy they didn't know. He came in from the outside.

The leaders had their own plans anyway."

"What plans?"

"Building a desert community. Which they never did. They would keep the members busy every spare waking hour. Work was their idea of controlling people."

"This outside man with the hypnosis program. It was rumored he was CIA?"

"Not exactly. You see, he was an 'independent researcher.' He was doing a study, he said. He made it sound academic. But to hypnotize people, to get them to be more loyal, doesn't seem like academic research. I think it was a front. Somebody was interested in experimenting on cult members. Who does that kind of research? People from intelligence agencies."

I had another conversation with Karen. She said, "I remember the man. He called himself Charles."

"The one with the hypnosis project?"

"Yes. I went out with him a couple of times."

"Socially?"

"He liked me. I let him hypnotize me. I wanted to see what it was like. He started flashing numbers on a screen in the dark. We were at the meeting room in the barn."

"Just regular numbers?"

"At first. Then he switched over to strange symbols. I'd never seen them before. They looked a little like Hebrew but they weren't. Maybe a cross between Arabic and Hebrew. I asked him what they were. Later he told me they were just warm-ups. Something to get me in an easy frame of mind."

"Because they didn't make any sense."

"That's what I think. You know, you get vague. These symbols flash by. It's like looking at calculus. What does it mean?"

"How long did the symbols continue?"

"About five minutes."

"That's a long time."

"I thought so. Then he put up the Seal of Solomon. The meshed triangles. He flashed that maybe fifty times. Different sizes, different colors."

"Did he say anything while this was going on?"

"Yes. He acted like a hypnotist. He told me to relax, to

focus on the screen and just relax. He said I was becoming calmer. I'm not sure if that was the word. But I did feel myself sinking into a warm feeling."

"And the Seal was flashing by on the screen."

"Yes. And he said I was a good person and part of a good group of people. Things like that. Praising the group. Then he said I was moving into the Seal. I should feel myself going inside the triangles to the center. Psychically moving. I went with it. I felt like I was moving in some space, through the air."

"Were you doing this on your own?"

"I surrendered to him. I let it happen. He took over."

"You went into the Seal."

"Yes. I told him I was there. He said that was good, and he said in the center of the Seal was a place of peace, and I could always go there as long as I was part of the group. I would always be welcomed inside the Seal, in the magical place. I think I dozed off at that point, for a minute."

"Was there any chance he gave you drugs?"

"No, I felt very clear, except I was fading into his words. I was being hypnotized."

"How long did you stay inside the Seal?"

"A few minutes, I guess. I don't know. While I was there, he said he was going to pass along a few secrets to me. I had to promise I wouldn't tell anyone. I don't remember this part too well, but he said I was now really in the group, I was in the place where the group was really located. I remember thinking this was a version of heaven. I was in the perfect place."

"He was hypnotizing you to feel this."

"Sure. He said that this was where I could have sex. I could be in this place and have sex, and it would be sacred. He said I could think about getting rich in this place, inside the Seal, and my thoughts would be magnified in power from this place. He said something about a swastika, too. He said it was a symbol of the rotation of the eight points of the universe. The universe was built on eight centers, eight psychic places of magic. This was a message I was supposed to remember and keep secret. He said the whole universe faced in differ- ent directions at different times, and he would eventually tell me what that meant, and how I could take advantage of that. But I had to be in the perfect place, inside the Seal, for any of this to work. He told me to go further into that space, into the center of the Seal. I did. I felt like I had the ability to do that, to follow his directions. He slowed them down, the Seals. They stayed on the screen longer. I was reacting to the colors and the sizes. Not in any way I can describe, but they were making an impression on me."

"Did he ever mention the CIA to you? After the session?"

"No."

"Did anything else happen in the session?"

"He pretty much left it there. I know he thought he'd be having a lot more sessions with me. But I left the group soon after that."

"The hypnosis sounded effective."

"It was."

"With more sessions, he might have put you under his control."

"Yes."

"Did he say anything to you about this method of his?"

"He said the advanced form of it was based on doing a personality profile on me. Asking lots of questions."

I told her that a psychologist named John Gittinger, who had once worked for the CIA, developed a well-known Personality Assessment System, as it was called, to measure people intelligence agencies might have some use for or dealings with. (PAS is mentioned briefly in Orrin DeForest's book, *Slow Burn: The Rise and Bitter Fall of American Intelligence in Vietnam.*)

"Well," she said, "Once, when we were out eating dinner, he said intelligence agencies had a way of looking at people based on their potential weaknesses."

"How did this come up?"

"I don't remember. I think we were talking about hypnosis and how it could be used."

"Did he ever mention the Nazis or Nazi symbols?"

"The swastika, like I told you. That's the only time. He did remind me about the animal sacrifices, though. A few times. He seemed to harp on it."

"In what way?"

"That I had participated in it. The suggestion was that I was a bad girl for doing it. He wasn't criticizing me. He was reminding me that I had done it. So I would remember. It was as if I had taken a silent oath. I was bad, and the hypnosis part could put me in the good place. That's what he was doing."

"During the hypnosis," I asked, "did he show any other images on the screen?"

"Scenes of farmland. A forest with trees and clouds showing through. Nature scenes. They were on the screen while he was talking. He was very calm. There was a picture of children playing in a big yard, too. Pretty children."

"Did he talk about these scenes?"

"No, I don't think so. They were just there. They were nice. Restful."

"Did he mention loyalty to your group?"

"It was more about going to the place in the center of the Seal. If I understood that, I would be loyal, because that was home. That was where everybody was. It was not only a peaceful place, a good place, it was a sensual place too. It was a place where sexual things would be more intense, where we could connect in a more intense way."

"A home away from home ... A world."

"Yes."

A statement from Charles Higham came to mind. Higham is a former *New York Times* reporter, a man not given to hyperbole. He authored *Trading With the Enemy*, the thoroughly researched history of a "money plot" involving elite players on both sides of the Atlantic, men who colluded before, during and after World War II — who essentially bet on both sides to win the War, and put their monies where their mouths were. Their concern was power, pure and simple. Higham called them The Fraternity. He wrote:

> ... the members [of the Fraternity] sought a common future in fascist domination, regardless of which world leader might further that ambition ... Several members ... [supported] ... a police state that would place The

Fraternity in postwar possession of financial, industrial, and political autonomy. When it was clear that Germany was losing the war the [American and British] business-men became notably more 'loyal' [to their own govern-ments]. Then, when war was over, the survivors pushed into Germany, protected their assets, restored Nazi friends to high office, helped provoke the Cold war, and ensured the permanent future of The Fraternity.

In Karen, was I looking at a person who had collided with a very minor fragment of that essence, who had met up with a far-down-the-line hybrid of Nazi and American intelligence in turn derived from a collaboration of power brokers?

As evidenced in Dean Radin's book, *The Conscious Universe,* the U.S. government has long been interested in what might be called psychic and/or New Age phenomena. Radin discusses funding for, and results of, the psychic remote-viewing experiments carried on at the Stanford Research Institute in the 1970s. The CIA has been notorious for investigating groups or researchers who claim to have the ability to demonstrate psychic phenomena. The CIA's interest, of course, is in collecting new "weapons" that can be used to gather intelligence, to spy, perhaps even to affect behavior at a distance.

Was Karen's group a slightly far-out exploring ground for a funded CIA researcher, who was told to go out and see what he could discover in a cult setting, with unaware subjects? Was this a testing place for trying out methods of "personnel control?

It made sense to me that this Charles, with his slide show and hypnotist's air, was establishing a psychic space — the center of Solomon's Seal — where the subject could "go." Undoubtedly, this would function as a place where control could be exercised, a pre-defined space whose landscape could be fleshed out, as a kind of artistic endeavor, if you will, by the controller, by the person who would by degrees dominate his subject.

It was a stripped-down example of the kind of space one could encounter in a cathedral, under the power of a priest, as a child, while the mighty organ played and the hundreds of candles flickered, while prayers were intoned in Latin, while duties were carried out to the letter in a slow but precise fashion ...

I spoke with a hypnotist, Jack True, in Los Angeles. Here is a quite relevant sample from our discussion, which occurred after I told him about my interviews with Karen and Avi:

Does hypnotism function as a security blanket?

It can. You can establish it like salt-water taffy. It'll do whatever you want it to. You can hypnotize someone to be three miles out in space and describe what he sees. You can have the hypnotic subject be a warm afternoon looking for rain. The usual constraints are off. It'll go anywhere.

But what about the subject himself?

The subject is hypnotized. Above all, you have to remember that. If he can sing like Caruso while he's under, that doesn't mean you can expect anything out of him when he wakes up. As obvious as that sounds, that's where people make mistakes.

But you can give post-hypnotic suggestions.

Yes. Just parlor tricks, unless you're a torturer and you're using drugs and duress and are hurting the person during the hypnosis and are giving post-hypnotic suggestions. But the usual kind of hypnosis is different. Post-suggestions wear off in a little while. He scratches his ass every time he sees a blue object, but only for a half hour or so.

What about a person who is hypnotized many times over a period of weeks and months?

Then you're doing something else. You're establishing a control-center, which is ordinarily the operator, the hypnotist. Everything refers back to him, but gradually. Gradually. That's how cults work.

You could have sub-centers too.

Yes. The operator, let's say, hypnotizes a person every week, three times a week, for six months, and during that time tells the person about a meadow in a forest where every-thing is peaceful and no harm can come. Then the meadow, even though it only exists in the minds of the operator and the subject, is very real, and the person can 'go' there. That's a sub-center. You can direct a person to go there and then you can begin to elaborate details about the way things are in the meadow. You can make up meadow-realities that will slop over into daily life.

A place.

It becomes a sub-center for control. The subject wants to be there.

Deceptive.

Sure. A nice spot in the woods, a relaxing feeling. But when the intent is ultimately control, you get something else in the long run. Anyway, it's a crock.

Why?

Because it's a hypnotic effect. What hypnotism shows is the potential of the mind to create while it's under the power of someone who has taken the role of "good authority."

And that person won't always be there.

The stage of child has to grow to adult. I don't mean hopes and dreams have to die horrible deaths. I mean the person has to outgrow being a subject for an operator. He has to some-how take over the reins of control and create for himself.

A lot of people feel more is possible under the control of the hypnotist.

Yes. They believe that outside themselves there is the answer.

Suppose you hypnotize a person a number of times and tell him that he will assume the reins of his own life, he will create what he needs and what he wants, that he will expand the power of his own imagina-tion to unheard of dimensions.

That's interesting. I've tried several versions of that. Because that's what you'd think is the bottom line on hypnosis. Get yourself hypnotized to become the king of the universe.

It doesn't work, right?

It doesn't work. Because the mind, the person knows what's going on. The basic fact is you're getting hypnotized by an authority to become your own master. But to become your own master you have to break the spell of your hypnosis. Break the spell. How can you increase the power of your own imagination unless you decide to do it, unless it's your show? First do that. Then come to me with talk about entities showing up and having Satanic powers and all that. First establish your own authority and begin to ...

... Begin to invent your own realities.

Exactly. Do that, know what it feels like to do it, then come to me with tales from the wild side. I'm not saying that non-physical beings don't exist. I'm saying that most control is established through various kinds of hypnosis, and the widest kinds are control of the information you're exposed to. Anyway, we're getting a little off the subject. In the case of this woman, Karen, she was given one session by an operator who knew what he was doing. He was showing her a place to go, a control center he called the center of the Seal of Solomon.

Have you ever run across that before?

Sure. Not that exact symbol used in this way, but the general pattern. You define a place where magical things will happen. See, she'll get her wishes when she hopes for them from that place. She'll get precognition when she goes to that place. Sex will be a lot hotter. Whatever you want. Do you want angels? I'll put you in a place called heaven.

There's nothing wrong with having a place.

What's wrong is having someone else put you there. See, there's a subtle dividing line between becoming inspired by reading a great novel, a great fantasy, and having a hypnotist put you in a place. Is a museum hypnosis? People like to tap dance and get fancy and say everything is mind control. That's baloney. A museum is an open space where you have the freedom to witness great things. Then you can do what you want to. If you get enchanted by Rembrandt and that takes you to the Bible and that takes you to Gnostic Gospels and that takes you to great historical lies and that takes you back to Rembrandt and that takes you to Leonardo, and so on, that's fine. You're on a trek. You're moving. But if I put you on a grassy meadow, and you meet every Thursday night with other people who know about the meadow, and everybody is reinforcing the hell out of this mythical spot, and everybody believes all magical ability comes out of that place and the enchantment given to it by a group and a leader, now we've got hypnosis. This Karen was put there. She was sucked in and then she was put there once. She went away, I guess. But another person may have stayed.

There are people who think hypnosis and creativity are the same thing.
Have you noticed the world is much more stupid as the years pass? Suppose I tell you a fantasy I have, all right? You listen to it, and you tell me because I spoke of a place that sounds to you like part of a brainwashing program, it's all hypnosis. For example, I like to think about Oz, and the people that inhabit it, because I read about it. You think it's weird and probably some crazy cult brainwashed me to think about it.

You're serious?
What do you think fundamental Christianity does? I'm talking about hardcore end-timers with a fixation on the apocalypse. They believe that God and heaven are no brainwashing program. No, no, no. They're real. Okay. Starting from there, they think that anyone who entertains or contemplates a landscape that has mythical figures in it that are not from the Bible must have been touched hard by Satan. Satan, the head of a brainwashing cult called Evil. Get it?

You run across people like this?
Of course.

They can't tell the difference between creating and getting hypnotized.
They can't make the separations because their lives are soaked through with a program. The hardcore end-times Christian, with some nasty racism thrown in, is the major program I know about. But it all comes back to, who did it? Did you become a Christian on your own? Did you read the books and ask questions and explore the stories and shape Jesus and work for the poor and help people, or did somebody stick you into it and keep you there and did you just accept it and go along with it like a gooney-bird soldier?

What did you think of this group that Karen belonged to?
Interesting. Did she tell you the name?

No. She wouldn't touch that with a ten-foot pole. Same with Avi.

It's several layers. The guy, Charles, he interests me. The hypnotist. He sounds like a hybrid. Semi-academic. A little of that background. But he has a taste for nasty stuff too. That's why he isn't sitting in a college teaching psychology. He can't get enough action there. He wants to push his particular envelope. Control people. Get that hit from them.

CIA?

Some intelligence outfit. A sub-sub contractor. A small fish.

As a member of this group, Karen was exposed to and bombarded by symbols. Symbols are one obvious and important aspect of the Formula of the Secret Society, one important part of the art that is made and used to control.

In Part 3, I'll take up the aspect of symbols. They are, by nature, slightly hypnotic.

PART THREE

47

Let me begin to flesh out the extremes of the Tradition of Imagination and the Formula of the Secret Society. They represent, I believe, the two greatest forces acting on this planet from the dawn of time.

The Formula of the Secret Society

We have the so-called action painters who improvise, as it were, inside the arena of the canvas, put on color rapidly and then eventually look for, or come across, "found objects" of excitement. We also have the great studied muralists, and Piero della Francesca was perhaps the greatest of them all. The Legend of the True Cross at Arezzo, with its section called King Solomon Receiving the Queen of Sheba, was built to last the ages. It is an architecture of spaces undulating slowly, turning inside out and throwing back an echo of its own figures. Piero found his perspective and proportions through a study of numbers, and he eventually retired to author works on the mathematics of painterly illusion.

Between these two poles of working, as it were, lie an infinity of artistic choices. The greatest of cults in the West, the Church of Rome, utilizing perversion as its major theme, took the vast, vaulted planned route to the exposition of its universe.

Perhaps no other secret society has approached the Church in its influence on the West. At its height, it was at least the equal of all the kings and queens of Europe. It could open a Holy Office of Inquisition on the continent, set up its own courts, try, torture and burn alive, at a chosen temperature, any human in its sight. A person not believing in its doctrines and invented entities could be labeled a heretic and banned from society or killed.

In a country like England, before the Roman Catholic influence waned, hardly a person would show his face in public prepared to cast aspersions on the True Church.

Since this Church owned one third of the land in England, it ruled vast numbers of serfs (slaves) who lived and worked on its estates. Thus, during the Middle Ages, the national forbidding of travel, for any lower-class citizen, from town to town without special permission was as much a Church enforcement as a secular regulation.

Of this life, Hitler and Stalin could only dream.

As one tries to piece together the historical influences and vital forces which produced such an immense imprisonment of medieval populations, it is easy to decide that events somehow conspired to make misery bit by bit. But the highest architects of the Church had their blank canvases. They invented the proportions of the works that would fill them. They at times may have massaged a bell of God, but they also made a Symphony of Torture. They created, and the work of art stood.

Consider this. "[E]very priest of the church had the right and the power to give orders to God, which God had no choice but to obey."

This power is alluded to or spelled out in a number of places. Father John O'Brien of the University of Notre Dame, in his book, *Faith For Millions*, unstintingly presents the fact:

> The supreme power of the priestly office is the power of consecrating [the body of Christ] ... In this essential phase of the sacred ministry, the power of the priest is not surpassed by that of the bishop, the archbishop, the cardinal or the pope. Indeed, it is equal to that of Jesus Christ. For in this role the priest speaks with the voice and authority of God Himself.
>
> When the priest pronounces the tremendous words of consecration, he reaches up into the heavens, brings Christ down from his throne, and places Him upon our altar to be offered up again as the victim for the sins of

man. It is a power greater than that of monarchs and emperors; it is greater than that of saints and angels, greater than that of Seraphim and Cherubim. Indeed, it is even greater than the power of the Virgin Mary ... the priest brings Christ down from heaven ... not once but a thousand times! The priest speaks and lo! Christ, the eternal and omnipotent God, bows His head in humble obedience to the priest's command.

Add to this the fact that the Church sets itself up with total control of the Genesis creation story. It declares ownership of the universe invented by a single God "on the face of the deep." So in a sense it even claims possession of the void.

Torture was handed out to heretics, those who would not avow belief in the Church and all of its inventions. It must be understood that such torture was cultivated as an art by Church practitioners. The application of thumbscrews, the suspension of the heretic from iron rings, the dislocating of arms from shoulder sockets, the feeding of foul meals and latrine water to prisoners, the burning of flesh — all this and much more were calculated to bring rebels as close to death as necessary for extracting full confessions of heresy.

"I blasphemed against the Church and God, and now I have seen the light."

For half a millennium, the universe created by the Catholic Church was the centerpiece of Western thought. After two World Wars, new artists aspired to take center stage. Their cosmos is less ambitious in its aspirations, but may become more enveloping in the long run. The theme? Global unity. The primary medium? Money.

Meanwhile, of course, the Church lives on. There are still, undoubtedly, Jesuits who dedicate themselves to the prayer of their founder, Ignatius:

"Take, Lord, and receive
All my liberty, my memory, my intellect,
And all my will —
All that I have and possess.
You gave all that to me.
To you, Lord, I return it.
All is yours.

Dispose of it according to your will.
Give me your love and grace.
Those will be enough for me."
Yes.

The pre-defined space run by Someone Else. The space is sketched out this way by Malachi Martin: "The Three Persons of the Trinity constitute the supreme hierarchy. The Pope and his bishops constitute a second major hierarchy. The General of the Society of Jesus and its Superiors, Major and Minor, constitute a third hierarchy. Within God's Heaven, there are hierarchies of angels, and within Satan's Hell, hierarchies of fallen angels."

And by some estimates a billion Catholics exist in this world.

This stands in stark contrast to the Tradition of Imagination.

48

I have received word through the Arizona address that Rachel Jenkins died six months ago. The address, a PO box, will be closed down.

Attempts to reach Carol Schuman have not been successful ...

49

Let me lay out in front of you some of the symbolism of the Holy Roman Catholic Church.

This is not an effort to show its entire pattern. I am mainly interested in sheer numbers and weight of symbols expressed in its religious art, expressed in cathedrals, in illuminated manuscripts and other properties of the Church. Keep in mind that although we may feel familiar with many of these symbols now, at their birth and for some time after — and always, for children — these shapes are door-openers. They make question marks in the mind, and wonderment, and then the high priests of Somesuch enter and explain the meanings.

That little explaining is the lobby, the vestibule, which of course is only a few steps away from the main events in the really big rooms.

Then the aspirant will want to study the subject in more detail, and, for that, there are more symbols.

This is all art. This is invention at work in the service of narrowing the imagination.

Start with a bare simplicity. The equilateral triangle.

Three equal sides and three equal angles. Three in unity. The Holy Trinity of God, Jesus, and the Holy Ghost.

This triangle has many spinoffs which stand for the same Holy Trinity. We have two triangles and a circle, or the trefoil, or two triangles and a circle interwoven, or the triqueta and triangle, a cross hung with a triangle on its shoulders, the fleur-de-lis, three intertwined fishes. The fish in turn can be traced to the five letters which spell the Greek word for fish. Those five letters form, in Greek, the first letters of the words in the phrase whose translation is: "Jesus Christ, Son of God, Saviour." I throw that in to show a glimpse of the far fields in which the manufacture of symbols takes place in order to attain a sensation of holiness.

What about symbols for God the Father?

A hand of God with thumb and the first two fingers extended and the third and fourth fingers closed. The three extended fingers are the Holy Trinity, and the two closed are "the two aspects of Jesus."

We also have a hand of God coming out of a cloud.

For Jesus himself, we have the good shepherd with the lamb on his shoulders. We also have the lamb. We also have the lamb resting on the Book of the Seven Seals. Or the lamb and a banner signifying victory. There is the fish, or a long sceptre ending in a sphere with a cross on top, or the sun, a tree branch, a fountain, a brass serpent, a pelican opening her own chest with her beak and feeding her babies her blood, the crucifix, a tree growing out of the loins of Jesse, who is the father of David, a vine, a lion, a daisy (standing for innocence of Jesus the child), a unicorn (representing the incarnation of Jesus), the Glastonbury thorn (the nativity), a shellfish shell (Jesus' baptism), the rose (the Nativity), a phoenix (resurrection), gladiolus flower (the word turned into flesh), a peacock (gaining immortality through Jesus), a butterfly (eternal life), the ox and the ass, staff of the shepherd, torch on fire, rosemary flower, three caskets, a five-pointed star, an olive, palm branches, pomegranate, crown and sceptre, a boat anchor, lit candlestick, cross overlaid with an X, five crosses together, a door, an eagle, the charadrius bird, a mermaid, a dolphin, a centaur, a swallow, horse and rider, the Judge, and various sacred monograms, each of which has several variations: Chi Ro; IHC; IHS; Alpha and Omega; Alpha, Mu, Omega; INRI.

The above list does not include specific symbols for the Passion of Christ, such as the lantern, the crown of thorns, Gethsemane, and the scourges. I have found 18 symbols for the Passion.

For the Holy Ghost, I have found 11 separate symbols, which I will leave unnamed.

Under a category called "The Word, Sacraments, and Sacred Rites," in F.R. Webber's *Church Symbolism*, there are nine symbols.

For the Blessed Virgin I find 39 separate symbols.

For the so-called Evangelists — Matthew, Mark, Luke and John — I have seen seven symbols. For the 12 Apostles, I locate 66 symbols, including as diverse representations as a rooster, three shellfish, a snake in a cup, an eagle ascending from a pot of hot oil, a windmill, a sailboat, a fish stuck on a hook, a snake thrown into a fire, a locust and a leather girdle, a tunic made of camel's hair. These are all in the form of shields.

Remember, I am only mentioning symbols actually used by the Church and its artists. These are not off the cuff.

There are nine official choirs of angels. For each of these types, we have various artistic depictions. The nine choirs are divided into three groups, each of which has three sub-types. The main branches of angels are the Counsellors, the Governors, and the Messengers. Under the Counsellors are the Seraphim, Cherubim, and Thrones. The Governors include Dominions, Powers, and Virtues. The Messengers contain the Principalities, Archangels and Angels. Each of these nine groups has its own named leader, style of dress, and symbols.

The Greek and Latin Fathers of the Church, eight of them, "figure very prominently in Christian art ..." I find 10 symbols for these men.

As for the Church itself, symbols abound. The ark, the ship, the ark of the covenant, the rock, the candelabra, wheat and tares, the mustard seed, and so on. I have counted 20 symbols.

Furthermore, through displayed art, there is an ingenious typing of stories within the Church, in which a key tale is not only pictorialized, but also symbolized by showing other versions of it. For example, the specific type of story known as The Epiphany might be referred to by art showing the visit of the Queen of Sheba to King Solomon — not a Christian adventure at all — or by the non-Christian Abner coming to see David, King of the Hebrews, or by Joseph's Hebrew brothers bowing down to him in Egypt. The Church holds that the real story behind all of these is: the Magi coming to see the Infant Lord.

In Church art, you would see all of these tales depicted — and all but one, the Real One, would have a symbolic meaning.

How many such official archetypes of Church stories exist? Well, there is The Annunciation, The Incarnation, The Nativity, The Presentation, The Holy Innocents, The Holy Family in Egypt, The Return From Egypt, St. John the Baptist, Our Lord's Baptism, The Temptation, The Sermon on the Mount, The Raising of Lazarus, The Transfiguration, The Triumphal Entry, Our Lord Weeps Over Jerusalem, Cleansing the Temple, The Last Supper, The Traitor Revealed, Our Lord in Gethsemane, The Betrayal, The Accusation before Pilate, The Crowning With Thorns, Our Saviour Mocked, The Scourging, Bearing the Cross, The Sacrifice on Calvary, The Seamless Coat (taken from Jesus by soldiers at the cross), The Pierced Side, The Virgin Mother's Sorrow, the Descent from the Cross, The Entombment, the Descent Into Hell, The Resurrection, The Woman at the Tomb, The Appearance to Mary, The Appearance to the Disciples, Thomas, The Ascension, Pentecost, The Second Coming, the Unbelievers, The Believers, The Church, Holy Baptism, The Holy Eucharist.

Again, each one of these story-types would be illustrated directly in Church art, but also symbolized by art which depicted other Biblical, historical, or mythological "versions" of them — which now would be co-opted and folded into the universe of the Church. A brilliant strategy to recast major events of history and pseudo-history: Call them SYMBOLS, and take them over. A rerouting of time into the One Major Train Station, the Church.

When I say a cult pre-defines a space and then claims that it is run by Someone Else, that the space contains a Pattern which must be studied — when I say a cult gives you an "elite special history" or "inner mysterious truth" as justification for its supreme elevation, this is what I mean. This is what I am talking about. This is the prime historical example.

This is how the citizen signs on to the idea that his own creation and creative imagination are not even important, or at best are bounded by the space set up by an elite.

I have not even taken into account the Church's absorbing of other non-Christian symbols and its wrapping them up in its own monuments.

The cross itself, for example, has many meanings. As an

alchemical and pagan object, it was often understood as a diagram of the four elements: earth, air, fire, and water. These elements were thought to be at war with one another. It was only by the introduction of the Quintessence, the life force which animates everything in the world, that the elements could be held from launching into chaos. Sometimes this life force was represented symbolically by the center meeting-point of the cross.

Let me add another fact. For saints of the Church, there are several symbols recognized for each. For example, a clay vessel and eight daggers belong to Saint Albert of Liege (1193 CE). An angel with a torch, some nails, and a stiletto belong to Saint Alexander of Rome (117 CE). I count 560 saints who each have these attendant symbols.

Does this give you some idea of the weight and extension of the Holy Church's symbolic endeavors?

Consider that none of these shapes, objects, animals, combinations in and of themselves immediately inform the eye or the mind. There is that moment or two or three of non-comprehension, of dumbness. Then the special meanings are supplied. The little bit of hypnotism is done.

When coercion also becomes part of the mix, you have a planet that generally teeters close to robothood.

50

Let us push forward this symbol-art of the secret society into a very strange venue, into the lowest venue of human activity.

Let us think about a secret society called the CIA. Let us widen that group and make it looser by calling it "departments of the U.S. intelligence establishment which have carried on secret mind-control experiments on humans."

Books have been written about the subject. Three of the most significant are John Marks' *Search For the Manchurian Candidate*, Alan Scheflin's *The Mind Manipulators*, and Walter Bowart's *Operation Mind Control*.

According to Alan Scheflin, these books were all begun from the same starting point: ten boxes of declassified CIA materials made public as a result of Freedom of Information Act requests in the mid-1970s.

The ten boxes of documents concerned a program called MKULTRA, which officially had been carried on between 1952–3 and 1964. Its purpose was to program or interrogate humans in such a way that they would not be able to resist, or know that the programming had been carried out. In effect, the secret intent was to make a robot who could act strictly on orders but who would not remember being given those orders. One who could not be de-programmed or discovered by "the other side."

One could command such a person to kill an enemy, to have sex with an enemy for blackmail purposes, to steal and store information, and so on.

One might also use the same methods to obtain secret information from captured enemies.

There are many opinions about the relative success of MKULTRA. I am not writing this book to argue that case.

However, it is clear that the Agency tried very hard to achieve its goals.

The following statement is part of a (non-CIA) memorandum dated June 27, 1994. It is written by "Advisory Committee Staff" to members of its own (Presidentially appointed) Advisory Committee on Human Radiation Experiments. This memo takes up the matter of an ongoing search into CIA records to see if the Agency had carried out illegal experiments on humans using radiation. The search was being done in conjunction with public hearings in Washington on the explosive matter of the U.S. government, in past years, condoning and sponsoring the perverted administration of radiation to U.S. citizens, "on a research basis."

The Advisory Committee Staff writes,

> In the 1950s and 60s, the CIA engaged in an extensive program of human experimentation, using drugs, psychological and other means, in search of techniques to control human behavior for counterintelligence and covert action purposes. The possibility that CIA itself engaged in human radiation experiments emanates from references in a 1963 CIA Inspector General's (I.G.) report on project MKULTRA, which was a program "concerned with research and development of chemical, biological, and radiological materials capable of employment in clandestine operations to control human behavior."

That is as clear and authoritative a statement as a novice needs to understand that the CIA did, in fact, run the mind-control project called MKULTRA. The fact that the above Committee subsequently did not find evidence that the Agency employed radiation convinced almost no one. The Agency, dedicated to covert operations, would normally and naturally behave covertly about exposure of an operation that would infuriate the public to the skies.

The most conservative of the original books on CIA Mind Control, *Search For the Manchurian Candidate*, reveals undeniable documentary evidence that the Agency was carrying out tests to induce amnesia in human subjects about its interrogation of them. This of course would also extend to attempts to program individuals to carry out assignments.

In other words, one strategy was to use drugs and other methods to obscure completely periods of time during which CIA hypnotists, programmers and interrogators worked on people.

On March 15, 1995, at 1 p.m., in the Executive Chambers, The Madison Hotel, in Washington D.C., Chris DeNicola and Claudia Mullin, patients of New Orleans therapist Valerie Wolf, and Wolf herself, began testimony to the President's Advisory Committee on Human Radiation Experiments.

Essentially, the three witnesses would allege that DeNicola and Mullin had been used for CIA-military radiation experiments which, however, were just a part of wider-ranging mind control "treatments."

Wolf had already forwarded to the Committee over a hundred pages of testimony on this matter. They not only included expanded statements from DeNicola, Mullin, and herself, they contained letters and testimony from therapists and patients around the U.S., many anonymously offered, recounting horrendous mind-control sessions, in some cases spanning decades. According to this testimony, CIA-military personnel had employed hallucinogenic drugs, spinning tables, flashing lights, hypnotism, physical torture, rape, threats of murder and abandonment, and the actual murder of other victims in their experiments. A purpose seemed to be the achievement of programming of sex-agents who could be used for blackmailing "enemies." Another, more inclusive goal was the inducing of multiple personalities in the victims. It was claimed that these artificial personalities could be slid in and out of awareness through trigger commands, like drawers in a file cabinet.

Wolf's pages of testimony, and the statements given by Mullin and DeNicola to the Committee, indicated that all of this had been done to children. DeNicola said she was four years old when her nightmare began. Mullin stated she was seven.

DeNicola, in her testimony, asserted,

I was in what looked like a laboratory and there seemed to be other children. I was strapped down, naked, spread eagle, on a table on my back. Dr. Greene had electrodes on my body, including my head. He used what looked like an overhead projector and repeatedly said he was burning different images into my brain while a red light flashed aimed at my forehead. In between each sequence he used electric shock on my body and told me to go deeper and deeper while repeating [that] each image would go deeper into my brain ... I felt drugged because he had given me a shot before he started the procedure.

DeNicola is talking about an attempt at establishing a slavemaster's control over her mind, in part by the use of images. So at the lowest level of secret-society human degradation, there is the use of non-literal images to program behavior. This is the lowest level of secret-society "work" to impress a universe on the mind of another person — with torture.

DeNicola, in an expanded version of her testimony, stated that her handler "used what looked like an overhead projector so that I could see the image. It was an upside down triangle called 'The Green Empire.'"

DeNicola continues: "He kept burning different images in my brain like triangles and other odd shapes."

An anonymous therapist, whose written testimony became part of the Committee record, wrote about the mind-control programming done on victims she subsequently treated: "Intricate programming codes [used] included Greek Alphabet, Kabbalistic terms, colors, numerology ..."

Another anonymous therapist lists "types of mind control programs," including "colors, symbols, numbers."

Even if one wanted to reject this testimony from top to bottom and call the whole thing fictitious, there would still be an obvious assumption contained in it that non-literal forms are to be used to program the mind.

This is precisely what secret societies, cults, and hierarchical religions do. This is part of their low, low art.

As I mentioned earlier, in secret societies, shapes and symbols have taken a pre-eminent place in the work of convincing adherents that the message of the cult is real and profound and beyond the normal scope of human knowledge.

In less coercive societies than the example above, authorities rigidly position all "official" symbols so that they convey a restricted meaning. More accurately, they combine a vagueness with a literal meaning in order to fix the mind. This hypnotic effect is key.

Take, for example, the universally known eye above a truncated triangle. Labeled as Masonic or ancient Egyptian, the combination of shapes would do justice to any decent surrealist painter. The viewer has a moment of non-comprehension. His mental computer doesn't make anything of the strange juxtaposition. He draws a blank. That blank causes a slight but definite vulnerability. At that point, he learns about the ancient building of great structures by "the original Masons," and the all-seeing eye and the work of the future in making a better world, etc. The aspirant tends to accept the explanation, no matter how foolish or simplistic, because he is slightly trapped by the non-literal symbol.

The lone triangle is used by many groups in the same way. The shape itself means nothing. It has no label. In that sense, it is a little unsettling. What is it doing, the viewer asks. Why is it sitting there alone?

Salvador Dali's famous melting watch could have the same effect, if self-appointed authorities began to attach arcane meanings to it. Why not?

Dali himself made a second career out of explaining his paintings. He very archly assured one and all, for example, that his grossly elongated lions really did imitate nature. For proof he supplied doctored photographs of lions in which their torsos began to look serpentine.

The surrealists reveled in the strangeness of shapes and combinations of realities. They really did open up unthinkable and marvelous universes. But theirs was essentially a revolution of cutting loose the anchor of fixed ideas.

The secret societies seek literal domination over the mind.

That is why they create art. That is their kind of work. They try to restrain the human mind from reaching freer levels of creation and imagination in which much wider versions of life swim into view.

They set themselves up against the Tradition of Imagination.

51

More on symbols

It now is clear to me that part of the Tradition of Imagination is the assertion that creation is a pre-eminent, or the pre-eminent activity of the human race.

The key is in how cultures look at their own collective present and their past.

In the West, many generations have been led to believe that religion is the major spiritual expression of civilization.

Who legislated that?

Suppose another activity had taken pre-eminence all the way along the line, coming down in time to us. Suppose, just to choose an example, human beings recognized that efforts to develop and practice real Magic have been the keynotes of civilization, from Sumer to New York.

Magic being, in its own way, a piece of the Tradition of Imagination — even though it is riddled with fakery.

Forget about whether the tradition of magic that did exist in alchemy, witchcraft, and works of the Persian/Egyptian magi is real or just a hope, a spark, a dream. The point is, is the Catholic Church really any more than that? And if not, then why shouldn't academies and cloisters of magic have grown up to be THE spiritual tradition of the West, instead of the Church?

The answer to that is, of course, simple. There are those who push hard and those who don't. There are those who use art to dominate large numbers of minds and there are those who don't. There are those who make wide Earthly power their number one priority, and there are those who don't. There are those who position their god far enough

186

away to withstand any effort to debunk his power.

Imagine for a moment that the striving to achieve what could be called paranormal magic — in all its glory — had somehow managed to become the central spiritual theme of our history. Where would we be now?

Suppose that magical tradition had been, for the most part, honest about its achievements and lack of same, and had painted a grand vision of a possible future in which humans could share in the joy of being able to "manifest matter, travel the realms, communicate over great distances by thought and feeling alone ..."

Where would we be now?

Suppose science and magic had been able to coexist, despite the debris of charlatanism that overlay magic and the willingness to follow institutional authority blindly that infects science?

Or what about this?

Suppose that art and artists had been revered more deeply, since the dawn of time, than the priests? Where would we be now?

I am saying that, in fact, the Tradition of Imagination has existed all over the place in history; it simply has not been pushed to the foreground. It has not been seen as a coherent human desire expressed in every time and every place.

And is it possible that, in the writing of history, figures who were presented as wearing spiritual robes of one Church or another were disguised from the future? Might they really have been, for example, magicians? Might their adherents, victors in a contest to see "whose gods were more powerful," have burned books, books that more accurately called their winning messiahs magicians?

Is popular history really a kind of crap shoot, or a heist, in which the weight allowed for one theme or another depends on who is shading the forms, coloring the figures, arranging the stage lights?

Of course it is.

But what is hidden by this machination is the sheer number of people who, through time, have really been thinking and hoping and desiring along a certain channel.

In the case of the unlabeled Tradition of Imagination, the number of people through history hoping and wishing for its brilliant realization has been gigantic, and if we knew it in our bones, if we, all along, had had the history to know it in our bones, and to know all the heroes, we would long ago have begun to step out into the light and claim our soulship.

It turns out, of course, that alchemy and witchcraft and magic all have had thousands and thousands of practitioners, and embedded in each tradition is imagination of a kind.. And there is a literature about Jesus, himself — the greatest symbol in the West — written by his opponents — in contrast to the Bible — which describes Jesus as a practicing magician. When all is said and done, men like Simon Magus and Appollonius of Tyana, both magicians, on-the-road conjurers who lived in the early Christian era, provided rather formidable competition to Jesus in the minds of people of the time. Reading over stories of the miracles they supposedly performed, one is struck by the similarity to stories about Jesus. The mind begins to bend as a new possibility is driven home: Jesus was another itinerant magician, and his followers won out in the struggle to make him a god.

You could say that the paranormal achievements of Simon Magus and Appollonius were exaggerated — Appollonius, for example, is claimed to have dissolved an entire wedding scene to prove it was all an illusion. It is easy to laugh this off. But then what keeps us from laughing off the works of Jesus?

There is no doubt that all these men were trying to create extraordinary realities.

That is in the Tradition of Imagination.

And in a reasonably generous appraisal, that is what counts.

But let us look a little further into Christ as the pre-eminent symbol of the West, the symbol that has been used to enchant, to fixate, the largest number of people in recorded history.

What happens when we slide out from under the curtains of the Roman Church, when we place the Bible aside and look at another sort of literature on this figure?

What happens to the power of the elegant and prodigious art that has been produced to glorify Jesus, what happens to the pre-defined space, the world, the universe, the pattern, the grand mural of the Catholic Church?

What happens to the Formula of the Secret Society at its highest pinnacle of success?

Morton Smith is the author of a book called *Jesus the Magician*. At the time of its publication in 1978, Smith was the recipient of uncommon praise from such luminaries as Hugh Trevor-Roper, author and Regius Professor of Modern History at Oxford University, and James Sanders, Professor of Intertestamental and Biblical Studies at the School of Theology at Claremont.

Trevor-Roper, dispelling any notion that Smith was merely cooking up a thesis in left field, wrote, "I marvel at Dr. Smith's exact and delicate scholarship. His method is as exciting as his result. Here is Jesus the magician, one of a swarm of Levantine magicians, before he was stylized in the form that we know."

Sanders asserted, "Smith's knowledge of the Greco-Roman world, Jewish and non-Jewish, in which Christianity arose and developed, is probably unsurpassed in scholarship today."

Smith essentially moves through a field dominated by centuries of suppression and censorship on the part of the Christian church, to flesh out a picture of the historical Jesus.

Smith writes:

... when we ask what people who did not believe in Jesus had to say about him [during his lifetime and immediately following], the answer is hard to come by. Almost everything we know about him is found in the works of his believers, mainly in the gospels, a little in the rest of the New Testament and other early Christian texts.

His believers not only wrote those texts, they also formed an organization, "the Church," that became strong enough three hundred years later to get the support of the government of the Roman empire and use it to suppress the works of anyone who did not agree with them. We are told that in AD 326 the emperor Constantine ordered that the books of "heretics" (Christians who held minority opinions) should be hunted out and destroyed. He evidently did the same for pagan works about Jesus ...

Yet enough fragments about Jesus, from divergent points of view, have survived to allow an assemblage of perceptions of his contemporaries "who did not become his followers ..."

Smith states that the world of Jesus and his contemporaries was "wholly mythological." That is, it was considered by its inhabitants to be full of angels, demons, and gods. The demons caused illnesses and plagues and wars. They could enlist the aid of humans who would perform miracles, "so as to deceive the many. The lower gods [demons] were the rulers of this age, and men [as well as women] who knew how to call on them could get their help for all sorts of purposes." That was the structure of belief.

It was also thought that Yahweh, the highest god, could bring about "disasters, sickness, etc., sent as punishments." For this, he could use demons or angels or human prophets.

Smith writes that most Jews assumed the god Yahweh would eventually "destroy or remodel" the world and "make a new order." The details of this revolution or apocalypse were varied, and there were many debates over which messiahs would take central roles.

In Jesus' time, any person who could help heal or allay symptoms of illness could be elevated to the status of "healer" or — depending on his message to the people — "messiah" or "revolutionary." Such appellations as "charlatan" and "brigand" and street magician also, however, waited in the wings, in case the healer was deemed to be a deceiver.

Some of Jesus' enemies said he "had a demon." They said he was "gluttonous and a drunkard." Frequently, Jesus' non-followers said he was a magician. This term had several levels of distinction, which were sometimes blurred by commentators. A magician could be "healing" only temporarily and by tricks, or through demons, or as entertainment in the marketplace. But he could be a magus, which meant he had both miracles and teachings of importance, about ethics, about the end of the world and the disposition of souls.

"Magician," however, normally implied that a divine messianic link to God was not present. There were exceptions to this. But when Jesus was accused of being a magician, the suggestion was clear: he was not divine.

Professor Smith compares the careers of Jesus and a near-contemporary about whom much is known, Appollonius of Tyana, the magician.

> ... both were itinerant miracle workers and preachers, rejected at first by their townspeople and brothers ... An inner circle of devoted disciples accompanied each. Both were credited with prophecies, exorcisms, cures, and an occasional raising of the dead. As preachers, both made severe moral demands on their hearers. Both affected epigrammatic utterances and oracular style; they taught as if with authority and came into conflict with the established clergy of the temples they visited and tried to reform. Both were charged with sedition and magic but tried primarily for sedition.

Smith goes further. From non-gospel and gospel sources, he isolates aspects of Jesus' life which place him in the tradition of magicians:

> After undergoing a baptism believed to purge him of sin, Jesus experiences the descent of a spirit upon him — the experiences that made a man a magician ... Then "the spirit drove him out to the desert," a common shamanic phenomenon. After visionary experiences there, he returned to Galilee where his new spiritual power manifested itself in exorcism, in cures of types familiar in magic, in teaching ... and in the call of disciples who, like persons enchanted, were constrained to leave their families and belongings and follow him alone.

With these disciples he lived the predictable life of

a traveling magician and holy man — a picaresque existence ... The company was supported by his success as exorcist and healer, which increased and was increased by his fame ... he began to initiate his disciples into his own magical experiences ... the larger text of Mark tells of a young man coming to Jesus by night, in the standard costume of an initiate, for instruction in the mystery ...

Smith calls the Eucharist a pure and traditional case of a primitive magician sharing his blood and body in symbolic form with his followers.

The self-appointed arbiters of history have chosen to blot out the magician's career of Jesus. They enshrined him as the Son of God and also supervised the subsequent accounts of his life. They have given us mural-art of a man artificially elevated beyond whatever his own creations actually were — outside the Tradition of Imagination. In that way, they obscured a real history, and turned a kind of artist into a bizarre figure intent on sacrificing himself so that humanity could achieve redemption. The life-force and imagination are surgically removed from Jesus. Instead we get the mandate for humanity to make a telescoped and narrowed journey through the surrendered body of Christ the Messiah. Toward an artistic invention called salvation.

Is there a lunatic myth to compare with this?

Subsequent official councils of the Catholic Church continued the artistry, more strange by far than any worlds of Surrealism or Dada. The body of Christ was honed and drained and polished into an object of suffering. If life was a veil of tears, and the fathers of the Church did their bit to make it so, then every human in the throes of soul-pain and body-pain could look to the image of the Christ who was so like them, in a way. The deity brought down from the shining gates of Heaven into their territory: the forest of despair.

"This god we can love."

The deception was complete.

Of course, by degrees, and over time, the Formula of the Secret Society became more complex. The liturgical and moral and enforcement possibilities blossomed. From the painter Giotto, through Fra Angelica to Michelangelo and Raphael, the illusion of the One Great One spread itself out for the throngs. Perspective, color-tones, dimensionality, the articulation of the human form — the magician Jesus was made into more things for more audiences.

Art, art, art. All is art.

52

I have pored over scores of planetary creation-stories from around the world. Humans hatched from eggs, warriors in communication with the all-giving sun, bogs of stagnant water hiding primordial land masses, coagulated cosmic dust, mother goddesses, gods in sky-terraces, caterpillars, a god making a man from clay and teaching it to speak and laugh and move. A god commanding sub-gods to make humans. A god placing his demands on the face of the deep.

There is always the suspicion that the central god referred to in a creation-myth may be a put-up job. In other words, He or She may be a coalesced and properly named entity made fit for obedient worship. Before the dressing-up, though, the original tale may have spoken of the creator as a powerful soul or a being rather than an explicit god.

We perhaps see a remnant of this in Herman Melville's account of his travels in Polynesia.

Led one day through interior jungle by a native guide, Melville came upon a small clearing set up with several life-sized sculpted idols. The wood had not been polished in some time. One idol was leaning to the side precariously. The clearing was covered with leaves and fallen branches.

When Melville inquired about the ramshackle condition of the sanctuary, his guide looked disgusted and said, "They didn't do anything for us," and he kicked the leaning idol, knocking it over, and walked on.

I would say we can place Polynesia on a list of places in space and time where the Tradition of Imagination held. There worship was not frozen by the cult-formula. The people moved through the spectrum of creation, paused for awhile in the worship aspect ... and then traveled on.

A soul or a being inventing the world is clearly not the same thing as a God creating it. A soul is more fluid. A God confers automatic and bureaucratic "legitimacy" on his work. "The world should have been made, and He made it. He knows what He's doing." The world is suddenly consecrated with a finality, and authoritative demands can be made and imprinted on the minds of those who inhabit it.

Religion confers an unchanging bound-in-chains God. Once again, what we are seeing is a freezing of the human race within one part of the dreamlike process we sometimes call art, or intuition, or dimensional travel, or imagination. "You have made your God. On that rock you must stand. No more versions. No more elaboration. That is not permitted."

We want to encounter/imagine/merge with/exit from gods and various other entities because we are all reaching out into infinite spaces. In the process of doing this, we begin to fathom what that infinite malleability called reality is.

Such a road may not be short, but shall we cover it over and abandon it in favor of a shaped and hardened and tailored myth, in which creativity is the exclusive province of a god? One who has had a shave and a haircut? One whom we made?

PART FOUR

53

This section of the book will be strange for some people. It recounts an experiment, the only proof of which is an internal victory won by the participant.

Also, there are questions. Is this experiment a kind of therapy for the imagination? A restoration of fluidity to "personal mythology?" A space for the exercise of freedom? It is all of these things and more. It is based on the idea that the Tradition of Imagination is more than just a hope. This Tradition is quite real, in which case none of us knows the powers within us.

Legitimate paranormal research suggests that this power is a far shore we can seek.

The results of imagination can lead us in so many different directions. "Psychologically," into expansion of our experience, into social and political change out of the swamp of conventional premises that threaten to sink us, off-planet into the universe around us, into capacities to make and unmake physical realities in fantastic far-reaching ways ...

It is all of this that the Formula of the Secret Society opposes. The Tradition of Imagination is not based on a premise of opposition, but it does leave all attempts to permanently narrow reality in the dust.

I wanted to do an experiment in imagination.

It occurred to me — and I'm not the first to consider this — that it might be interesting to have a person create or invent a dream with his eyes wide open. Why? Because dreaming is one of the most compelling things we do, in terms of energy and deep grasping of the forces of life within us.

What might this experiment show?

It might begin to transform the conscious dreamer in some way. It might increase his confidence in relying on his own imagination.

I felt that, for these objectives to be attained in a serious way, however, it could take a year or more of steady work with a person.

But perhaps I and another person would begin to see a "mythological shift" in a shorter period of time. A shift from assumptions about life based on obvious myths to something less categorized and more personal.

I found a volunteer, and without knowing exactly what I was aiming for, I jumped in.

I want to warn the reader that the substance of these waking, invented dreams may seem unusual when they appear in print. They should be no stranger than dreams we've all had while asleep. But there is a tendency to discount dreams automatically as frivolous and absurd, because they break all the rules of ordinary life, all the rules we hold to be the center of "real" existence.

These dream-accounts may seem to go nowhere, to produce no tangible result, to fracture their own fragile story lines. They may seem, therefore, childish.

But I maintain that these criticisms are precisely what hold us back from the unabashed creation of the strength and power that lie inside us. We have all graduated with honors from the school that teaches us that the highest honor is to be normal.

Additionally, there are people who steadfastly maintain that the imagination should only traffic in "nice" images. These self-appointed censors are quick to declare that a "bad" image produced by the imagination will most certainly lead to bad behavior. In fact, it is just the opposite. I believe the suppressed imagination is the key to crime, violence, and repellent actions.

Let the brief excerpts from the dreams recounted here soak in a little. Consider what effect they may be having on the person inventing them. And remember, these are inventions. They are, in a sense, instant works of art. (Each of Ginger's sessions was about an hour — so what I'm setting out here is just a fraction of what happened.)

Ginger is an emergency-room nurse who is an ex-nun. She still has a fascination for the Church, and she prays every day. She told me she felt she needed "a new outlet."

I told her this was not therapy.

"I don't want therapy," she said.

In my introduction of the experiment to Ginger, I eliminated entirely the strategy of most religions and secret societies. I didn't describe the cosmos in any way, or postulate gods or saints or nirvanas or flying angels. I didn't describe a psychological landscape replete with the Unconscious or sibling conflicts or parental issues or childhood sexual fantasy. I didn't offer any significant symbols or shapes or legends or myths or "secret histories." And I most certainly didn't offer dream analysis and "what dreams really mean," which to me is the fastest way to ruin a good thing.

The first experiment was this: I told Ginger to imagine a dream of worshipping God.

Ginger immediately invented herself in heaven walking along the edge of a cloudbank. She proceeded to a small house that was empty inside. She walked through to the back door and out into the sky again. Large cumulus clouds. Two angels flanking God sat in large chairs. God himself sat on a silver throne.

Ginger started laughing. She walked right up to the edge of the silver throne.

"God is about fifty years old," she said. "He's wearing a gray robe. His hair is light brown. He hasn't smiled so far. In fact, he looks irritated. His eyes are blue. He has a long nose. British. I walk around to the back of the three chairs. There's a bird there, a green bird with a yellow beak. It has a bowl of seeds next to it. It's pecking on it. I talk to him: God, there are a lot of people, and I count myself as one of them, who has doubts about you. He stands up, turns around and looks at me. He's pretty angry. He says, 'You come all the way here with that? How did they let you in? I don't answer questions from ordinary people. You have to be a movie star or a politician to get an audience with me.' God, I came here because I've been a believer. But now the air is letting out of the tire. I think you should stay invisible. 'I am invisible. Do you think this representation is me? Do you think I inhabit this form?' God, you're talking to me. You must be here. I don't want any proxies. 'You don't mean anything to me, even if you are a nun. What do I care about what you think?' God, this is how kingdoms fall. With a single crack in the armor. 'Nothing falls, unless I let it.' So you're just a dictator. 'I'm God.' Who gave you the right to set yourself up? 'Nobody! I took it.' You mean you came across a big empty place and you planted your flag. 'That's right!' Then I think you've got a lot to learn. A lot of people down there think you're holy. 'That's their problem.' I'm getting down on my knees and worshipping him. He's God. It's beautiful. God sitting there. He really has a beautiful face. I feel like I could marry him. I love praying every day. You know, I like to worship. He just became a green goat. A soldier in armor sitting on a wooden chair in a castle dining hall. He looked like a snake. God, why did you say you were human in appearance? 'I never said that.' It's implied. You look like a snake. It's ugly. It isn't right for a God to look like that. 'Why not? Aren't you giving me too much adulation? Who says I want any? I'm tired of all you people and your stupid ideas.' No you're not, God. You like having us around. You don't want to be alone. I can worship an ant or pray to a garden or a traffic jam on the freeway. But you'd rather I worship you ..."

All Ginger said at the end was, "That's very interesting."

54

Ginger had been on the ground in Vietnam. Never seriously wounded herself, she had seen men come in blown apart from jungle forays. She had been part of one impromptu rescue mission behind enemy lines.

Ginger wanted to invent a dream about Vietnam, so she did. She was back in the jungle. A soldier, Mark, was lying on the ground wounded. There was enemy fire. A few other American soldiers were firing back.

Ginger said, "I feel hatred. Fear. Like a monster is present. Cold. A massive warrior in the sky. His right arm is ripped from his shoulder. Blood falling into the trees. A man floating in a bubble of blood up toward the sun. The bubble breaks from the heat. The man inside it speaks about war and the flight of people out of unnamed countries. He severely berates the President of the United States for the death and destruction in Vietnam. Talks about big business and oil profits in Southeast Asia, and the worthlessness of human life. There are swamps full of lizards and men with green faces who live underwater. They pull soldiers down into caves. Their faces are changed into monstrous shapes. An underground sun. Shining an eerie blue. Fred keeps firing his rifle at the sun. Small planets or asteroids. Like ships. Men tumbling off and floating. Bodies hacked to pieces flowing down a huge tube. Soldiers at the receiving end desperately trying to glue the pieces together ..."

After the session, Ginger said, "You know, it's almost as if what I imagined happened there was more important than the memories of what did happen. What I imagined unloaded something from my mind."

"What didn't happen was more important than what did?"

"Imagining all those events, flashes, whatever ... it was as if they held more feeling than the real events. I got rid of something."

55

A week later Ginger wanted a healing session. I hadn't done one in several years.

She lay down on my table, and I put my hands on her shoulders. I felt an electrical movement. Then I sensed a parade of shapes and symbols, as if they were coming out of her body. Circles, squares, triangles, ornate shield-type designs, intricate flutes of color, the Masonic seeing-eye and triangle, and various other flowing shapes embedded in larger squares and circles. A procession of stars of different sizes and composition, some quite simple and others built up with interior lattices.

I responded by imagining a host of similar shapes and placing them in Ginger's body.

A back-and-forth flow began, which lasted for a minute or so. The sensation was like a spectacular conversation.

After the session Ginger told me that she felt a tremendous energy in her body. Her eyes looked very clear.

When she left, I sat down and thought about what happened.

I was reminded of the spring of 1996, when I was living near the beach in Santa Monica. I had begun a series of drawings I called Imaginary Languages. Using black acrylic paint, I had made rows of large letters on six-foot panels of thick cardboard. These letters weren't from any language I knew. They were spontaneous improvisations which jumped off from the point of Chinese characters.

I stood the finished panels around the room and left them for several months.

One day, I was lying down looking at a panel I had set up in front of a large window. I imagined that the letters really were part of a language; that they weren't just shapes. As I continued to look for several minutes, a change occurred. I began to "read" what was there. What came through was definitely not literal meaning as we understand that. It was a series of feelings which existed in a range that did not correspond to what we take as human emotion.

A rule of this language was: Any shape can have a meaning.

Briefly, I was in a register where the shapes on this board spoke to me. Then the sensation flickered off. It was thrilling. The language was more aesthetic than English. The meanings were of distinct feelings and sensations I was not used to. It was as if I had just been introduced to the bulk of the light spectrum which is not visible — but can be just as definite in its imprints as those colors we see every day of our lives.

This in turn reminded me of a night twenty years earlier when I had been driving through Hollywood with the radio on, listening to a symphony by the American composer Roy Harris. For several moments I was no longer listening to music. I was a telegrapher at my outpost receiving a message. Every nuance and shift of the orchestra told me something new, except that it didn't translate into English. It spoke of rivers of changing feelings, and I as the telegrapher was receiving the moment by moment transmission. The Harris symphony had gone from being a kind of rhythmic canvas of moods to a glittering and glowing story coming straight at me, straight at a new sense-perception faculty that had just been unwrapped from its package.

In the case of Ginger and her session, the river of shapes and symbols had gone from her to me, and then from me to her, back and forth, back and forth.

I'd had a glimpse of a much larger arena, in which all energy between two people travels back and forth and is a language that is understood perfectly by both parties. Perhaps the human need for healing is the result of that dimension of experience being shut down.

Just as many religions try to curtail fluidity and freeze humans on the aspect of worship, so these societies use shapes in a frozen way as well. They make them stand for various secrets and values and "vital meanings." We are held in a bit of awe when we see these shapes displayed, perhaps because just below the surface of our experience lies the whole panorama of language unspoken, a range of life unlived, a beauty forgotten.

We are capable of speaking and hearing on that marvelous plane. We are capable of using an infinity of shapes to convey fluid and changing emotions and sensations. But we have closed ourselves to that. The realm of art, though, is still alive, and it is the door into the wider world where all our experience would change, would become art and life at the same time.

I have spoken with an Egyptologist who has worked with the ancient hieroglyphic language for twenty years. I asked him whether he ever experienced the glyphs on another level, whether the shapes themselves affected him in his studies.

"There are three levels," he said. "Start with literal meaning of the symbols. Then go to the dimension the pictographs add to that meaning because of their representational quality. A bird, a snake, a human figure, an eye. The third level is artistic. It has to do with the look of the language. Once in awhile that kicks in. It's hard to describe, but you feel like you're reading drawings and getting messages from them."

"Are the messages literal?" I asked.

"Not in the ordinary sense. They make me feel the way I do when I'm walking around in an art museum. It's a marvelous effect, overall, but I can't really explain it."

The Tradition of Imagination.

There are many glimpses and hints of the kind of aesthetic language I encountered. Of course, the ancient Egyptian and Chinese characters. Pictures which, over time, became words or letters in those alphabets.

Look at the paintings of Paul Klee, Kandinsky, Mark Tobey. Listen to music that takes up a position vacillating between façade and emotion: Satie, Debussy, Mussourgsky, Monk. Tantalizing fragments of languages from different realms.

Classical Greek tragedy combined dance, poetry, chant, story, character. There is no doubt in my mind that somewhere in time and space existed a kind of art which brought all the various elements together. As in ancient Greece, where we taste that melding, there would be a civilization which followed that road but went much, much further. The art so inclusive, so bled into the fabric of the culture that it was truly insepa- rable from living.

In such an atmosphere, a true transformation would take place. The emotions which rule the lives of people would instead be loomed into experience so that, moment by moment, a kind of ecstasy would take hold. There would be no need for symbolic ritual to fill a void. People would not be so hungry for experience that they would gather around the structure of a secret. The cult, the religion, the oppressive forces of a society would drop away into the richness of the ongoing unrolling Adventure. Symbols would appear and bend and twist and ride and march and fly and decay and filter through nooks of etheric feeling as frequently as the leaves move on the trees.

56

Ginger tried to help me find long-term practitioners of Tibetan deity-visualizations who would talk about their experiences and progress.

So far we've had no volunteers who are passionately dedicated to the "ultimate" outcome of that work.

Ginger became interested in this subject after reading John Blofeld's comments on dream as a very deep version of creativity. She located an interesting section in Stephan Beyer's remarkable book, *Magic and Ritual in Tibet*.

First of all, Beyer, writing about a more complete version of Tibetan practice than John Blofeld — although probably reporting about a different sect — describes four stages of attainment that can be reached doing deity-visualization.

Beyer is informed that in the fourth and ultimate stage, a practitioner "has attained a complete control of appearances ... he is able thereby to empower the appearance of anything he wishes."

Such a person would be "the owner of the universe, for he understands and is able to manipulate the very processes that create the cosmos ... To gain such contemplative control of reality is the work of many lifetimes."

Beyer therefore implies that a long-term school for such attainment has existed on the planet, in Tibet. Mark this off to paranoia if you want to, but to me it is hard to say the invasion of Tibet by China was only about land and human resources. The living Chinese Maoists would surely rankle at the aims and straight-on spiritual practices of their sophisticated neighbors.

Beyer traces a roughly parallel Tradition of the Imagination in the West, through surrealism back into alchemy. Both of these movements have suffered from criticism based on the suspicion that they somehow try to avoid the "arduous work" needed to attain spiritual or artistic worth.

Surrealism and alchemy have also been accused of courting the Faustian taboo: trading virtue for power. Indeed, in many circles, both fundamentalist and liberal, power itself is viewed with alarm, as if it basically and intrinsically implies destruction.

In Ginger's third dream-session, she dramatically illustrated a version of this conflict. She chose to imagine a dream about power.

The intensity of conscious dreaming is widened by speaking with, and as, the people and qualities that come to life in the dream — a device originated and utilized as therapy by Fritz Perls and J.L. Moreno. Ginger fell into it naturally.

Here is a brief excerpt from her third imagined dream:

"I'm in a supermarket at night. It must be 2 or 3 in the morning. The lighting is very bright, and there are hardly any people around.

"A man approaches me. He's wearing a robe. A shock goes through me. He has tremendous sexuality. He takes a package of rice off a shelf and tears open the cellophane and scatters it. The air turns blue.

"I feel his energy-heart inside my belly. This isn't his ordinary heart. It's very wild, like an animal.

"I devour this energy. I take it into my eyes, my mouth, my belly, my shoulders.

"Now I'm in another aisle. I begin looking at cans of vegetables on the shelves. I have them float up and move out into the aisle. They bob along in the air and down toward the far end of the market. I make a chicken appear. He breaks open big bags of grain and starts eating. But his mouth is a dog's mouth, and he darts out and takes in scoops of grain at a time. He looks at me and I force him with my mind down to the floor. His whole body is pressed hard against the concrete. A man comes walking around the corner of the aisle. He's a clerk. The dog is now a chicken. I let him up and he struts away.

"The clerk says, 'What the hell is this! Where did the chicken come from!'

"I tell him I made the chicken.

"He looks angry, nasty.

"By concentrating I lift the clerk up off the floor and glue him against the kitchenware rack. He can't move. He's wiggling like a fish. I let him go and he drops on to the floor. He's sweating.

"He says, 'Goddamn you! What do you think you're doing?'

"I turn out all the lights in the store with my mind. I start turning them on and off quickly. Then I leave them on. The store manager walks toward me with an ax in his hand.

"I appear as a religious figure to these two guys. I'm wearing a robe, a white silk robe. No shoes. A beard. I spring a large gray beard. I turn my eyes sparkling blue. I put a haze around me. A gold aura.

"The clerk screams and freezes. The manager throws a can of food at me. I melt it in mid-air.

"The clerk starts crying. The manager says, 'You're the devil!'

"I say, 'Look at the register.' We all walk to the front of the store. Behind his desk the manager opens the register drawer. It's full of gold and silver coins. They spill over. He glances outside the store. In the parking lot is a new black Porsche.

"'It's yours,' I say.

He looks at me.

"'Do you want a different color?' I ask him. 'Red?'

"I make it red.

"His face is breaking into a grin.

"The scene changes.

"I'm in a huge building, futuristic. A bunch of people like me are arrested. We're all in a courtroom. A judge is sitting there. He's thinking that we're troublemakers. He's thinking we have to be put into a box. He has to make an example of us. He's talking to me. He's saying, 'This has to stop. I'm going to start a propaganda campaign. We're going to discredit all of you. Every time something bad happens, a train wreck, a bomb, a crash, we're going to blame it on you people. By the time we're through no one will want to use powers. They'll stink like rotting corpses. People will like being peaceful and happy in a little world.'

"I say, 'You can't stop what I do.'

"'Of course I can,' he says. 'I can make people hate you. You disturb the tranquillity of the state.'

"'They'll find out. I'll turn your soul inside out so everyone can see it. Like a dirty rag.'

"'Try it,' he says. 'They'll see what I want them to. They want order. Something pleasant.'

"The judge's eyes fall from his head. Ashes begin to blow out of his eyesockets. The roof of the courtroom creaks. It caves in ...

"Now the judge is a priest. I take him to a small room and I make him lie down in a bathtub. I run water over him and his vestments dissolve. He's naked. I bring in a small sun and I set it near the ceiling. It shines down on the priest and his white skin slowly starts to turn brown. He's weeping. He's swearing and weeping at me, but in a low voice. It's almost like a song, like a song being sung by the whole Church. I'm bathing him, cleaning debris from his body, from the wars. The wars of attrition, of killing bodies and spirits. All this will have to come back to life. All this is going to come back to life ...'"

57

This was Ginger's fourth imagined dream. She picked the subject. Night.

"I'm in a dark place, maybe a car on a lonely road. It's funny, but as soon as I start to invent it, it has a life of its own. It begins to talk back to me. All right. Anyway, now I'm in a dark theater. There are players on a stage. There are no people in the seats. I can smell cigarette smoke from years of rehearsals. The players are going through a scene. They are young and earnest. They want to do it well. The director is an old man who sits in a rocking chair. He has a shawl over his knees. He looks like Winston Churchill. He's falling asleep. He looks very comfortable. He doesn't care about other people being around. He just dozes off. Now I'm dreaming his dream. I'm asleep and I'm inside some kind of dark space. I can't figure out what it is.

"This is weird. It's a bed. I'm inside it. I'm crawling through the springs and the cotton material of the mattress. There are two people above me, a man and a woman. They're on top of the bed. I'm very small compared to them. I'm very small. I'm crawling through the mattress and I can sense them above me.

"They're having sex. I'm part of some energy that's wrapping itself around them. A *Gulliver's Travels*. Anyway, we're or I'm wrapping this energy around them. Now I'm in a tunnel.

"Another shift. Now there are Indians in headdress. They're all explosions of light.

"I'm in a kitchen. I'm baking bread, and the ceiling is beginning to split open and plaster is falling through. The plaster is falling all over the kitchen counter. I don't care. I just roll the dough. The rolling makes a sound, it's like coins in a metal machine ringing. The dough is turning silver and I'm standing next to a window. Outside the window it's sixteenth-century Amsterdam and people are walking along the canal. The canal is silvery in color and it's overflowing. A man is standing on one of the canal waves. He's wearing a black robe and there's a large red star on his back. He has a sword. I walk out of the kitchen into the street and there he is sitting at a chair in a cafe. The water is running around everyone's ankles but nobody cares. It's warm water. The water, all of it, changes to powder, mountains of it. People are putting it into glass jars and sealing it and running with the jars into houses along the street. The powder is red and orange and silver. I take a jar and open it and pass a handful to the magician in the black robe. He smiles and nods and filters it through his hands and smells it and then eats a bit. He nods as if he recognizes it and then he leans his head back and grins. His teeth are very white. The wrinkles at the corners of eyes dissolve and he stands up and takes off his robe and now his face is on the body of a large dog. He trots away down the street into a bakery and I follow, and the back of the bakery is missing, there's no wall. We're looking at the black sky, we're standing on the flat edge of a planet. The stars are very brilliant. The dog looks at me. Now it's a dog with a dog's face. We both run to the end of the bakery and leap off into space. Singers drift by us as we float. They're singing something I can't make out. A woman is giving birth to a child and a group of girls is watching this. It's all happening in space. The dog says to me, 'It's a long night.' I ask him what we should do. Now he speaks to me telepathically. He tells me that we don't have to do anything, we're all floating around in a circle, and in the middle of the circle — which we keep getting closer to — is a town, a summer town. I now feel apprehension, as if I'm going to be baptized in some kind of hick church. I don't want that kind of water. So I turn the church into a lemon grove, and the dog and I are walking through it. He trots into a small cottage. I follow. On the walls are polished plates, copper plates, and guns. Rifles, pistols, machine-guns, antiques and new guns. I walk into the next

room. A man in army fatigues is sitting in a chair. He looks at
me, as if to say, I can use those guns any time I want to, I can
kill you. I watch him get madder and madder. I place one
eye in the center of his forehead and he starts beaming out a
ray of blue which is quite, quite beautiful. He tells me he's a
rebel.

"Beings in an energy-state, without bodies, are talking to
one another. This is a very long time ago. I don't know how
many there are. But they're from all over. They are saying
that separation from the all-inclusive main harmony is a
coming trend, so to speak. They are saying that perhaps a
million years into the future — although they don't quote
figures — that's just a feeling — we will see beings who
become isolated individuals to pursue a new path, to find a
new type of reality, to explore a different basic situation, for
the first time. This will be troublesome, because it may involve
an exercise of power against the present state of harmony. In
that case, what will the rest of us do? Will we abandon our
oneness to take on this threat? It can't be ignored. It has to be
dealt with. It reminds me of a choir. A hundred singers dedicated to the joint effort, and three people who want to mangle
the beauty. Anyway, power becomes in this assembly an issue
for the first time. Everyone is sharing existence on a very
conscious and rich series of levels. We are all totally plugged
into one another. There is no need for trying to figure out
anything because we are tuned into everything that is. There
is no need for struggle because we are there, we have it all.
We can sense the harmony at any moment. It doesn't go away.
It's a steady hum. It's much more than that. It isn't just
a sound, like a prayer or a mantra. Those are pale, pale
reflections of what it's like to exist with many hundreds of
thousands of others in a Oneness that is completely and
voluntarily open. There is no coercion. No one makes demands
of any kind. But among a few of us, an appetite grows for
new experience. It's very difficult to figure out what to do
about it ..."

Ginger commented: "They sure as hell didn't teach me
about this in Church."

58

In her fifth dream-session, Ginger imagined a dream about gold. The topic was, again, her choice.

"I'm standing in a large cave under the floor of the Indian Ocean. There is a parade of pirates and adventurers coming in and out. They get here through a literal hole, a series of holes into the bottom of the sea. They transport chests full of treasure, and I sift out the purest gold, which I can recognize by sight. I'm aware that, to get to me, these pirates have already engaged in wars of ... spite, rumor, gossip, accusation, physical violence. This is a vicious world they live in. It reminds me of the world of political relationships, a world that would completely deteriorate into chaos if cooler heads didn't prevail. The trouble is, the cooler heads are the ones who wield the real power. The petty squabbling crowds of rumor-mongering fools say they want to build a better world, but in the end all they want to do is tear people down. In this dream, the pirates are open and nasty about it. They don't try to cover up their foul natures.

"The gold is lying in heaps on my wood table, a very sturdy table. I hold a chunk in my hands and feel its vibration. A slow electrical impulse goes through my body. I feel I'm preparing myself to teach others about gold. I'll show them how to feel the nuggets and necklaces and decide which is most pure.

"I see huge factories of the future standing on platforms in the middle of the ocean. The day is warm and sunny and the birds are singing. They float on the waves. A very poor man walks up a long concrete approach to a salamander, a giant one, which is guarding the entrance to a ... villa. The poor man removes a nugget of gold from his pocket and the salamander flicks his tail, as if he is being sexually aroused. The poor man begins to weep and shout and he takes off his filthy clothes. All his old friends come up to him and he ignores them. He gets on the back of the salamander and they crawl the whole length of the side of the villa and approach the swimming pool. The salamander turns black and begins to die. He is the old age passing into obscurity. A parade of machines comes into the pool area. These are gigantic structures. I'm unfamiliar with them. One begins to break apart the swimming pool and suck up the water through large tubes. Another machine unloads earth into the empty hole, and sprinkles seeds. They grow up into very high stalks. Corn ears. A machine with a hundred long metal arms reaches out and picks up a column of water out of the sea. It seems to 'look' at the water, and powdered minerals begin to fall from the column and blow away into the air. The water is now clear. People circle around it and drink and bathe and jump inside and swim. The machine with the arms continues to process the column and remove minerals and other substances from it. At the horizon I see a machine that looks as big as several factories. I can hear it adjusting itself. The sounds are faint and not unpleasant. I can barely make out huge lines of products that are coming out of one side of the machine. There are no humans inside it. I realize that under the sea are several cities which are uninhabited and manufacture products for human use ..."

I showed this account of Ginger's dream to a reporter I've known for some time. He said, "That's ridiculous. No water-processing system would work that way." Then he remembered that this was a dream. Then he remembered it was an invented dream spun by a person who was awake. He was a bit nonplused. "Well," he said, "there are a few people who think automation will go a lot further than it has, especially in Japan."

A psychologist I showed the account to began to discuss Ginger. He went from "symbols for personal issues" to "archetypes in conflict, that sort of thing."

I read the dream over the phone to a sculptor of mobile structures I know in downtown LA. He laughed.

59

What kind of world is it in which I can come up with this curious idea of the invented dream and bring someone in and ask her to experiment with me in inventing her own "culture" and her own images — which she can discard at will or save? It is this world, which, over the last ten thousand or twenty thousand or hundred thousand years has brought itself to the point at which there could be an unprecedented freedom. No completely autocratic and dominated society could permit such experimentation. No small society with a single overarching religion could allow this to happen. In those cultures, stories would be immediately woven into a central myth-structure which would be called True. Here and now, we live in a world we have liberated to a great degree for the imagination, but we don't use the imagination. We amazingly let it lie fallow.

After Ginger's session with its huge factories and machines, I wrote down a few Buckminster-Fulleresque notes:

Now we have the technological means to answer the question, what is technology for?

It is for the building of a groundbase zero of guaranteed survival for every human on the face of the Earth, now and forever. It is for the groundbase from which human imagination can fly and become whatever it can be with as much power as it can create. The histories of societies show that such power is not friendly to autocratic rulers, even though that very power is what is needed to save those rulers from eventual destruction at the hands of their subjects.

A groundbase zero gives birth to the time and space for the one quality which is kept, to a degree, under wraps while the planet evolves to this point: human creation. The man and woman and child who must think about nothing else except work, a job, to survive is burying that imagination because it is too spilling-over, too exuberant, too free for the circumstances of economic life. But as automation becomes the rule rather than the exception in industry, an opportunity arises. A new power can replace the old.

Instead of the same faceless power-mad rulers of high IQ and no apparent soul running the show, making war and peace and reparation and re-configuration of land and human resources, we can give way to our own cumulative ingenuity and, without making a One World Corporation to be the new God, we can have these transnational gargantuan companies create enough food, clothing, shelter, education (unlimited), healthcare, and transport for every human being on Earth. Groundbase zero. That's what it is.

We can do this, by making a real economy of companies that employ people and sell products made by their machines in such a way that anyone can afford a groundbase zero of his/her own, for the wage earnable by a minimum number of hours every week at a job.

Imagination. Invention. Unlimited.

Ginger said to me, "There was no question in my mind when I saw those huge machines that ran industry in my dream ... there was no question that they can exist. They already exist, in a sense. They just need the concentration of the people who can build them. The skill and the know-how are already here. The whole thing is here."

This need not be a massive socialism or a massive runaway capitalism. This would have to be voluntary direction taken by companies and by huge numbers of people who could graduate to other goals, other visions.

60

In Ginger's sixth dream, she began with the idea of multi-dimensions.

"I'm standing in a room that has a sparkling marble floor. I'm watching a film about fish of the Great Reef. I'm also running down the side of a mountain wrapped in blue fog. As I move, my legs take on the pattern of a gazelle. Longer and longer leaps. At the same time I'm laying out on a metal table the energies of the mind of the Freudian analyst who is devoted to translating every impulse into a childhood sexual experience. The energies of this analyst's mind look like a funnel flower. At the top is the vast number of experiences of one patient and they rain down inside the stem, the funnel of the flower, finally into a black box. The box is the Oedipal night. When the baby tried to make love to his mother and gain power over his father ... this model is repeated and sustained over and over for all time, until one day the analyst wakes up and says, 'This is me. This box. This is what I am doing. This is what I'm harvesting again and again like the most boring concerto ever conceived ... '

"The gravity in the air of my living room speaks to me. It says, You could be me in your next life. Don't think it's impossible. You could be pulling and pushing in one place and feeling the entire network of gravity throughout the solar system, throughout the universe. You could be that, a local moment that is never noticed that is part of the whole wheeling show from Earth to the end of time.

"Now a wisdom voice speaks. It says, You are witnessing an attempt to organize and flatten consciousness on your planet. The elite groups responsible for this are moving by degrees into a century of corporate control. Economic entities will, in this version of reality, decide who survives and who doesn't. The availability of work, food, and so on will come under their sway.

"Now God One talks. He says, I created the universe in all its glory and you owe me whatever I ask for. If you don't get down on your knees and live the life I tell you to, I'll flood the whole Earth and get you to die and then be reborn to relive the whole show from scratch. That's how we do this. We junk the surface of the planet and then we rebuild it again. That way you can't progress too far.

"God Two shows up. He says, Don't buy that nonsense. He didn't create the universe. You did. The distance between where you are now and you knowing that is the first great leap. The distance between knowing you created the universe and being able to do it again is the second great leap. Let's not kid ourselves. Let's admit the truth ..."

After the session, Ginger said, "Suppose we imagine a culture, a civilization in which the myth-structure that under-lies it changes every day at 1 p.m. Now we're talking about an advanced thing, I think. That's what this imagining is, from a certain point of view. Instead of a bound-up religion, I'm forming a brand-new state of dreamhood every time we have a session. The old part of me says, Wait, go back, don't accept the new, just find the truth and stick with that. The new part of me says, The truth is the proliferation of dreams, the art of it, the invention, the beauty, the weirdness, the shifts, the freedom. There is a temptation to stay with the thing you thought was vital yesterday even though you don't like it today. That temptation asks you to sculpt a whole civilization out of a few images and keep it that way. I can understand that, especially when the lack of food and the lack of heat and so on were the main fears. But now we have something different. We can use this stability to go to the next step of our evolution."

61

If the invented dreams of Ginger seem "weird" and inconsequential, think about this. The political left and right in the U.S. are both quite aware that, under whatever name, more and more power is accumulating in fewer and fewer hands on this planet. The left and right cannot agree on anything substantial. They fight. They debate. They make deals. They argue, but the march of power beyond them goes on.

The left and the right are glued to their philosophies and their labels, and they do not like each other's attitudes.

What do we call the corporate power-elite that is taking over the reins of this Earth gradually, which will continue to do so for the next hundred years? Do we call it Satan or Friendly Fascism or Collectivism or Socialism or Runaway Capitalism?

In truth, the failure to join sides and unseat this creeping power structure is a failure of the imagination. It is literally a failure of the right and the left to be able to imagine different worlds. They are locked in their philosophies because, at bottom, they cannot imagine their way out.

That is the truth.

They are not good enough artists. That is their failure.

Even their corruption, their sell-outs and their capture by various lobbies and elites would vanish if they had the imagination to see beyond that, AND if they had enough experience in truly using the imagination to rely on it , if they could in truth steer by imagination for the good of everybody, come hell or high water.

62

In Ginger's tenth dream, she chose the subject of death:

"I'm in a grotto. I'm talking to a greenish yellowish person. I can only see his face. We're having a friendly chat. He is telling me that I've done well, that I've arrived at a way station where things are checked over. I ask him, what things? He says, just the general condition of my energy. Are there any leaks, for example. He says I'm ready to pass on to the next place. I tell him that I'm surprised I'm so so lucid after dying. I say I wonder whether I'll have to be reincarnated in a body back on Earth. He says that's up to me. I can go anywhere I want to ...

"I'm on a battlefield with a sword. My horse is lying nearby with a lance through his side. I'm looking around for the man who stuck him. Flags are waving. Scarlet banners, smoke, the background of gray stone mountains. Armor. We're all wearing armor. Swords clashing. Bright steel, polished. I knock a man down and feel a thrill course through my body. I feel I'm on the right side. I can't remember what this particular cause is, but it's right and the enemy is evil. I stab a man coming at me and he goes down with a shout. Horses thunder by him. I run toward an embankment near a stream where another fight is going on. Here everyone is on foot. I strike a man on the top of his head with the flat of my blade and he goes down like a supplicant. Around him on the ground I notice other men. I still feel great spirit in my veins — the spirit of being on the right side in a battle that has a goal, that has a good motive ... but I see these dead men and they all have strange markings on them. Their skin is discolored in places. I see brown and gray splotches on their cheeks, long furrows of rashes on their arms. Their ankles are swollen and some are punctured like balloons, and fluid is oozing out. I walk from group to group and I see these men. They're all marked and ill and dead. But it's not an illness I'm used to. This is unfair, this is wrong. This isn't a battle for honor and cause and idea. This is subversion in some strange way. I don't even know which side these dead men represented ... a group of riders comes this way. They're the lead scouts for a larger group behind them. Small potentates sit in chairs on ornate frameworks. Some frames are carried on the backs of horses, others are carried by foot soldiers. At the front of each frame is a man who holds in his hands a scroll, full of printing. Actually, it's a testament on a wooden roller. And he reads in a foreign language the creed of the Great Country. It's an entire ideology. There's poetry in it, and reference to duties. Behind these frameworks is a stagecoach drawn by very tall horses, and the King and his retinue of a hundred all sit in rows of seats in the stagecoach. The King is the absolute ruler of one of the sides in this war — it really doesn't matter which side. I don't know anymore. Now I look at those dead bodies on the ground and they're turning black and rotting like old fruit. I realize the bodies are from both sides. The King in the stagecoach has no favorites. He's an actor. He lives his whole life as the chief of a country, but in fact he's something more. He's a link in a chain of powers that sprawls all the way up into the sky. They've spread this disease, this fungus that rots from the inside out among the soldiers who have a kind of spirit about why they're fighting. The cause I was fighting for is a dim memory. Why am I standing there waving a sword? ..."

63

After Ginger's 20th session, she said, "I don't know what would happen if we did a session every day for ten years. How much could I begin to use my imagination?"

64

How awake can we become to the pre-defined spaces in which we live our physical, material, moral, emotional, energic, and spiritual lives? To what extent can we create these lives by our own imaginations, rather than by using our inventive powers to fit into a tight blueprint of reality?

In particular, the answer to the second question is up for grabs. I know of no system or practice or strategy which can claim to have brought home the ultimate bacon in this regard.

What is the ultimate?

Can we say that the solid matter and the space and time of this universe is basically a construct of our imaginations? And if so, can we demonstrate that some human somewhere has the power to override, so to speak, the universe and play a new tune?

A Tradition pointing in these ultimate directions has existed for a very long time on this planet, and it has been masked over.

Reviewing the scientific evidence concerning paranormal powers, we can see there is no escape from the fact that people have been altering the shape of the universe as we know it. They have been operating outside the normal constraints of space and energy and matter and even time. This is a strong clue that we have the creative capacity to "make things anew."

65

The Tradition of Imagination

Centuries before the birth of Christ, the marble island of Crete was built into palatial homes by its inhabitants. Deviating from the vast echoing gods of Egyptian sculpture, the Greeks arrived at an art of human dimension, in which the fluidity of the carved figure was articulated as never before. The Greeks often struggled against their beloved gods, and tried to steal their fire on several fronts, but in most confrontations the people fell to superior power.

In Greece, at the time of Pericles, "every third [free] man ... was a sculptor or a sculptor's assistant. But today, Greece is barren of artists."

The Tradition rises and falls, and appears in all places.

From Sophocles to Rimbaud, from Imhotep to Ravi Shankar, from Sappho to Nicola Tesla, no attempt at codifying it has succeeded. This is a Tradition without system.

It does not sit on any single person's shoulders. It is built from the ground up by human creators. It stands as the alternative to the Formula of the Secret Society, in which more and more power is taken into the hands of a few.

Ginger's 23rd dream took up the subject of creators:

"... They're trying to kill him. He's running with fire up to the top of a hill. They're circling around him like dogs. He floats up off the ground toward the sun. The sun is small and gray. It's heading toward night. Horses come racing across the sky dragging a child. She's running to keep up, and by a miracle she does. She flies into the man's head and he stops in his tracks with the fire-torch. She's dissolved into his mind. He starts weeping and then his face is transformed. He becomes ... I don't know what it is. It takes in the essence of the little girl, but she's no little girl. She has a plan. Whole civilizations unfold from his head, the blueprints. He's standing in the middle of a desert now, and palaces begin to form around him. Marble palaces. He sees a long stone road and it forms on the sand. Now the little girl is standing there too. She's a woman. She looks ahead of her and a mountain rises up in the sky, a cone of a mountain made out of glass. Inside it sits a king, a man who wants to take all the structures and run them as a machine, with little people doing all the work, the maintenance. He wants to set up a reason for this. He wants people to think there is some reason they all have to work for him. Day and night he ponders this. How to pull this off ..."

66

Suppose we could reduce down a thousand homilies and speculations and blurry statements from the field of psychology — and say, simply, that the repression of imagination causes violence.

Suppose that is really true.

Then we are talking about something at the core of our problems, a kind of invisible disease that moves from generation to generation on rails far beyond the gene-centered view of what a human is.

When we look at the holocausts of history, the enslaving and murdering of millions of Africans in the establishment of slavery in the Americas, the wars of ancient Egypt, the destruction of Crete, Constantinople, all the way up to the present, when we look at the forcible securing of thousands of regimes in nations all over the world from the dawn of time, we are talking about a collective repression of the creative capacity in humans which, beyond suffering due to loss of loved ones, beyond personal pain, has a pain of its own — which can result in the harnessing of energy for violent purposes, rather than for innovation in making a world closer to our real desires.

The Tradition of Imagination is found and then lost and then found again. Its essence is so marvelous and liberating that we tend to discount it. A perfect example is the work of A.S. Neill, author of the 1960 book, *Summerhill: A Radical Approach to Child Rearing*, named after Neill's own experimental British school.

At the time it appeared, and for a decade, the book caused ripples in the areas of the social sciences, and certain artists including the American author Henry Miller praised Neill to the skies. Deservedly. Then Summerhill was discarded by educators as an "interesting, isolated phenomenon," much as a cancer cure using so-called natural medicines would be dismissed by the central medical research establishment.

Neill, following down in action what he took to be the major principles of Freud and Wilhem Reich, had started, in 1921, a live-in school, Summerhill, in England, which catered largely to rejects from the tight, buttoned-up British school system.

Neill operated on the idea that if you allowed students and faculty to participate, by vote, in the running of their own school, they would be more real, more alive. And then if you gave students, with no tricks, the license never to come to classes until they were ready to learn, they would live out their childhood fantasies to the hilt.

A child might play in the fields and the mud with his companions until he was fifteen — every day — and then finally school would begin to interest him. At that point he would come to class to stay.

Playing in the fields was not organized by teachers or counselors. It was kid-play, with its wild changes and acting of roles and pretending and the rest of it. Free-form.

Imagination.

Neill said on many occasions, "If you stop a child from living out his successive layers of fantasies until he tires of each one, if you try to cut that process short under any guise, the child will not grow up."

Very uncompromising, and Neill was extremely acute when it came to observing the deceitful ways massively uncomfortable adults would try to derail this living-out process.

Neill's book shows that his students would, in fact, come to a point at which they wanted to learn. At that juncture, twelve years of education might be telescoped into two or three years, without stinting. The classrooms at Summerhill were not remarkable. There was no effort made to "interest" the child in a subject through special aids. Neill forbade this. He saw that when a child wanted to learn, the teaching became easy, and when he didn't the introduction of seduction was a cruel thing.

Neill essentially proved in his school that the imagination

is the core of a child's world, and that it manifests in an art
which engages the child right to the end of his fingertips.
Playing is the medium. Play. And the child is a supreme actor.
Thwarting that process, during which a whole string of fantasies is enacted, you repress the imagination and repress true
maturation.

The freedom Neill created was, and is, a brilliant sun. And
it finally illuminates the creativity of a child, and how the
rigidities of character form — from the dampening of that
inventive spirit.

Neill saw what he did as nothing more than giving what
educators would now call "a developmental approach" to the
underlying ideas of Freud and Reich. There is a subconscious.
It holds fantasies. The child wants to act these out. Let him.
Let him make the unconscious conscious. Let him take that
road to the end. He will, in the process, naturally get bored
after a shorter or longer time, and he will move on.

This was also the idea of the brilliant American psychologist, J.L. Moreno, the founder of psychodrama. In a classic
case, one of his patients, a teenager, thought he was Jesus
Christ. The child was from a large family. So Moreno assembled
the other family members and convinced them to play, every
night at dinner, the roles of the various apostles. To go along,
in other words, to the hilt with the "psychosis." For several
months, the family cooperated. Their son was Jesus? All right.
They would help. They would join in. At the end, the son
just tired of the whole thing and dropped it. No analysis, no
office visits, no attempt to modify behavior. Nothing. Just
the brilliantly obvious.

Allow the imagination to blossom.

That way the Christ is not crucified.

That way, instead of a person's imagination — his dream
of being Jesus — hooked up to one or another structure that
promises relief but gives bondage, it is hooked up to a piece
of theater, creation, art, in which the family become the
apostles and the drama is completed.

The work of Neill shows that, for a child, the imagination
is the master key that creates fantasies, roles, games that

unroll a carpet of inner time into the world around him. The child, thus empowered, can literally play himself into maturity. Evidence that the imagination is wise, that it leads toward a richer life.

In her 34th dream, Ginger chose the subject of children. She had taught school briefly in a community in Canada where, for a year or two, the environment was modeled after Summerhill:

"I feel like crying. I always feel like crying when I talk about this. The children and their parents. I see the parents circling the children, trying to destroy them, trying to rip out their souls. It's a long winter afternoon, and the parents can't take it anymore. They can't stand the laughter; the playing of the children is driving them crazy. Day after day the kids have nothing but freedom. They roll around in the dirt and the snow and they build structures and they pretend God knows what! It's their world. Worlds. They keep making them up as fast as you can figure out what's happening. That's the beauty of it. The kids are playing on the hillside. They don't care about anything else. They're happy. This is the terrible thing. This is what's driving the parents toward murder. They want to murder their own children. I can feel them. They want to take their children to places where the clothes are all laid out and look the same. Uniforms. Armies. The children go right into the army and they're beaten if they refuse to obey any order. They're sent right to the battlefield where they 'honorably' serve their country. This is insane! Fodder! I'm up on the hill with the children. I'm yelling out to the parents — stop! Don't do this! Let them play! They'll go on for years playing! Let them! They'll eventually stop and come inside. When they come inside you can teach them. They'll want to learn. Just teach them what they want to learn. Have patience. Even if takes twenty years, they'll want to learn. When they want to, teaching them is so easy. There's no pain! Don't you understand? There's no pain! Let them play! They're just trying out their bodies and souls and minds in the world. It's wonderful. They love it. Give them that.

Just give it to them. Don't get nervous. Don't take it away. Don't kill them. Don't approach them here. Leave them alone. Get away.

"I see whole groups of parents, like a society of parents from all countries who hate this and they're walking across the plains like the old pioneers, except now they want to kill their children the way they themselves were broken, they want to stop their own children, they want to take their souls. This is the reason for all the genetic research, all the labs, all the ... they're trying to create perfect children who obey every command. They can't stand the pain in themselves of seeing happy children. They're afraid of the freedom. We don't need those covered-wagon pioneers now. We settled the West! Now we can give these children freedom. That was why we settled the whole thing. That was the purpose. Doesn't anyone remember? That's why the kids worked alongside their parents in the woods, chopping trees and hunting and planting and all that. So that now we can let them play. Don't you remember? The freedom. The children will want to learn. They'll do it.

"Night comes down. I see a huge building, it's a Congress of some kind, and the waves coming out of it into the sky are nasty and cruel and painful. I mean painful to the people inside. Not free. They want to go to war. They think war is the only answer to the whole civilization. If we don't kill the people we disagree with, then how can we live? This is the insanity. The children have no insanity. They just want to live out their fantasies. They're actors. They're all wonderful actors. They have so many roles they can play ..."

67

In her 35th invented dream, Ginger gave me a different slant. She said, "I want to use a symbol to represent the thing I'm dreaming about. I want to bring the symbol into being myself and assign the meaning to it. I've thought about it. I'm going to call it Upward Delta. Upward Delta means change toward infinity, toward unlimited capacity, toward a consciousness we don't yet fully understand. People might disagree with that. They might say it's a meaningless symbol, but for me it has great meaning. People might think that existence is all matter, but that's their invention, really. I know that much. No one else has to agree with my symbol or my dreams. They can invent their own."

This was Ginger's dream:

"I'm moving as Upward Delta would. In an ascension. I get to clouds in the sky, at about 30,000 feet, and the air is cold, but I'm feeling fantastic. I come across a palace built in the air. It's more a structure of beams and square arches and vertical columns. It's open. The materials are gold and silver and copper. This is quite gorgeous. I walk through it and feel like I'm exploring a lost continent, a place where people once lived in a frank, honest way, and their existence was beautiful for that reason. The columns are charred in places, the remains of wars fought over territory.

"I keep ascending past that to a red palace. This spreads out in every direction, a series of domes and balconies and steeples and minarets. It pulsates. The interior is empty. I walk through it. I realize that this is a focusing apparatus for rays of energy that come in from outer space. But this outer space is etheric, it's not on the same level as the physical universe. The major purpose of the etheric planets is transmission of energies. I'm receiving the rays as they are focused

233

and modified by the red palace. A healing is taking place on the atomic level. A reinvigoration. I move out of that place and ascend higher. There are actually a series of palaces of different colors, and each one functions as a focuser for energies coming in from different spheres. All of this has to do with healing. I decide to move through these to a higher elevation. Now I see a blue spherical structure. Windows and balconies are cut into the sides of it as it floats. I suddenly decide that I'm going to change this. Without even knowing exactly what the sphere is for, I'm going to change it into a green and black sleek object that is half-machine, half-life, a kind of huge cat that moves through space, through the night. Now I change that into a floating ship. The ship is used for ... I'll have the ship used for the transformation of energies. It takes biological emanations from cell-molecules and turns them into wave lengths that can penetrate the tissue and bones and heal disease by reshaping the electromagnetic fields around the diseased tissue. Wave lengths that cut huge holes in the fabric of space and reveal great fountains of energy that fuel several different universes. Animators ..."

68

Ginger, in her 38th dream, stuck with her symbol, Upward Delta. "It won't be in the dream itself,' she said, " but I'll be referring to it in my mind:"

"I'm changing into a tiger, and that tiger is sitting at the top of a tree that spans hundreds of miles. I jump off from the tree and sail out into a white blinding light, a sun that you can live inside of. I turn that sun into a moon, that moon into stars that sit in the black sky. I unroll a long cloth and stretch out on it under the stars and fall asleep. In my dream, I form mud into a riverbank and water runs past my mouth. I move out on to the river and swim with it up a hill toward the sky. I swim between huge clouds and small villages into a gray wall of fog. Inside the fog I see an attic of a palace and I jump through an open window into the attic. I turn myself back into a human and wander through the rooms where books are stacked against the walls. A naked blue god stands in one of the rooms. His body is perfect. I reach out my hand and exchange hands with him. Now I take his other hand and it slips on to the end of my wrist and he has my other hand. His eyes float out into the air of the room and they settle on my eyes. I see gleaming silver cars move by the window of the room. The god asks me if I have died. I tell him that there is only this place and that place and this form and that form, and I am a formmaker ... the Upward Delta is a way to remember this."

69

In her 39th dream, Ginger said:

"I have Upward Delta, a triangle, inscribed on a stone wall, a very smooth wall on the side of a building that stands below a larger stone structure. The larger structure is a pyramid with a ball on it. The pyramid is ... I'm making the pyramid into a seething mass of wild energies, and they hold the sphere on top. Earth. Our planet is held on the point of a pyramid of energies. The Earth occasionally bounces up off the pyramid point, and I bounce it higher into the blue, into the black space. It takes a collective breath on each one of these high bounces. I'm floating and turning upside down above the Earth and I'm drifting much higher into a heaven of gold angels that float around. I ascend higher through this place into a series of green castles. I congeal the castles into one. I compress them. I force the green substance up into a high, high building that touches the clouds at the top of the realm. I float up to the ceiling of the realm, which is made out of a linen cloth, a white cloth, and I cut through it with my hand and float outside ..."

70

Ginger sent me a letter several months after our last session, which was her 41st.

"I feel I've taken over the reins in a certain way. When people belittle the imagination, they're jumping back from fear. I can see every significant institution I've been part of in my life now as someone else's solidified dream. Not mine. Why they would want to keep control of other people is beyond me. Anyway, I'm writing down my imagined dreams every day now, accumulating a sheaf of them. Who knows how far this can go? I see no limit on it. Occasionally I find myself focusing too much on the meaning of the dreams, rather than on the adventure of inventing them and feeling them and seeing the images. At those times, I realize how programmed we all are to what you call The Pattern. We think that finding It will somehow do the whole job of liberating us. I'm beginning to see that the truth is far different.

"My grip on the Vietnam war is unshakable now. They sent us because we would go. Whether it was about oil in Asia — whatever the real reason, we — on both sides — picked up weapons and went there to kill each other. That's a hell of a dream, and I can tell you that's what it felt like during my tour. No government or institution can tell me now that I owe them something special, because I know what they're doing. They're trading on history, which is a long road of leaders trying to get people to jump. I'm not jumping anymore ..."

At the level of the psyche, I believe there is a debate among ourselves. There are those who feel that forces outside us are the primary creating agencies of this world, this universe,

237

this life. Then there are those who hold that our own imagination, our own invention, is the ascendant key. All the way along the line there is the temptation to interpret Pattern as the explanation for life, when Pattern is the swirl, the deposit, the fossil left by life, by us, as we seek to extend our consciousness — or, shrinking back from that, as we seek to wall in and control others.

This series of invented dreams I have presented — and Ginger's sessions were each an hour, so the versions printed here are only excerpts — these dreams are an effort to make a beginning along a modern road of increasing the scope, the power, the dimensions of the imagination.

Whether I or you like Ginger's dreams is beside the point. They are hers. What would yours be?

The Tibetans have made the purest statement of their hope and intent: that the imagination is the prime source of creation in all realities. Can we find a way to the realization of that? Can we go the distance?

I see no reason to shrink back. And I am certainly not interested in an argument about the merits of one system versus another. We need people who will present and experiment with every method they can conceive.

The future is there to be made.

PART FIVE

71

(All quotations in this chapter are from the compelling 1980 collection of essays called *Trilateralism: The Trilateral Commission and Elite Planning for World Management*, edited by Holly Sklar. That book, if it has a political slant, is toward the left, so drop any notions that I am pawning off some version of globalism as the Work of Satan. In fact, clear the decks of as many ideological preconceptions of global power as you can. I hate to disappoint doctrinaire readers, but global power is as politically neutral as the Church of Rome. Which is to say, elites will ally themselves for a moment with whoever can help them, and will label themselves whatever will pragmatically advance their goals — but their real desire is domination. They take it; you name it.)

What about today? In the big picture, how can we interpret the so-called status quo? Is there an art here that tries to freeze us into a state of submission? If so, what could be the hidden agenda?

If power is the capacity to create, those transnational corporate elitists in the secular realm who achieve massive control over the lives of others are missing an important part of the equation. They ply their repressive trade as if it were the piling up of blocks.

Domination and dominion crowd out a sense of invention at the highest levels.

When they collaborate with one another to influence the course of nations, these men favor the inevitable "add-on" philosophy of simply bringing more into the fold. More money, more natural resources, more political leverage, more cheap/slave labor.

They expand from one million to a hundred million to a hundred billion of *something,* but the paradigm-landscape essentially remains the same. In part, the substance of their art is in advertising. They fashion, for the masses in the industrialized countries, a generic excitement, a universe which appears secure, which seems to promise continued comfort.

It is important to understand this type of universe-making, because it is the up-to-date version of God, of how things are run.

Multinational corporations, governments, banking institutions, and the clubs they form are, by my definition, a network of constantly evolving, constantly solidifying, constantly learning secret societies. They show the public various benign faces, but they conceal an agenda whose congealing purpose is the making of global rule and uniformity. This is not spoken about. It is a goal 180 degrees away from the seeming goal of global unity.

Coming out of World War II, it was easy to believe that the fate of nations rested on the ability of world leaders to forge agreements that would bind them together.

The piecing together of such a structure was attractive to industrial corporations and banking institutions. They signed on to solid trade pacts and the lending of huge sums in order to resurrect trading partners out of the rubble of Europe, out of the humiliation of Japan. All would be well. World-wide production and sales of goods of every type would soon soar. Anyone could see the dimensions of the new money-world over the horizon. How could isolationism last in the face of fleets of oil tankers? How could economic separatism prevail when massive airline operations, speeded-up planetary communications, and mind-boggling plastics and electronics industries were taking over the limelight?

Indeed, comprehensive planning for the postwar world had been taking place for some years.

The privately based U.S. Council on Foreign Relations' (CFR) War and Peace Studies Project, starting in September of 1939, formed up to come to an understanding about the desired shape of "a new world." Five study subgroups, made up of a hundred influential American men, including eventual

CIA director Allen Dulles, initiated a six-year project of research. These men made lasting links with "at least five [U.S.] cabinet-level departments and fourteen separate government agencies, bureaus and offices ... The aim of the vast undertaking, to which the Rockefeller Foundation alone gave over $300,000 in a six-year period, was to directly influence the government [in U.S. postwar planning] ..."

The CFR "initially proposed during 1941 and 1942 the idea of international economic institutions to integrate the new world order ..." The International Monetary Fund (IMF) and the World Bank, eventually created at the Bretton Woods Conference in New Hampshire in 1944, resulted from the combined efforts of CFR members, the U.S. Treasury Department, President Roosevelt's cabinet, and the Department of State.

The IMF and the World Bank would be used to stabilize national currencies, fund industrial development in chosen countries — often through outside U.S. corporations — and, eventually, command the vital affairs of debtor nations who couldn't meet their loan payments.

CFR director Isaiah Bowman, in May 1942, asserted that the United States needed to establish a United Nations. He, along with four other CFR members, became the substance of a secret six-man committee set up by Secretary of State Cordell Hull in January 1943. This was named the Agenda Group, and it planned the United Nations. Its proposal-draft would closely resemble, in many ways, the final UN Charter negotiated at the international meetings at Dumbarton Oaks in 1944 and San Francisco in 1945.

In fact, the CFR-controlled Agenda Group was, in effect, "the coordinating agency for all the State Department post-war planning ..."

Of course, the public was quite unaware of this vast and illegal influence by the CFR over our postwar affairs. And this was not through inattention. The CFR did not court public support or publicity. It was only interested in obtaining results.

Nine years after World War II, a new group of major players emerged in Europe. Named after the Holland hotel in which their first meeting took place in May 1954, the Bilderberg Group has "filled, to some degree, the need to coordinate the transnational system of the West." Like the CFR, its emphasis has been on foreign policy. In 1957, it played a major role in manufacturing the consent that brought the European Common Market into being.

"Participants in the [Bilderberg] meetings over the last twenty-five years have included most of the top ruling-class actors in the postwar history of Western Europe and North America ..."

Bilderberg's first chairman, Prince Bernhard, had gone to work for the German chemical cartel I.G. Farben in the mid-1930s, at about the time Farben was throwing its considerable weight behind fledgling leader Adolf Hitler. Bernhard was given a position in department NW7, the Farben intelligence section. In 1937, he married Princess Juliana of Holland. They sat out the war in Canada, where the Prince busily raised funds for the Dutch Army and acted as a military liaison with allied groups opposing Germany.

Bernhard, like many other elite players, was acquainted with all sides of the action.

A 1966 Bilderberg prospectus sums up one of the group's major thrusts:

> In the early fifties enthusiasm for, and confidence in, European unification justified the expectation that an economically and possibly a politically and militarily integrated Europe would be in a position to speak with one voice with the United States. There was every reason to expect that Bilderberg's activities would considerably facilitate and help to consolidate this process ... the prospects of achieving the desired economic integration became increasingly gloomy ... [but] the [Bilderberg] organization has continually adapted to changing circumstances ...

Judging by the current state of Europe, Bilderberg's patience has paid off. The continent is much closer to a unified political status, and even though there are dissidents, one would have to say, particularly with the election of Bilderberg British Prime Minister Tony Blair, that the future looks quite promising for elite interests.

Clearly, both CFR and Bilderberg have continued their pursuit of power, with the strategy of bringing nation-states under the aegis of comprehensive institutions created for that purpose.

Bilderberg, the CFR, and the similarly non-governmental Trilateral Commission — created in the U.S. in 1973 — have continued their push in the international arena. It has become clear that, even when competition develops among or within these groups, there is a gigantic prize to be won. Continued cooperation will lead to unprecedented world dominance by the few over the many.

These powerful men have seen that, for them, it makes no sense to stop at the level of trade treaties. The mandate should be to bring about global control to the degree that global populations will stand for it. In that setting, inevitable backslidings and defections can be nipped in the bud by members of this "Club."

The public face put on this kind of "progress" has been: let's have peace once and for all. (Let's establish UN and other regional peacekeeping forces for that purpose.) Let's bring to fruition the great human longings — the end of hunger, triumph over disease, economic opportunity for all. Behind that benign face is quite another attitude. Take, for example, the much-applauded UN effort to bring health to the continent of Africa. After ten years of research on American and international cartelization of medicine, I (and many others) have come to the conclusion that the UN has done everything but actually solve the centuries-old African health crisis. That situation is based on two factors: dirty water and the lack of food caused by the corporate-government theft of good growing land from the people of Africa. Any medical agency worth its certificates and its oaths would long ago have begun a massive material and PR effort to solve these problems — which are the basic cause of chronic illness and death on the continent of Africa. Cleaning up the water is not, by the way, an impossible task. Not at all. But UN health efforts somehow manage to focus on other things which do not bring about the greatly needed result.

The art of politics, at the highest levels, is to give a human voice to people's great historic longings, and to keep hammering on the idea of ever-constant, forward progress. However, behind that light will hide the agenda of global control.

As early as 1979, how could one avoid shaking his head at the potential power of an organization, Bilderberg, whose steering committee alone consisted of: the head of FIAT, Giovanni Agnelli; David Rockefeller; Baron Snoy et d'Oppuers, the Secretary-General of the Belgian Ministry of Economic Affairs; Victor Umbrecht, director of the Swiss pharmaceutical giant, Ciba-Geigy; George Ball, managing director of Lehman Brothers; Lord Eric Roll, director of the Bank of England, and chairman of the Common Market Trust; Emilio Collado, Exxon executive and J.P. Morgan director; and Otto Wolfe, German industrialist.

Wolfe, Rockefeller, and Agnelli also served as executive committee members of the Trilateral Commission.

Going back even earlier,

> President Kennedy "virtually staffed the State Department with ... Bilderberg alumni" — Secretary of State Dean Rusk, Undersecretary of State George W. Ball, George McGhee, Walter Rostow, McGeorge Bundy, Arthur Dean — and Paul Nitze at the Pentagon. Furthermore, many of the Trilateral Commissioners in the Carter Administration [were] also Bilderbergers, including Vice-President Mondale, Secretary of State Vance, National Security Advisor Brzezinski, and Treasury Secretary Blumenthal.

Not all Bilderbergs or CFR members or Trilateralists have signed on to the same policies at every important juncture. Debate, particularly at Bilderberg meetings, can be lively. But the sheer weight of collective control that can be exerted, as decades pass, by men such as those mentioned above, is beyond simply dangerous. As more political and economic power comes into their hands globally, the vision of an elitist future is easier to see — and there is less reason for disagreement among them.

Meanwhile, Bilderberg, perhaps the world's most dominant club, maintains, as well as it can, the objective of not drawing the attention

> of the greater population to Bilderberg activity ... Bilderberg's existence is often denied, even by foreign ministry officials. Apart from planted newspaper articles, no Bilderberg publications are available to the public. The extent of media blackout is remarkable ... [In 1967, press Baron] Cecil King, chairman of the International Publishing Corporation (which was the largest daily circulation press in Britain) and chairman of the Newspaper Proprietors Association, requested his fellow proprietors to see that "on no account should any report or even speculation about the content of the [current Bilderberg] conference be printed."

The above quotes about media secrecy concern the 1960s and 70s. Today, not much has changed. Public pressure to reveal the location of yearly Bilderberg meetings has made it more difficult to maintain concealment. But no articles — except as a result of infiltration — appear that detail the substance of these conferences.

The Trilateral Commission has, at least on one occasion, shown a more careless attitude toward press coverage of its actions. This astonishing, through-the-looking-glass 1978 exchange between reporter Jeremiah Novak and Trilateral Commission members Karl Kaiser and Richard Cooper shows how much control apparently resides within the unelected private Commission:

> *Reporter:* Is it true that a [private Trilateral] committee led by Henry Owen of the U.S. and made up of representatives of the U.K., U.S., West Germany, Japan, France, and the EEC is coordinating the economic and political policies of the trilateral countries? [The Trilateral countries are U.S., Canada, Belgium, Denmark,

France, Ireland, Italy, Luxembourg, Netherlands, Norway, Spain, U.K., West Germany and Japan.]

Cooper: Yes. They have met three times.

Reporter: Yet, in your recent paper you state that this committee should remain informal because to formalize 'this function might well prove offensive to some of the Trilateral and other countries which do not take part.' Who are you afraid of?

Kaiser: Many countries in Europe would resent the dominant role that West Germany plays at these meetings.

Cooper: Many people still live in a world of separate nations, and they would resent such coordination.

Reporter: But this committee is essential to your whole policy. How can you keep it a secret or fail to try to get popular support?

Cooper: Well, I guess it's the press' job to publicize it.

Reporter: Yes, but why doesn't President Carter come out with it and tell the American people that economic and political power is being coordinated by a committee made up of Henry Owen and six others? After all, if policy is being made on a multinational level, the people should know.

Cooper: President Carter and Secretary of State Vance have constantly alluded to this in their speeches.

Kaiser: It just hasn't become an issue.

At that time, the mix of corporate and government members of the Trilateral Commission was quite chilling. A very partial list included major executives of General Electric, CBS, Time, Exxon, General Motors, Bank of America, Ford, Coca Cola, Bechtel, Mitsubishi, Cargill, Rio Tinto Zinc, Bank of Madrid, Shell Oil, FIAT, General International Bank of Western Africa, Midland Bank, Belgium National Bank. More? The Prime Minister of France, the Japanese Minister for Foreign Affairs, the West German Minister of Economics, the British Secretary of State, the President of the United States, the U.S. Secretary of State, the head of the AFL-CIO, the head of the U.S. Federal Reserve Board, the head of the Council on Foreign Relations (CFR), the head of the Bilderberg group.

Although the Trilateral Commission has many plans and activities, at the top of the list would be making the world safe for transnational corporations — including banks who naturally want to invest capital, unimpeded, in any country in the world. All this is subsumed under the buzz-term free trade.

The translation of this apparently open policy is another matter entirely. The trend is toward more control by mega-corporations over the lives of people everywhere. As these corporations get stronger, make up a larger part of any local economic sector, they become "kings of survival" for people who need jobs to live. The same corporations exercise more and more influence over governments — and this means obtaining land and resources for a song in places where people have lived and farmed for centuries.

Under pressure from the International Monetary Fund to pay off loans, countries will bend more easily to transnational corporate requests for land, resources, and by implication slave labor.

The theme is: More and more power falling into the hands of fewer people.

One could call this the end-game of free market capitalism and applaud it as the natural outcome of survival of the fittest, but that would be a delusion.

What we have here is a coalescing of power through illegal collusion, manipulation of free enterprise, and the hijacking of governmental functions by groups formed alongside such governments: CFR, Trilateral Commission, Bilderberg.

Those who argue about socialism vs. capitalism entangle themselves in words that no longer fit the reality: powerful men and their institutions are gaining more and more control of this planet, under the aegis of co-opted governments, international financial organizations, and global corporations.

If unchecked, what kind of world will emerge?

A more robotized obedient one.

If survival can be made into a carrot/stick for every human

on the face of the Earth, and if this carrot can be held out by a smaller and smaller number of corporations, then human behavior itself will take a quantum leap into a caricature of itself.

People will become blinder than ever to the misfortunes of others. They will affect satisfaction and happiness, and come to equate these qualities with fitting into the slots of their jobs. They will seek to understand more exactly what is required of them by their bosses, and they will conform to those demands in greater and greater detail.

Does this sound familiar?

The new world is a matter of degree, not kind.

Meanwhile, this network of power, this confederation of men who discover, every year, how to wield more control over the lives of Earth's six billion, uses its imagination to construct a universe whose message is:

"We are moving forward. Progress is good for everyone. Life is better. Regardless of glitches, everything is all right."

That may sound like an uninspired form of art, and it is. It's not Michelangelo, but it works. And the glamour of the advertising world supplies the glitz.

This elitist art-strategy works because it is a version of what we all are already creating in our civilized hearts: a future that succeeds for everyone, exciting new times, true human progress, a sense of reliability, a platform from which to launch great adventures.

Why wouldn't we accept the same message from other people, particularly from our leaders?

The only flaw is, they are using that message to soothe a world as it falls further under their sway.

Is this universe-making on the part of these power-brokers completely conscious? No. These men are also talking to themselves, trying to reassure one other that all is well. Like most humans, they need that reassurance because they are cut off from the deeper levels of their own imagination. That is the problem. That is the real crisis of faith.

72

The general consensus among economists who care to look is that about 300 transnational corporations presently control 25% of the world's productive capacity.

Read those numbers again.

73

Just to do a little updating, here are some members of the CFR and/or the Trilateral Commission from recent times:

"... Fed Chairman Alan Greenspan, former Chairman Paul Volcker ... Cyrus R. Vance, Bobby Ray Inman ... CBS chief Laurence A. Tisch, anchorman Dan Rather, NBC chief John F. Welch Jr., anchorman Tom Brokaw and David Brinkley, ABC chief Thomas S. Murphy and anchor Diane Sawyer, PBS's Robert MacNeil and Jim Lehrer, the *Washington Post*'s Katherine Graham, CNN's Daniel Schorr, *U.S. News*'s David Gergen ... Al Gore, National Security Advisor Anthony Lake, Secretary of State Warren Christopher, Secretary of Defense Les Aspin, Secretary of the Interior Bruce Babbitt ... Secretary of Health and Human Services Donna Shalala.

"Between May 30 and June 2, 1996, the Bilderberger Group met in King City, near Toronto, Canada. Attendees included President Clinton's senior adviser George Stephanupolos, Defense Secretary William Perry, Henry Kissinger, Lloyd Bentsen, and David Rockefeller."

74

This chapter presents a speculative sketch of a person who may be an elite controller type, behind his apparent good works. Is he high in the ranks of those men who increasingly see their way clear to sculpting "their kind of Earth" in the 21st century?

Consider this statement attributed in 1988 to Prince Philip, Duke of Edinburgh, consort to the Queen and renowned champion of ecological causes. The statement stands as a monument to weakness sitting at the heart of great wealth. It is also, in a way, Philip being creative. I believe it represents a prevailing thought — if the walls could speak — of many among the super-rich:

"In the event that I am reincarnated, I would like to return as a deadly virus, in order to contribute something to solve overpopulation."

One wonders whether Philip sees himself as a wealthy virus who would somehow retire to his castle for a bath and a late dinner after inflicting death on several million valueless humans.

On a similar note, here is a wry (?) statement made 35 years earlier by Bertrand Russell. It reflects a sometime level of imagination among the British intellectual elite:

"War, so far, has had no very great effect on this increase [in world population] ... but perhaps bacteriological war may prove more effective. If a Black Death could spread through the world once in every generation, survivors could procreate freely without making the world too full ... The state of affairs may be somewhat unpleasant, but what of it? Really high-minded people are indifferent to happiness, especially other people's."

Men like Philip apparently omit from their memories the history of "overpopulated" nations whose pasts have been dislodged and crushed and dominated by foreign interests, colonial interests, *before* bleeding out into a horrible state of economic misery. Viewing this endgame misery, the Philips of this world warn that attempts to help put things right may result in just too many people being successfully born and surviving. In other words, worse overpopulation.

I know I am jumping ahead several large steps, but follow me.

Consider the following as serious thoughts in the mind of a human being:

The desire and willingness to destroy populations.

The concentration on population-reduction as an experiment.

Scenarios for reducing population drastically through experiments.

This is the art form of certain human beings, and I am not making a trivial point.

This is the limit of their imagination.

This is the shape of their imagination, yes, but this is also the serious limit to which their imagination has been taken.

Here is a statement attributed to Prince Philip (University of Western Ontario, Canada, July 1, 1983):

"For example, the World Health Organization Project, designed to eradicate malaria from Sri Lanka in the postwar years, achieved its purpose. But the problem today is that Sri Lanka must feed three times as many mouths, find three times as many jobs, provide three times the housing, energy, schools, hospitals and land for settlement in order to maintain the same standards. Little wonder the natural environment and wildlife in Sri Lanka has suffered. The fact [is] ... that the best-intentioned aid programs are at least partially responsible for the problems."

Sri Lanka's problems started long before malaria drugs were dispensed, and those problems were not entirely separate from elite foreign intervenors.

In his 1988 preface to *Down to Earth*, Philip wrote what, under a certain light, would appear ominous:

"... as a boy I was made aware of the annual fluctuations in the number of game animals and the need to adjust the 'cull' to the size of the surplus population."

On at least several occasions, Philip has said that the survival of a species is the thing to be desired, and the deaths of individuals within a species are unimportant. It also seems clear that he views animals and humans as just "different species."

Philip wrote the Introduction to a section in *Down to Earth* called "The Population Factor." He speaks of control of the numbers of animals on the planet, and then switches over to humans. His statement has an odd whiff:

"Predation, climatic variation, disease, starvation — and in the case of the inappropriately named Homo sapiens, war and terrorism — are the principal means by which population numbers are kept under some sort of control."

Background: if having a friend and business associate like Prince Bernhard of the Netherlands could be counted as a reference-point for his own attitudes, Philip, it should be remembered, has worked for many years with a man who had labored for the notorious Nazi cartel, I.G. Farben, in its intelligence section. Farben, as one of the major leveragers of Hitler, eventually, after Bernhard's departure, set up concentration camps as factories for the production of synthetic oil and rubber, and used and killed many prisoners as "temporary employees" in these factories.

Philip, as consort to the Queen of England, is linked into enormous power which, among its more obvious avenues, uses money and home-grown corporations and banks to buy companies on a global basis.

How does a Duke with connections at the highest levels of business maintain his celebrated position that in a few years the world will be destroyed by overpopulation and pollution unless we forestall it, while some of the very men who, for instance, belong to his Club of Isles, must be busy fomenting that pollution?

The Royal Family business and/or personal connection to Dutch Shell, Imperial Chemical Industries, and Unilever makes it quite hard to accept Philip's sentiments about saving the planet as altruistic.

It is reported that a stated aim of the Club of Isles is the reduction of world population to under a billion. If so, how could that be done, except by genocide?

How does a Duke whose family is tied so closely to vast petroleum interests renounce pollution without explicitly renouncing his family's judgment? Have you heard such a ringing declamation? I'm willing to be proven wrong, but I haven't heard a thing.

Can we infer what kind of world the sort of man I have been describing in this chapter would want, would work for? Whether this man is Philip or someone else, I am convinced he exists and that there are others like him.

This kind of man wants a world that is like a golf course. He lives on the fourteenth fairway and he also lives in a castle on top of the nearby mountain. There are very few cities left on the planet. There are many pretty towns in which artisans perform their wonderful tasks for low but reasonable pay. The machines of industry are spectacular and they are hidden underground where a technician class of worker ensures their efficiency. The population of the planet is down to 600 million and wildlife are flourishing. So are the plants and flowers and trees. The streams are clean. The air is fresh. The smog and the old cars are gone. Vehicles run on water.

In this setting, one can live the very good life and indulge whims, for one is the feudal King of his domain.

How do you cure the kind of imagination that really wants that world? Does merely stepping on it do the trick? Perhaps, but not in the long run.

In the long run, we are talking about education — and not in the familiar sense. We are talking about something new and extensive which, for the first time on this planet, gives the imagination so much free-ranging exercise that the owner of an imagination turns out to be able to conceive world solutions as something far different from wars and plagues decimating populations.

In the long run, we need a planet full of people like that.

75

The Tradition of Imagination personified.

In 1940, R. Buckminster Fuller knew and said that business and government could walk another road. He had calculated that we, as a race, had enough technology to provide every human on Earth with more than the essentials of life: housing, clothes, food, transportation, unlimited education and health care.

Fuller pointed out that the alternative would be incredible dislocation and unemployment-disaster as industry became automated.

"There are two ways to look at the same thing," he said. "You can be out of a job, or you can be on full scholarship."

For Fuller, full scholarship meant being charged with the job of trying to come up with really bright ideas that would push human progress along.

This was not some vague dream on his part. He actually envisioned a world in which every human would be liberated from sheer toil and from living on the edge of survival. Liberated into what? Into whatever would constitute true human advancement, as defined by each person.

Fuller presupposed that technology actually existed for a reason. At one time that reason may have had everything to do with competition or wealth ... but what do you do when humans have so brilliantly succeeded that their technology now allows the whole race to survive? What do you do when the largest corporations cannot go full-bore on production, because their capability to turn out products is too great, would cause drastic oversupply, would force prices to collapse overnight? What do you do when the brilliant technology of automation will, in the next fifty years, eliminate the need for millions of workers all over the world? What do you do, in other words, when you thought you were playing chess and now you discover you are playing tic-tac-toe?

You see the board and you know how to win, tie, or lose.

At that point, you can choose, as major power players on this planet have, to run screamingly from such realizations and pursue your former goals. Or you can find a confidence in your own imagination and begin to envision a new level for the world.

This is the crisis.

This is where the failure of imagination, and the fear of relying on it, will bring the whole house down.

It is clear that massive corporations can find ways to supply the essentials of life to the planet and help end war and disease once and for all. And they can still make a profit. They don't have to engage in excessive collusion to accomplish this feat, and they don't have to make governments even stronger in the process. They don't need to wheel out a global government. And national economies don't have to be placed under the rule of a Transition Commission to a Better World.

That "Commission" is what we have now, as sketched in over the last several chapters, and the deception is obvious. It is not about better, it is about more domination and control.

The truth is rather ruthless: without a background of trust in one's own wide-ranging imagination/process, one will always opt for the solution that preserves the status quo. Oh, you might tweak that status quo a little and call it wonderful, but you will be afraid to imagine and then try anything truly new. Why? Because you have no experience in doing it, in finding out that you don't end up falling down into a dark abyss permanently.

If not sooner, it should be apparent now that the Tradition of Imagination is not about parlor tricks. We are talking about the future of the planet.

To cite only one of a host of examples, it was a failure of the imagination that led America to draw back from its own space program. In 1982, I carried out an extensive set of interviews with scientists, including the Galileo Jupiter-probe engineer, Ted Clarke, from Jet Propulsion Lab. He, among others, remarked that orbiting hotels and space colonies were far from sci-fi fairy tales. The technology was here, the projects could be begun immediately. We could eventually outfit ten or twenty space-cities and, through gravity assists, send them out of the solar system on thousand-year journeys.

Implementing these and other ideas would incidentally guarantee full employment in this and a number of other countries, to say nothing of the sea-change in the minds of our people. It is called inspiration.

Fill in the details yourself.

We have, for some time, been a nation that is lingering in still waters. We have largely forgotten what a great journey would be.

76

The Tradition of Imagination.

New ideas.

What follows are two quite brief interviews with people who, in different fashions, embody the Tradition of Imagination. The result of their work reveals ways of decentralizing power — economic power, political power, energy-power.

This must be understood: to bring about a successful decentralization of power on this planet could virtually end the hegemony of the ages-old Secret Society Formula. To make this happen, we need technology which can function at the level of the individual in such a way that he/she gets off the central energy grid. This technology must also make it possible to maintain and update infrastructure at local levels, without reference to large corporate and government bodies. And finally, there must be a coherent plan which gains the support of many, many people to drastically reduce the weaponry on the planet — without simply leaving that force in the hands of governments, armies, or police.

Ted Clarke Interview

Ted Clarke is a man with vast experience inside the U.S. space program. He has worked for 28 years at the Jet Propulsion Laboratory in Pasadena, California, as an engineer, scientist and technical manager on the Mariner Venus/Mercury, Voyager, and Galileo space missions.

The following excerpt is taken from several conversations we have had over the years, starting in 1982, through the early months of 1998.

In 1978, you lectured in front of a group of builders, construction people.

Yes. I told them about orbiting hotels.

As a dream?

As a reality by the end of the 20th century.

Is this true?

Of course. The technology is there. These men were exhilarated to the nth degree by the prospect of working on a program like that. The first popular move into space. I mean, their feeling was so high it was incredible.

People are inspired by space.

When the Pathfinder mission landed on Mars, do you know how many hits they got on their website?

No.

A billion. One billion.

This takes me back to the lines around the block in the 70s when Star Wars first appeared. A friend of mine went to the opening of the film on Hollywood Boulevard, the first day, the first morning, at 11 a.m., on a weekday. The place was packed, and she said that the instant the large print began rolling on the screen — "In a galaxy far, far away" — a roar began building in the theater. No one had seen a frame of the movie, and a collective roar started and kept going all through the credits.

The politicians won't take the hint. They're too worried about the length of their term in office. They only want to fund space projects that come to fruition during the time period of their terms.

No reliance on imagination.

It's a tragedy.

What gets me is, a real space program could mean full employment, and not just in this country.

No one fully grasps the extent of what a real space program would be, but you're right. You're absolutely right. Here's a real commitment to space. You build a domed city every thirty or forty years. You take a space platform out to the asteroid belt, and you use materials there to build the city. Many, many people have the experience of contributing to this. It takes several trips out and back to build each city. Let's call it ten thousand people — they are the final number to take off.

Take off where?
    With gravity assists, you can get outside the solar system. You direct each city to a system like Bernard's Star, where we think there is a planet. Every thirty years, we send out a domed city with ten thousand people on it. Self-sufficient. We send fifty cities in all.

Is there a stated purpose to the mission?
    Damn right. To rendezvous at Bernard's Star, at that system, around the same planet, and compare notes on the evolution of, say, fifty societies.

How long would the trip take?
    About ten thousand years. That's a space program! Do you understand? Not a shuttle going around the planet. Nothing wrong with that, but the reason it's a winner in the NASA sweepstakes has to do with the politicians again. They're scared to fund anything you have to wait a long, long time for, to see results.

Ten thousand years? That's fantastic.
    Isn't it?

And it's doable?
    We can do that. It's reachable.

You're talking about space as the ultimate diversifier.
    Sure. You get many, many societies operating on their own. This isn't a monolith.

It decentralizes.
    The broom sweeps clean. No way you can pre-determine what a domed city is going to evolve into in ten thousand years. Some of them will fall under the influence of lunatic dictators. But for how long? And what about the others?

You feel we're potentially in a renaissance. That's a word you use.
    Yes. What do you call it when every citizen is inspired by

great dreams like this, when the implementation of those dreams means full employment and full-on excitement at the level of the mind? This is what I'm talking about.

And it breaks the stranglehold of being held under the sway of one way, one central theme, one giant bureaucracy.
No question about it. And we can do it.

You've mentioned an article in the Michigan Quarterly Review ...
Yes, in 1979. Spring. Stanley Rosen compiled the quotations and experiences of some of the American astronauts who went into space. A surprising number of them had profound transformative experiences. Mitchell, Irwin, Harrison Schmitt, the last man to be on the moon. You see, a lot of the astronauts came back changed. They had seen the Earth from space. It was like a spiritual awakening. Or, if you don't like that language, call it a psychological shift of great proportions. They felt a great desire to eradicate the false differences between people, to unify the planet in a true way, to end the stupidity of war. Just for starters.

Are you saying that this is what many civilians would go through if they took a week off and traveled to an orbiting hotel?
That's what I'm saying. And they wouldn't just sit on it when they returned. They'd spread the word ...

77

In my mind, I pair up Paul Glover and Stephen Dunifer. They are both innovators squarely in the Tradition of Imagination. Dunifer opened Free Radio Berkeley on April 11th, 1993, a 24-hour-a-day local station dedicated to the First Amendment and issues of community concern.

This is a microwatt FM station, which jousts with an ambiguous FCC regulation concerning licensing of stations under 100 watts. The FCC apparently never thought anyone would open a sub-100 station, so they didn't extend their control over such stations — Dunifer and his co-workers simply slipped onto the FM dial between already existing programming.

You can buy equipment which makes it possible for any person to start his own radio station for under $1000 — and cover the area of a small city.

Multiplication and diversification of realities.

Decentralization of information, to the maximum.

In 1997 there are hundreds of microwatt stations burgeoning all over the country. Sensitive political issues, among others, are explored at a depth impossible on conventional radio or television.

In 1996 I was interviewed twice by a coastal California microwatt station, and in those five hours I spoke about the pharmaceutical/medical monopoly, its abuses, its toxic drugs, with a specificity impossible on 99.99% of American radio.

Dunifer is currently in court with the FCC, which is trying to shut him down on behalf of the federal government. The case has dragged on for a year and a half.

Meanwhile, the proliferation of microwatt radio is making it harder and harder for the federal government, even with a favorable court ruling, to take major action against these broadcasters.

CBS. NBC. ABC. CNN. They stand for a basic centralization of information. Their hegemony is fading from a new threat which could truly shred the whole corporate system of info-control in the U.S.

Do some of these microwatt stations, in their provincialism, in their anti-human attitudes, broadcast falsehoods, do they sometimes represent offensive points of view? Of course. Which is worse, that or the death of freedom?

Paul Glover once formed a group in Los Angeles called Citizen Planners, which as a model constructed blueprints to show how a square block in the Boyle Heights district could be completely recycled and rebuilt to provide free food to residents, community spaces, no cars, cleaner air. Now, in Ithaca, New York, he has founded a private money system called Ithaca Hours. After several years, 350 businesses, several thousand individuals, a bank and a hospital are accepting the paper money of Ithaca Hours. Fifty-two spin-off systems around North America have taken Glover's start-up kit and begun their own private money systems.

Several years ago I asked Glover how he himself uses this non-federal paper money.

"For example, I pay my rent with it. My landlord takes it and gives it to two carpenters who build additions on to his properties. The carpenters could pass it along to local farmers for produce, and so on ..."

Aside from existing as independent from the U.S. Department of Treasury and the Federal Reserve, local currency, as it's called generically, seems to have a profound psychological effect on some people. It helps them change their work to something closer to the heart. They plug into a local group of friendly people who will be more prone to pay for their service or product.

Paul Glover Interview

You've invented a system of money called Ithaca Hours. How did that happen?

I quit watching television in 1969, so unofficial ideas occur to me. But the existence of the system is to the credit of the thousands of participants who have explained it to one another and who have earned and spent it [Ithaca money]. They are the pioneers.

Your bills, the money itself, are called Hours.

Yes. One Hour equals one hour of basic labor. Professionals are entitled to charge multiple Hours per hour, but this reinforces the idea that everyone's hour of labor has at least a minimum dignity.

Give me an idea of the range of professions and businesses that have signed on to the system, that use the money.

Over 2000 individuals have earned Hours, and 350 businesses accept Hours, including a bank, movie theaters, bowling alley, restaurants, health clubs, and even the hospital.

I take it this money is not backed up by gold or silver. How do you decide when to print more of it — and how much to print?

U.S. money has not been backed by gold since 1933 nor by silver since 1969. We print Hours as we need more of them for disbursement ... issuance of Hours must be systematic and fair, reflecting the quantity and variety of goods and services that Hours will buy.

What does the U.S. Department of Treasury have to say about the existence of this money?

They and the IRS, FBI, Secret Service have all been contacted by the media, and have repeatedly said there is no prohibition on private paper money as long as it does not look like dollars, as long as it is regarded as taxable income, and as long as the smallest denomination has at least $1.00 value.

What keeps you from lining your pockets with Ithaca Hours?

I've lived here since 1953, and many of the Hour users are friends of mine.

From reading the newspaper you put out, it seems that some people see Ithaca Hours as a chance to do what they've always dreamed of all their lives. Why does this system of money liberate them?

[Conventional] bank loans are available at interest, only in large quantities, for narrowly defined practical projects. This money [Hours] is lent without interest charges, and new businesses find a ready pool of customers who have discretionary local money to spend.

Ithaca Hours does increase local commerce. This includes farmers.

Food is our directory's largest category. At the Farmer's Market, 55 of 100 vendors accept Hours ... [which] stay in our region to help us hire each other. While dollars make us increasingly dependent on transnational corporations and bankers, Hours reinforce community trading and expand commerce which is more accountable to our concerns for ecology and social justice ... The Success Stories of 300 participants published so far [in the *Ithaca Money* newspaper] testify to the acts of generosity and community that our system prompts. We're making a community while making a living. As we do so, we relieve the social desperation which has led to compulsive shopping and wasted resources.

Ithaca Hours can be reached at Box 6578, Ithaca, New York, 14851, or by e-mail at hours@lightlink.com.

78

The Formula of the Secret Society

There is a principle that has arisen in global politics, particularly over the last fifty years. It is inclusion, inclusion of all points of view. But with a catch. Through non-confrontational negotiation, through finding what the other person wants, or will settle for, an appearance of success can be attained.

This *appearance* is art, and it is one of the major created spaces of the global elite which the public is enticed into accepting and inhabiting.

In this way, for example, international interests can converge on the Dominican Republic and simulate the coming of democracy to that troubled country. In Panama, a mirage can be created in which colonial interests seem to recede in favor of "home rule." To a degree, the same can be said about South Africa. But in these and many other cases, the underlying economic game holds the fort. The multi-national corporate power remains intact, and the more "progressive" home government — which may put in place a soft version of the First Amendment, which may permit a variety of political parties — nevertheless assures a very low minimum wage, incredible tax-free havens for foreign businesses, and carte blanche to the multinationals to grab mineral rights, dig up the land, and pollute it to the hilt.

This softer approach has proven to work in many cases.

It is the policy of the Trilateral Commission.

It is what they urge in all cases.

After all, given enough time, with attrition, some opposition rebel leaders within a Third World country can be bought off, or can be bought off to a degree, and if the diamonds and the gold and the oil are still being dug up and processed and sold by the same elite corporations, does anyone really care?

This Trilateralist policy, of course, does not preclude the use of force when necessary, but it pushes it back on the agenda.

As our technological age shrinks the planet and dissolves barriers, another factor emerges. Warring political and economic elites begin, gradually, to discover common interests.

A process repeats itself over and over. I call it upward funneling. I am simplifying and distorting, but here is how it is played. Ten powers try to steal and chew on and own the same piece of valuable meat. From this struggle, three winners emerge, and they are funneled upward in the power stream. Somewhat bloodied and dazed, they look around and see a higher level of atmosphere, of sky, and they also see one another. They soon concur that there is no point having another battle, because, come to think of it, the potential spoils are so great down below that they can join up and share them.

Not only that, but way out there is another group of corporate dogs which is slathering and looking for meat. A battle will sooner or later take place at that level: Why not strengthen the group at home before launching out to take on this tough foe?

And then the next fight does take place, and from that one, two dogs emerge victorious, and they are funneled even higher in the power stream, and from their new elite skypost they see a larger territory of potential exploitation, and they see each other. Why go for the throat now? Why not join up ...?

Upward funneling — and then pretended inclusion of lesser opponents — as time passes, as the planet shrinks, becomes the order of the day.

This is the game.

Greater territory owned by fewer and fewer.

Is this is a conspiracy? Does it involve front groups and alter egos and deception and betrayal and so on?

Of course.

Only a senseless idiot would fail to notice that.

But it has an organic aspect, it evolves out of conflict and out of cooperation.

The groups who are the emerging controllers become more clearly defined over time. And their methods become more refined, more deft.

In this light, consider my comments on a continuing Nazi agenda. At first glance, the existence of such a thing appears to linger, if at all, on the outer margins of power and society — or only in the secret labs and halls of military intelligence operations. And perhaps that is its position. But over time, the process of conflict and cooperation brings more and more power toward the center, and sooner or later, many players see that there is much to be won by working together. Why let ideology cause permanent rifts?

So even that "far-out" sinister despicable Nazi power can be brought into the fold of major players. Not without enmity, not without conflict — but in time, it is possible.

And what is the art, aside from the inclusion-scenario, that assures major players gain concealed control over more and more lives?

No vast ritual is needed here. No fresco-ceilings, no tall fish-hats, no satin robes. In fact, just the opposite art has occurred. A minimalism. It is blandness that takes over; that is the art-form. Respectability. Legitimacy.

These are the foundations of the art of the evolving secret society — whose agenda of control remains the same.

Not cathedrals and wafers and wine for blood and cherubim, but instead invocations of human rights and free elections and adequate medical care, and Capitol Hill and the State Department and being interviewed on Meet the Press, good lighting, well-tailored suits, sponsorship by well-known multinationals ...

It seems to be simple, but remember, it wasn't until a hundred years ago that industrialism, a middle-class, and bureaucracies began to swim into view together in this world.

All that set the stage for an elite that could play peek-a-boo behind the columns of respectability. Until then, there wasn't quite the combination of a business-government clique and a large audience living above the dire poverty line.

Thailand. Malaysia. South Korea. Indonesia. Almost unprobed in the press, a virtual takeover of these countries is occurring. In what sense? Their economies are not simply being bailed out by the International Monetary Fund and the World Bank. They are being hijacked after a long period of punishment through manipulations of money markets — which has helped cause their financial viability to quiver on the edge of disaster.

Is that too strong an assessment? Is that too conspiratorial a judgment?

Perhaps it is.

Let's imagine the reality is 30% of what I've just asserted.

Even in that case, we are witnessing a strong trend, and it will continue over time, as these nations are brought into the center of the financial network that envelops global trade and foreign investments. These Asian countries will not be permitted to exist arrogantly on the edge. The key is supra-nationalism. Elite international economics rests on the premise of corporate structures that supersede national loyalties.

"Swim in our ocean or die."

If you were to say, "Well, there are financial forces outside this global machination," I would not disagree. But again, my point is, over time, those forces and these forces and the other forces over the hill will come into conflict and upward funneling will take place and the winners will ultimately work out their differences, and behind the art of respectability and blandness and "concern for human beings," they will emerge stronger and in more control than ever.

That is the awareness that has long ago taken hold among the major players of the major elites.

How far might this control go? At the extreme?

It might go into engineered genes and into the serious tinkering with neurotransmitters and synapses of the brain.

Oh, you say, the idea of that level of control is absurd.

All right, I'll agree with you, just for the sake of argument. Today. But what about tomorrow? Still absurd? What about ten years, twenty years, fifty years from now? Still absurd?

Think about it.

The outcome is not decided.

The game is afoot.

79

Experimentation is part of the reason for the creativity of humans. This is a bottom-line activity of the human spirit.

The invention of the United States was taken by the founders to be an experiment in freedom, and, to the extent that freedom was truly built into the system, it was and is such an experiment.

The invention of a religion has always been viewed by its founders as experimental. Will good fortune come to believers who worship in a particular way? And later on, will the religion "allow" its founders and their minions to control large numbers of minds?

A company, a business is an experiment which is created along a certain pattern. Will it work? Will profit be made and maintained?

There are experimental shadings in a marriage, a family, a home.

Think of the thousands of communities, large and small, which have been created by humans since the dawn of time on this planet. Each one was a test, an experiment.

We must face the fact that, along with creation, invention, there is always the aspect of experimentation. It is a basic impulse of a soul — to see what happens when he/she creates a certain thing. A whole life can be seen in this way.

"What will happen if I live this way and take on these traits and invent these circumstances?"

Of course we tend to assume that our choices are forced by external events into a particular series of shapes, but there is another level at which that is not the case at all.

We must come to grips with the fact that the imagination has an infinite range of inventions it can bring about, at its own choice and desire and whim.

We must also accept that many of these imaginative potentials are on what we would call the dark side of life. In other words, experimentations which would involve the destruction of certain realities which are held to be inviolate, the breakup of which would cause pain.

It is in art where such events can be experienced without interfering with other people's freedom. A war of great devastation is not necessary. A surrealist painter like Max Ernst can bring variant set-pieces of reality into clashes and conflicts and meetings at a level far deeper than any high-altitude bombing over a major city can. And the meaning of his painting is soaked through with more profound effects for consciousness to consider. It is in art that emotion can be expressed and portrayed and felt in both its purest and most multiple ways.

As always, imagination and its expressions hold the key.

Now pretend you are a controller.

Pretend you are one of those shadowy figures who, behind the scenes, collaborates with like-minded manipulators to stage wars, take over the finances of nations, maintain poverty and derail progress in countries "not slated" for significant economic participation in the world community.

This is your creation. This is your level of invention.

Well, there is always a reason for creation. The soul doing it at least suspects he will like the outcome, will find out something from the outcome, will explore new territory with the outcome.

But after thirty or forty years of being a controller, what do you get from the creation of pain for others? You get control. It comes back to you over and over. You get more and more clues about what it is like to live in a world of people who are controlled, who are robotic, who are at your call.

What is the end of this kind of creation?

At what point do you begin to see where it is all going?

When do you decide that you have found out enough about that?

When do you begin to open up your imagination to other worlds, worlds, say, of abundance and freedom?

The controller, at one level, is dumber than what he takes to be the dumbest beast. At that level, his imagination does not take flight into constructing possible realities in which non-control, diversity, freedom, the flourishing of art all bring about a different world.

At that level, he is the very kind of crude boor he says he abhors and must control.

PART SIX

**Further reflections on the
Tradition of Imagination
and the
Formula of the Secret Society**

80

Hello, Richard Jenkins.

What I'm about to write gives credence, finally, to what he said to me: that history has a lineage of healing that is not based on a single method. Yet is a tradition.

Here it is.

In the book *Rolling Thunder*, the now-famous American Indian medicine man of the same name tells the author, Doug Boyd, about how healing works.

"I want to warn you," he says, "not to copy me, but work out your own method. Our people tell us to be original. If you can watch the method, though, and the way I go about it, maybe that would give you some thoughts about what to follow, what it's all about. Then you work out your own substance, your own songs, your own prayers and things go with it. It's not good to copy."

This is Jenkins to the hilt.

When I discovered this quote by Rolling Thunder, I realized that The Tradition of Imagination had been alive in Native Americans — which possibly means indigenous people from the tip of Alaska to Tierra del Fuego. In other words, among some but not all, healing was taught as Rolling Thunder describes it: watch me, see what you see, don't model yourself after me, find your own way, be spontaneous, be an artist.

Time and time again throughout my life, the discovery of people who operate in this way has driven me out into the realm of imagination, when I had been feeling, for a time, that everything was down pat, the framework and the rules and the guidelines were all in place, and life was a trip on a train along the already built rails.

What are we to think when suddenly it becomes possible

that a whole continent — two, in fact — have contained, for perhaps fifteen thousand years, a people among whom a highly individual form of healing-creation has been practiced? A non-system.

We are to think this: there are many areas on this Earth where the Tradition of Imagination has been overlooked and left out of the history books. There are many instances of the Tradition which, if recognized at all, have been left as isolated cases — and not hooked up together.

So what?

So this: the true picture would give us a wholly different past and a different feeling and assessment of the human core and the human life.

81

Today I saw a four-minute film never promoted by NASA. It was taken by the Galileo craft during a one-day period starting at six in the morning on December 11th, 1990. At the time, the spacecraft was 1.3 million miles out from Earth and moving away. What you see, for several minutes, is unprecedented. The Earth actually turning below the craft. Rotating around its own axis. Why did NASA refuse or neglect to promote this film to the public? After discussing the question with Galileo scientist Ted Clarke, who was at a loss to explain it, I came to the conclusion that this film has been kept out of sight because it might trigger too much imagination, too much wild surmise, too much hope.

The more times you watch this film, the more marvelous it gets. Not just the storms, or the rust shape of Australia appearing to jut out from the blue and white background, but the blue and white itself, the wraparound muscular energy of the Earth, showing up in whorls and shoulders and vortexes as the rotation goes on.

The little dried-out nasal skeptics of this world, who sell their souls for the chance to snap at the heels of any human with real adventure on his mind, will try to make rules that keep spontaneous life from appearing without notice.

But they will fail. They will definitely fail.

I asked Ted Clarke why he put out so much effort to get this film made to begin with, against so much lethargy and opposition of officials.

"Because I wanted people to dream," he said.

82

That there is no history of an event may, in the long run, prove to be more important than everything we can find buried in the stones of the past.

That's certainly the case with the implications of Rolling Thunder's message.

Let me give you another example which, by this time, should have an impact.

There is a set of monk-dug caves in northwest China called Dunhuang. Some of the greatest painting yet produced by humans is contained in the hundreds of rooms of those caves. 460 rooms remain from perhaps an original thousand, after the wear and tear of Gobi desert sand, centuries of it.

The Buddhist painting and sculpture at Dunhuang was done by outside artists and, in some cases, by resident monks. The work, begun in 360 CE, spanned ten centuries and several dynasties. The middle Tang is considered by most scholars the major epoch of Dunhuang.

What was the daily life like in the communities of these artists, from generation to generation, during which time 2000 statues of Buddha and 50,000 square meters of mural-painting were made? By daily life I don't mean the meals and the laundry and the divisions of labor. I mean the making of great art, on the spot?

A major Chinese scholar at UCLA, to whom I directed this question, said, "That's very interesting." In other words, no one to his knowledge had taken up that matter.

Blind spot of enormous proportions.

Dunhuang may be the longest-lived artistic community in the history of Earth. Add to that the fact that the quality of the work there was, at times, breathtaking by any standard — perhaps even equal in moments to the floating paradises of Piero della Francesca.

Although religion was the motive force behind the work, that was clearly left far behind by some artists — just as was the case in the Italian and Dutch and German Renaissance periods.

This being so, how did creation, imagination itself move to the fore within these endless caves, within these stone rooms, many of which were cramped and dark?

Dunhuang was one of the major events in the history of humankind. From decade to decade, wall-painting, sculpture carved into the walls, and walls cut out into sculpture and painted transformed that dark universe.

The Getty Conservation Institute has recently been doing some research and excellent preservation there, but I have heard nothing about an attempt to plumb the collective life of the greatest artists who spent time at Dunhuang.

For a parallel, imagine that waves of most of the recognized painters and sculptors of every stripe in America — and many unknown artists — traveled to New Mexico and lived for a thousand years painting and carving the insides of mountains.

When history leaves a gigantic hole, when history arranges its priorities so that such holes are left, we realize, by degrees, the unspoken truth.

What was not reported, what was ignored, was buried, in the long run, because we could not muster the perspective from which to see how vital it was — and is.

How do we speak about the overlapping personal orbits of brilliant Chinese artists who lived at Dunhuang at the same time, when it doesn't even occur to us that such a subject or "category of interest" could exist?

And how can we then think that human creation and imagination have really been reported?

We know that, by their omission, we are admitting to their vast thunder.

83

In the 21st century, the challenge will be to decentralize reality. If every human could rise to the level of harnessing his/her imagination at ten percent of peak power, at five percent of peak power, the lives of all of us would change radically. We would begin to truly live. A "spontaneity of time" would occur. We would naturally and creatively, in many different ways, shed our attachments to the Central Machine of civilization. That Machine, as part of its guts, feeds its singular reality, so to speak, for massive consumption. If we all stopped eating that, controlling us would be impossible.

84

The secret behind secret societies and cults and hierarchical religions is the artistic creation of a universe which is then frozen for mass consumption.

The pressure of major elites, in government, in war, in power-struggles, involves the slowing down of the imagination so that a central mural about reality can be set in concrete. From it, an agenda can be spun off. The agenda inevitably involves control of large numbers of people. Why inevitably? Because the slowing down of the imagination and the solidification of a pre-defined universe for the masses already point in that direction.

85

There is no way around it. A true collective evolution of humankind cannot be engineered by a trick of mass hypnosis or mass spiritual uplift or mass revelation. No, what is necessary is the liberation, for each individual, by each individual, of his own imagination to greater and greater degrees of power.

86

Monopolies work only when imaginations are sleeping.
But a better world is only the beginning. People fall back on Authority time and time again when their own exploration of creativity, invention, imagination is not enough to sustain them, is too daunting, is too simplistic. We need to overcome that and take the full ride.

87

What might a page torn out of a teacher's notebook from the year 2020 look like?

"From 9 to 10 today I took the six-year olds out to the park to continue the *becoming* exercises. Becoming a tree. Merge your mind with the tree. Then think like the tree. Look at the park as if you were the tree ... This exercise is now in its third year with this group. Three students are describing very clearly out-of-body experiences. They are detailing landscapes at some distance from the park.

"From 1 to 2 the six-year-olds invented dreams for each other, working in triads. From 2 to 3 they focused on creating in their minds new worlds, new inventions and societies on this planet. This latter exercise they have been doing for a year now. Some of their creations are quite detailed.

"From 3 to 4 the after-school volunteer group of 15-year olds continued their individual work creating, for lack of a better word, 'deities,' beings who have great scope and consciousness. This is an ongoing exercise with this group. It is in its fourth year. The beings created tend to pass on wisdom and to exude great energy and happiness. We alternate periods of creating these beings and getting rid of them — so that attachments don't grow too strong, and also so the students feel first-hand that they can deal in any way they want to with the products of their own imaginations.

"Our weekend volunteers are concentrating on paranormal work. We have twelve children who regularly demonstrate telepathy among themselves, move physical objects with their minds. Two children have materialized small objects in full view of the other students in the class, and on videotape.

"It is important to note that these capacities, as time passes, become more and more stable. The children themselves are beyond stability. They are very happy, in general, and they have enlarged their sense of adventure because they feel they are on a fantastic journey.

"I would also add that some children, in their work, seem to encounter, from time to time, other beings who do not have bodies, or who have energy bodies. As these experiences accumulate, the students can more clearly differentiate between what they themselves are creating and what they are encountering that is already there. These non-physical beings are not treated as masters or Gods. They are appraised and communicated with as souls who are in different form and space.

"Fixation upon mythical names and descriptions of non-physical beings has long ago faded away, in the light of real experience, to which creativity seems to be the key.

"Group work, for example, on imaginatively constructing so-called entities like God and Satan brought out and dispelled a certain amount of fear and confusion and dissolved, on occasion, into uproarious laughter. These stock entities are if anything 'fun things' for the children now, like pets or fairytale characters.

"The children are, all in all, amazingly confident. This, I believe, is because they can create realities, and that changes everything.

"Another of our weekend projects, initiated by several older students, involves what they call world-invention. This has several levels. There is an ongoing study of available and soon-to-be available technology. For instance, the development of better and more portable and much cheaper energy packs is bringing off-the-grid self-sufficient living into sharper and sharper focus for more people on the planet. The weekend group considers this vital, and they want to speed this process along. Their thinking is that independence in living enables people to focus on their own untapped capacities. Such independence is, of course, already making serious changes in government and corporate life in every country of the world. The group feels that as long as major technology can be produced at the individual level, every person will have sufficient leverage to make a life without the need to depend on a huge centralized government-corporate-media Machine.

"As we all know, many groups around the world are working on non-polluting energy technologies. The demise of the oil stranglehold on society was seen to be the result of a breakdown in an elite program to monopolize fuel. As cold fusion and hydrogen technologies came to the fore so quickly, the stranglehold was essentially squashed, although the elite tend to maintain an attitude of, if we can't own the farm we'll burn it down. They should be attending school with my three-year olds.

"The world-invention project has many aspects, and the weekend group is already linking up with groups in the U.S. and other countries.

"Of course there are people taking an old-fashioned position, attacking us for what we are doing. They claim all sorts of dire consequences will result. They don't really know the first thing about what we are up to. We have voluminous reports on what has happened since we placed the imagination at the center of education in a really serious way — for the first time in history. Since the academic performance scores of these children are through the top, and since by any psychological measure they are simply tremendous people, we are on remarkably firm ground.

"I have to emphasize that this is not a program for placing certain images in students' minds. That is the furthest thing from our objective. That is in fact an old view of imagination. A backwards lunacy.

"We have been approached by the military to work with them in training their personnel. They want to use creativity as a weapon in war. 'Psychic warfare.' We turn down every such request, and we always will ..."

88

The Tradition of Imagination

Twenty years ago, while working as a tutor and a minor administrator at Santa Monica College, in Santa Monica, California, I proposed two plans to the College. One was very informal, and the discussions never came to the official level. I wanted to see the College utilize the good weather of Southern California and become a world-class center for alternative energies, starting with solar.

I wanted to see many of the buildings of the College transferred over to state-of-the-art solar. The instructors in that subject would have students crawling up inside the buildings and seeing first-hand how such a system could operate.

But that would just be the beginning. Ozonated water systems replacing toxic chlorine, wind-power demonstration projects, solar-powered College vehicles, urban organic gardens, alternative fuels for cars, including the controversial but workable H_2O — global conferences on energy held at the College, a center for alternative energy established featuring reliable and unbiased testing of alternative fuels.

As I say, that conversation never rose to the official level.

I did, however, meet with the College president to discuss another project of mine. I offered to resign my position, to be rehired as a consultant on art. My job would be to visit the local studios of painters and sculptors and secure their work on loan and consignment, to be hung on the miles of bare corridor and office wall-space at the College — on a rotating basis, with new shows every month. In that way, struggling artists would gain recognition, their work would be seen and bought, the College would be saturated with art, and a new community spirit would take shape.

I was told that the insurance premiums for such a project were prohibitive. I felt that behind the president's objection was a distaste for allowing anyone else to re-shape the College atmosphere. The controller didn't want to relinquish control.

Some years later, during a lecture in Santa Monica, I used this story as an example of missed opportunities. It suddenly struck me that I was literally looking at a hole in space and time, a place where a different reality could have entered and generated several new futures. The image of the hole was exceptionally vivid.

Reality is malleable. There are an infinite number of places in which a new seed-reality can be inserted.

This fact should be the entire basis for education.

Not the prevailing policies of insurance companies.

89

There are those people who are opposed to free creativity, to wide-ranging imagination, to the development of the power of the imagination as a fundamental capacity of the human being.

They are particularly opposed to placing such capacities directly under the control of the person who has them and not in some external agency. These people speak of dangers, and of course to them the biggest danger is freedom.

We should recall that the most oppressive regimes of the 20th century, when it comes to art, were the Nazis and the Soviets. They characterized creation as something that needed to be legitimized by deriving from an ideology.

Social Darwinism, Freud, Marx, and most religions of this century say or imply that the imagination is rooted in a tainted impulse, whether that be the need for tooth-and-nail survival, a clinical neurosis, bourgeois leisure, Satanic influence, or an unhealthy appetite for excessive freedom.

These are all expressions of fear.

In particular, I have found some Christians who automatically associate imagination with Satan, under the rubric of: an idle mind is asking to be captured.

I categorize all efforts to discredit imagination ultimately in this way: the discreditors have never truly developed their own imaginations in a free atmosphere, and they have no confidence in that hidden core of themselves.

Opponents have said or implied that freedom as an experiment has failed because it was responsible for, among other things, the holocausts in which slaves were brought to the New World from Africa, Jews were killed in the ovens of Auschwitz, the atomic bomb was dropped on Hiroshima, the environment has been decimated by big corporations, the ownership of guns has proliferated in industrialized countries. Since freedom caused these conditions, it must be abandoned and we must substitute for it a communal sense, a community-feeling. Individual freedom must be phased out. And since that is the case, we must throw out wide-ranging creativity as well, because, after all, creativity is part of freedom.

That is a pose of being against the imagination, and it is based ultimately on fear.

Freedom, power, and imagination are three qualities or aspects that feed into one another, and they are the irreducible core of what a human being is. No one knows what the limit of the imagination is when all three aspects are present. Our choice is this: we can deny and subvert these core-essences in the coming century and substitute a mechanical model of humans, in which case our world collapses and becomes a slave planet. Or we can take courage and go to the heart of the issue, and build a society on what we are.

90

There is an extraordinary quantity of brain research in science journals covering the past fifty years.

The premise of some of this research is that areas of the brain or chemicals of the brain are responsible for controlling behavior and emotions and thoughts.

As the years pass, for many people distinctions between "brain" and "mind" seem academic and absurd and petty.

In fact, that arena of discussion will influence to an alarming degree the shape of our planet in the next twenty years, and from then on.

The slippery slope goes this way: if the brain is the mind, then thought can be managed by making physical and chemical changes in the brain. Therefore you and I can be "taught" to think in certain ways and to avoid thinking in other ways.

There is a further implication. If the brain is the mind, then we already are thinking in predetermined ways. The brain unfurls, at any given moment, a chemical blanket which gives rise to thoughts and feelings and we follow, like dogs after bones, what those thoughts and feelings imply in the way of action.

And if this is so, then what we take to be our imagination, our creativity, is another "outcome" of the brain's state. Nothing to get inspired about. A delusion, really.

But if mind is something separate from the brain, if it is a word we use to label a landscape of thoughts and feelings and imaginative creations which we can manufacture, as it were, and amplify or dampen or discard or recall and press back into service — if the mind is really a series of infinite spaces in which we can create what we choose, then we are not merely atoms and electrons and quarks to be experimented on, we are artists who, perhaps through inattention and self-fogging, have misplaced our true position in the scheme of things.

Research which seeks to alter brain states can and will affect us mightily, because we are inside and outside and around our bodies and we aren't ready to maintain that residence while dealing with massive tranquilizing effects or sudden re-wirings. We need healthy brains.

It is unsettling, to say the least, that brain researchers as a group do not believe that the mind is beyond the brain. They proudly wallow in the certainty that their sense of self, their moment-to-moment awareness of color and thrill and days and nights and music and admirations and respects and the infinite rest of it emanate as projections of brain chemistry. As if that were possible. That is like thinking that a waterbug on a small rock in the Mississippi River can make the River.

The Tradition of Imagination doesn't need Lilliputians sticking needles in brains.

Here is a 1937 quote from Nobel Laureate in physiology and medicine, Albert Szent-Gyorgyi:

"In my search for the secret of life, I ended up with atoms and electrons, which have no life at all. Somewhere along the line, life has run out through my fingers. So, in my old age, I am now retracing my steps ..."

And then there is a statement from Leonardo da Vinci:

"If the painter wishes to see beauties that would enrapture him, he is a master of their production, and if he wishes to see monstrous things which might terrify or which would be buffoonish and laughable or truly pitiable, he is their lord and god ... In fact, therefore, whatever there is in the universe through essence, presence or imagination, he has it first in his mind and then in his hands ..."

Now, it may be possible through the administration of enough brain-affecting drugs, such as, say, Thorazine, to make it not occur to Leonardo to think that thought of his — and perhaps after radical brain surgery or by the manipulation of synapses, the great master might not want to paint anymore. He might want to become a dog. But that does not mean that the brain is the mind. It simply means that by enough coercion, a soul called Leonardo occupying his body can be shunted off into strange gestalts and closets of feeling.

Even if the degree of brain manipulation, through lasers or chemicals that selectively affect cells, is refined, the fact that it can "change the thoughts of a person" in no way implies that the brain is the mind. Anyone can change thoughts by administering minute amounts of toxic substances to the bloodstream.

What is left out of this whole equation is the fact that the mind is part of an embrace, a dance, an adventure in which you take up the existence you find here, in the physical world, and what comes with it: a body, a brain, certain feelings, and so on. Naturally, a scientist can devise ways to prod a tiny piece of that embrace and cause a ripple. But that does not mean that the mind is a brain and life is only atomic particles.

It means nothing of the kind.

I am not talking about a remote specialty tucked away in small labs of universities. When I say brain research, I am talking about — along with gene manipulation — the obsession of the coming century. I am talking about a long slow rain of thinking among scientific elites that, more and more, life appears to be nothing but process carried on by particles in which no one is at home. There is no you, there is only electrical impulse and chemistry and illusion and this sort of thing.

To actually articulate this position and take it to its logical conclusion makes it seem absurd. But in some form it is the fall-back position for any researcher who tinkers with the molecules of the brain for the purpose of control over a human.

91

The Tradition of Imagination.

Suppose this is a page torn out of the *Washington Post*, dated July 1, 2037:

"Today, in a heated floor debate on Capitol Hill, Senator Graham Ingersoll asserted that recent history has caught the government unaware. 'We are largely becoming a nation of independent individuals and small groups,' he said.

"Because of developments in energy technology," Ingersoll stated in a prepared message from the Progress Caucus, it is now a given that every American can, for a nominal price, obtain energy packs powerful enough to supply all of his or her domestic needs for the foreseeable future.

"Not only that, but through micro-tech engineering innovations of the last twenty years, infrastructure itself is now buildable and maintainable on a local basis, by small groups of citizens, without reference to major corporations or government agencies. This," Ingersoll maintained, "is the end result of a revolution that will allow maximum individual freedom without limiting technological progress."

Ingersoll went to say that the old paradigm, in which large corporate and governmental organizations oversaw progress and protected the standard of living, was obsolete. "With the demise of that guideline," he said, "we have also rid ourselves of the need to sculpt one 'official' flow of information to our entire nation. In other words, realities will proliferate as never before ..."

If such a future does come to pass, it will be because thousands of people put their imaginations to work,

overwhelming the corporate strategy of forwarding technology that always seems to require large organizations to
implement it, to control it, to dole it out.

92

Beyond the experimental sessions with Ginger, I want to do many experiments in the realm of the Tradition of Imagination. Why? To confirm and convince, to show that human creation has the potential for greater power and scope than any of us would suspect.

For example, referring to an earlier citation, how does a human being alter the location of water molecules with his mind? Consider another well-known study, by Dr. Herbert Benson, which showed that practitioners of certain types of yoga/meditation could raise body temperature with their minds — how is this done? (See Benson, Herbert, et al. 1982. "Body Temperature Changes during the Practice of gTum-mo Yoga." *Nature* 295 [21 Jan. 1982]: 234–236)

There are several possible answers. A person "pushes" or "agitates" molecules (of air? of tissue?) into more intense motion — which results in heat.

If so, then that leads to a further question. What is he pushing the molecules with?

Is he creating a flame under the molecules? Is he manufacturing or inventing energy, which in turn stirs up the molecules in question? In any case, he is the author of energy which suddenly comes into existence. That is a staggering assessment. In a moment, we overturn every cosmological theory from Lucretius to Aristotle to Newton to Einstein. Why? Because none of them admits that a human being can, out of nothing, create energy that has the immediate characteristic of affecting physical-universe matter. All views of the universe as its own system are demolished.

All right, then. Let us suppose that a human being creates heat with his mind by pushing already-existing molecules with thoughts which are not energy. That view is also a disaster for all models of the physical universe. To say that an absence of energy stirs present energy to higher temperatures defeats the foundation of all laws of motion. Can the absence of a car run over a pedestrian? This prospect would cause physicists and logicians to suffer psychotic episodes.

Perhaps we want to posit the existence of a "non-material but positive mind-force created by a human being," to make things sound a little softer. Alas, this euphemism seems only a thin cover for either of the paradigm-destroying scenarios we have just described.

How about this? Sitting in my living room, I mentally reach out into the air and take molecules of oxygen and transform them into hotter oxygen and move that into a small pot of water standing on my kitchen stove and raise its temperature by two degrees. Well, what does "transform" mean? What does "take" mean? They also add up to creating something from nothing or moving something with nothing.

Even quantum physics, with its sumptuous ideas about subatomic particles coming into existence and being destroyed on a moment to moment basis, can't fit this "heating-up" event of human creation into its fold, without making up vastly bizarre tales of randomly accidental overloads of heated particles being reborn, where just an instant ago unheated particles were the case.

Paranormality, as shown to exist time and time again in the laboratory, cracks the paradigms of physics wide open. The imagination as a creative force will not be denied, and it will make room for itself at the expense of whatever "objective" theories we have devised to explain existence.

The so-called indeterminacy principle, which has been used by various thinkers to show that precise location of matter is a pipedream of the past, only begins to touch on the real situation. We do not merely alter the location of particles of matter by the act of observing them with instruments which emit beams of light. That is sub-kindergarten. No, we change the position, temperature, location, shape, motion, velocity, and character of matter. And we do it with our imaginations. This is the story. This is the crumbling of the assertion that the universe, at all levels, is stolid, is repeating, is its own entity, is our "definer."

I find it interesting that in 99.9% of the other-planetary UFO stories coming down the pipeline at the end of the 20th century, we hear no wise advice from ETs to go to the well of our imaginations and make our world and ourselves far more marvelous. I hear nothing of this kind.

I wonder why that is. Could it be that we filter all such "ET encounters," on whatever level they occur, so that the result places us in the role of wide-eyed awestruck children under the sway of unfathomable events?

Several years ago, I was told a story about several reporters and a scientist who went to Uganda to study the AIDS situation there. In one hospital, they saw two patients who had been diagnosed as HIV-positive. These patients were quite ill and the prognosis was not good. A few weeks later, a team of researchers came through the hospital. They were doing a study on the accuracy of HIV tests in the country. They discovered that the two very ill patients had never been HIV-positive. Those tests had falsely registered on other factors. The patients were informed; two weeks later they had completely regained their health and were discharged.

We blithely call this the placebo effect.

Scientists are rather comfortable with it. They can invoke a passive model, a stimulus-response hypnotic model of human process. "Varying diagnoses automatically set into 231 or health."

But when we shift the focus to consciously chosen and pursued imaginative creation, an uncomfortable shudder runs through these same scientists. They do not take kindly to the idea of the human being as undetermined agent of his own universe. That stings. That brings in a whiff of freedom, a situation without an anatomy. To admit this, indeed to usher this non-formula to the forefront of the pantheon of life, throws a giant X into the careful equation.

But there is no way around it. Behind our drive to master the machine-age and bring yet greater machine-ages into being, we are artists. We are doing things and operating on levels beyond the capacity of our machine-serving paradigms to offer explanations.

The Tradition of Imagination.

PART SEVEN

93

I believe that what people refer to as the CIA is one of the most dangerous complex secret societies in the world. Bred on too much money and too much secrecy, it has expanded to resemble separate kingdoms with little or no accountability. Since this is not a book about the CIA, I'm not going to take on the task of exploring each one of these kingdoms.

But think about this. What do you call a group that over the course of fifty years has been toppling regimes, training national police forces in torture, looting S&Ls, running an extensive mind-control superproject, helping import ex-Nazi war criminals into America and collaborating extensively with them, apparently assisting in the transport and importation and sale of illegal drugs, running propaganda campaigns designed to create and exacerbate conflict among political groups within foreign nations, exploring and funding all sorts of university and private research into consciousness for possible use in controlling people's minds, paving the way for multinational corporations to expand their operations into foreign countries — thus considerably aiding the economic ruination of those nations — infiltrating the American and foreign press with significant numbers of reporters who are compromised, who slant news, who omit vital news, who protect the Agency from harmful exposure, who keep the American people from knowing what is going on behind the scenes in their own country ...

What follows now is information from an official transcript of testimony about the CIA's MKULTRA (mind-control superproject).

The date is August 3, 1977. A Joint Hearing is laid on by the U.S. Senate Select Committee on Intelligence, and the Subcommittee on Health and Scientific Research which is under the Senate Committee on Human Resources.

The place is room 1202, Dirksen Senate Office Building, Washington D.C..

Presiding is Senator Daniel K. Inouye, chairman of the Select Committee on Intelligence.

The official stated object of this Hearing? "PROJECT MKULTRA, THE CIA'S PROGRAM OF RESEARCH IN BEHAVIORAL MODIFICATION." This project covered a large number of experiments whose purpose was to exercise control over the minds of human beings through the use of drugs and other means. As mentioned earlier, the motive for this involved the possible programming of American agents as psychologically unbreakable "robots," and, in general, the possible creation of mental blank slates which then could be impressed with whatever realities were deemed important.

It is very instructive to read through this obviously selective — but still startling — one-day report on the CIA's activities. What is not said is ultimately more important than what is revealed. Immediately, we hear Senator Inouye assure one and all that "we are focusing on events [MKULTRA] that happened over 12 or as long as 25 years ago. It should be emphasized that the programs that are of greatest concern have stopped ..."

In the next sentence, Inouye states, "We also need to know and understand what is now being done by the CIA in the field of behavioral research to be certain that no current abuses are occurring."

This back-and-forth theme will be repeated several times during the August 3 testimony. "We assure America that this horrible business has been ended ... we have no idea what the CIA is now doing."

Senator Kennedy follows Inouye with this bombshell:

Some 2 years ago ... [t]he Deputy Director of the CIA revealed that over 30 universities and institutions were involved in an 'extensive testing and experimentation' program which included covert drug tests on unwitting citizens 'at all social levels, high and low, native Americans and foreign' ... At least one death, that of Dr. Olsen, resulted from these activities ... Perhaps most

disturbing of all was the fact that the extent of experimentation on human subjects was unknown. The
records of all these activities were destroyed in January
1973, at the instruction of then CIA Director Richard
Helms ... no one — no single individual — could be
found who remembered the details, not the Director
of the CIA, who ordered the documents destroyed, not
the official responsible for the [MKULTRA] program,
nor any of his associates.

Kennedy goes on to state that one person, by filing a
Freedom of Information Act request (author John Marks),
did manage to shake loose "additional records" on MK-
ULTRA. These records, Kennedy says,

reveal a far more extensive series of experiments than
had previously been thought. Eighty-six universities
or institutions were involved ... The Central Intelligence
Agency drugged American citizens without their
knowledge or consent. It used university facilities and
personnel without their knowledge. It funded leading
researchers, often without their knowledge ... many
researchers, distinguished researchers, some of our most
outstanding members of our scientific community,
involved in this [MKULTRA research] network, now
really do not know whether they were involved or
not ...

Kennedy seems to be affecting a bit of innocence on behalf
of scientists who suspected or knew who they were working
for, whose money they were taking, but kept themselves in
ignorance.

After Kennedy, Admiral Stansfield Turner, then-current
1977 "squeaky-clean" Director of the CIA, read his prepared
statement into the record. Turner and the Committee are
clearly on friendly terms, and Turner is later praised by the
Committee for his cooperation in a "search for the truth."

Turner begins by saying that the 1953–1964 MKULTRA
program had involved "among other things research on

drugs and behavioral modification." He then mentions the "drug-related death of Dr. Frank Olsen," who in 1953, while "a civilian employee of the Army at Fort Detrick, leaped to his death from a hotel room window in New York City about a week after having unwittingly consumed LSD administered to him as an experiment at a meeting of LSD researchers called by the CIA." An MKULTRA victim.

Turner readily admits that the destruction of MKULTRA files in 1973 is not the only reason the program has such a murky past. It was CIA policy, he says, quoting a CIA report, "to maintain no records of the planning and approval of [MKULTRA] test programs."

Nevertheless, some financial records have been uncovered, and they reveal heretofore hidden information about MK-ULTRA. There is evidence, for example, of "single subprojects in such areas as effects of electroshock, harassment techniques for offensive use, analysis of extrasensory perception ..."

No fewer than 39 subprojects are identified as probably or definitely involving human testing on the behavioral effects of drugs.

Al Brody, a long-time member of the CIA, then testifies that he has no knowledge of the Congress ever being informed about the existence of MKULTRA at its inception — or funding the program. There is no follow-up on this.

Senator Kennedy remarks,

Admiral Turner, this is an enormously distressing report [in general] that you give ... an activity which took place in the country that involved the perversion and the corruption of many of our outstanding research centers ... [concerning research] done with American citizens who were completely unknowing in terms of taking various drugs, and there are perhaps any number of Americans who are walking around today on the east coast or west coast who were given drugs, with all the kinds of physical and psychological damage that can be caused.

A destructive, chaos-causing cowboy operation. This

August 3, 1977 Hearing impresses the reader more and more, as it continues, with the fact that the CIA, an official government agency, was turning its guns on and maiming American citizens.

Under questioning, Admiral Turner tries to say that CIA programs similar to MKULTRA — the MKSEARCH and OFTEN and CHICKWIT programs — involved no human experimentation. After a nudge from Senator Kennedy, Turner admits he has not thoroughly read the history of CHICKWIT, but it was basically a Department of Defense project in which the CIA "participated."

However, on page 169 of this same August 3, 1977 Hearing report, there is a short description of MKSEARCH, OFTEN, and CHICKWIT. They clearly involved the evaluation and testing of "drugs and chemical compounds" at Edgewood Arsenal Research Laboratories — compounds "believed to have effects on the behavior of humans ..."

The final paragraph on page 169 states, "There is a discrepancy between the testimony of DOD [Dept. of Defense] and CIA regarding the testing at Edgewood Arsenal in June 1973. While there is agreement that human testing occurred at that place and time, there is disagreement as to who was responsible for financing and sponsorship."

This gives the lie to Senator Inouye's opening general assurance that the "events" under scrutiny by the Committee "happened over 12 or as long as 25 years ago." This hearing, again, took place on August 3, 1977, and the human MKULTRA-type testing at Edgewood is dated June 1973, only four years earlier.

There is no follow-up on this.

Senator Schweiker then points out that a series of MKULTRA experiments took place — under arrangements with the Federal Bureau of Narcotics — in which LSD was tested "surreptitiously on unwitting patrons in bars in New York and San Francisco. Some of these subjects became violently ill and were hospitalized ... If you happened to be at the wrong bar at the wrong place and time, you got it."

Senator Inouye takes Admiral Turner back to the matter of the death of Dr. Frank Olsen. MKULTRA subproject 3 was either the umbrella under which this death occurred, or it was carrying on tests exactly like those which resulted in Olsen's death. It is established that the men who ran subproject 3 continued to do so "for a number of years" after Olsen died. Inouye asks Turner if these men were ever punished or fired. Turner later supplies the Committee with a letter which indicates that these men, who were, in 1977, no longer working for the Agency, had never been fired.

Senator Schweiker engages Admiral Turner in a hide-and-seek conversation about a hospital location or annex, the building of which the CIA had paid some monies for. Human testing had been envisioned. Turner says he's not sure testing was ever done there. The name of the facility is not mentioned. Turner doesn't seem to want to mention it. But Turner or someone else supplies that information to the Committee and it is inserted into the Hearing record. The facility is the Gorman Annex apparently connected (administratively) to Georgetown University, and it was dedicated in March 1959. The insertion states, "Of the several MKULTRA projects conducted at Georgetown, only one involving human testing covered a time span subsequent to March 1959 ..." Therefore, there was ample opportunity to do MKULTRA human experiments in the Gorman Annex. The insertion now becomes explosive: "Authorization to contribute CIA funds toward construction of the Gorman Annex is contained in Subproject 35 of MKULTRA. Recently discovered material indicated that Dr. Geschickter continued his research for sleep- and amnesia-producing drugs under Project MKSEARCH through July 1967 at Georgetown University Hospital ..."

Geschickter was well-known as a CIA contractor. He worked at Georgetown. At Gorman Annex? Hard to prove. Does it matter? The CIA-Georgetown-Gorman connection is suddenly very solid. Amnesia-producing drug research. A hallmark of MKULTRA-type experiments. After all, one of the first requirements of chemical mind-control is the ability to question or program individuals while they are drugged, so that they will not remember that the programming occurred.

Admiral Turner is skittish about revealing the details of this Gorman Annex-Georgetown program. In part, this is no doubt due to the prestige Georgetown University and its hospital enjoy in government circles. But there is something further. Turner is led to the edge of a precipice by Senator Schweiker, who reads him a statement from a CIA document about, clearly, the Gorman Annex and the Georgetown Hospital: "The facilities of the hospital and the ability to conduct controlled experimentations under safe clinical conditions using materials with which any [CIA] agency connection must be completely deniable will augment and complement other programs recently taken over by TSS, such as ..." At that precise point in the document, Senator Schweiker remarks, there is a deletion made by the Agency. He wants to know, what are these other programs recently taken over by the CIA's TSS (technical services) people? Schweiker is very interested, because if he knows what these other programs are, he'll have a good clue about what was to happen in the Gorman Annex, what the CIA intention there was. On his own, Admiral Turner coughs up the answer.

"[The deletion read] QKHILLTOP. It doesn't help you, but — "

Schweiker replies, "Can you tell us what that is, or is it still classified?"

Turner replies, "I don't know, and I assume from the fact that we deleted it, it is still classified, but I will get you that answer, sir."

The answer is supplied in the Hearing record, as a later addition, on page 171, the last page of the Hearing transcript:

"QKHILLTOP was a cryptonym assigned in 1954 to a project to study Chinese Communist brainwashing techniques and to develop interrogation techniques ..."

Let's see. The use of materials at Georgetown, a stone's throw from the federal government, materials which the CIA must be able to deny any connection to. LSD? Radioactive minerals? Other mind-bending substances? Experimental amnesia-producing compounds? The use of materials to assist in developing interrogation techniques. Tests on Americans.

To make it even stranger, Schweiker then asks Turner if experiments at the Gorman Annex (or perhaps Georgetown) involved terminally ill cancer patients as subjects.

Turner says, "Yes, it does appear there is a connection here, sir."

A number of exceedingly cruel experiments using radiation on cancer patients have been uncovered in subsequent years.

There seems to be no follow-up on any of this. No follow-up on Dr. Geschickter, "deniable" MKULTRA-type materials or drugs, Gorman Annex funded by the CIA, cancer patients as test subjects, amnesia-producing compounds ...

In the closing dialogue with Admiral Turner, Senator Kennedy presses hard for the Agency to question Sid Gottlieb, one of its key managerial figures in MKULTRA. Turner comes across very lamely at this point, stating that Gottlieb no longer works for the Agency, has already testified to Congress, and should rather be the focus of a Justice Department investigation, since the CIA has no jurisdiction to carry out domestic intelligence operations.

Indeed.

Kennedy mentions a CIA MKULTRA project which involved two safe houses that were in operation for eight or nine years. Untold numbers of unwitting Americans were drugged and "studied." These houses were clearly set up as brothels, and the johns were given LSD and who knows what else in their drinks. Again, a random attack on Americans by an American intelligence agency. Kennedy states that Gottlieb had signed many of the documents relating to this project, but then somehow Gottlieb could not remember its history when testifying before Congress. Turner backed off this subject.

In an Appendix to the Hearing Record, a fragment from the "Inspector General's survey of MKULTRA in 1963" offers a rather astonishing rationale for secrecy in the overall MKULTRA program:

"Research in the manipulation of human behavior is considered by many authorities in medicine and related fields to be professionally unethical, therefore the reputation of professional participants in the MKULTRA program are on occasion in jeopardy ...

"A final phase of the testing of MKULTRA products places the rights and interests of U.S. citizens in jeopardy."

This remarkable admission is followed by another summary:

"Over the ten-year life of the [MKULTRA] program, many 'additional avenues to the control of human behavior' were designated as appropriate for investigation ... These include 'radiation, electroshock, various fields of psychology, psychiatry, sociology, and anthropology, graphology, harassment substances, and paramilitary devices and materials.'"

Not only the range of materials but the mandate was broadened to include the general field of behavior or mind control. The program was moving far beyond ordinary insanity into super-insanity. The intent was miles past "protection from our foreign enemies." There was the feeling that MKULTRA would include, operationally, the idea that any person could be a threat to a prescribed way of life and must therefore be probed to understand what would control him.

This official point of view could serve as a functional definition of psychosis.

The Appendix to the August 3 Hearing continues to flesh out the astounding parameters of MKULTRA. Reading, one cannot escape the conclusion that the CIA was infecting every stratum of American life, in this one program:

"The research and development of materials to be used for altering human behavior consisted of three phases: first the search for materials suitable for study; second, laboratory testing on voluntary human subjects in various types of institutions; third, the application of MKULTRA materials in normal life settings." (This final phase of testing involved, for example, the administration of LSD "to unwitting nonvolunteer subjects in normal life settings by undercover officers of the Bureau of Narcotics acting for the CIA ..." The rationale was, to observe the full range of MK materials and their consequences, you must go into "the field" and give them to unwitting people in the middle of their lives.)

The Appendix continues:

The search for suitable [MK] materials was conducted through standing arrangements with specialists in universities, pharmaceutical houses, hospitals, state and federal institutions, and private research organizations. The annual grants of funds to these specialists were made under ostensible research foundation auspices ...

The next phase of the MKULTRA program involved physicians, toxicologists, and other specialists in mental, narcotics, and general hospitals, and in prisons. Utilizing the products and findings of the basic research phase, they conducted intensive tests on human subjects.

This section of the Appendix-report mentions an early MKULTRA research project at the Addiction Research Center in Lexington, Kentucky, a prison where drug offenders were serving sentences. From this population, volunteers were found and experimentally "administered hallucinogenic drugs." For their participation, the prisoners were "provided with the drug of their addiction."

A number of well-known jazz musicians ended up at Lexington in the 1940s and 50s. The public was unaware that this MKULTRA project was the "rehabilitation" doled out to some of these men.

As the Appendix spells out the true range of MKULTRA, the saccharine and symbolic questioning of CIA employees by the Committee on August 3, 1977 is driven home. Better to have jumped into a full-scale investigation of the effects (past and ongoing) of MKULTRA on every level of American life. But that was not to be.

There is, of course, other testimony about the CIA on the Washington record, but I present the above as an example of the depths to which the human imagination can sink, when it is lashed to a secret society whose aim is lowest-common-denominator control of the mind. This is the Formula of the Secret Society at its most squalid.

It is no accident that the kind of people who belong to this cult pay no homage to the wide and free exercise of the imagination. That tradition is strange to their senses. They recoil from it. They have no confidence in its power. It is their abyss, and they struggle instead for the eternal continuation of the institution called slavery.

What about the assertion that the CIA was closely bound in its thinking, attitudes, and projects with Nazis? That the

CIA was/is a secret society joined at the hip with a continuing Nazi agenda?

Of course the above MKULTRA program reveals some of those ties, stemming in part from Nazi experiments on human prisoners in the death camps.

There is much more.

In Linda Hunt's shocking 1991 book, *Secret Agenda*, the degree of complicity of the CIA in Operation Paperclip, which brought Nazi scientists and intelligence operatives over to the U.S. as employees, after World War II, is spelled out.

Frank Wisner, a top CIA manager, "operated out of the State Department ... His considerable influence in the State Department meant a more favorable climate [for Paperclip] ... [Wisner] helped ... obtain visas for Paperclip scientists."

Hunt details a U.S. Army project carried on in the late 1940s and 50s at its Edgewood Arsenal facility in Maryland: "...the chemical corps, using Auschwitz documents as a guide, conducted the same type of poison gas experiments that had been done in the secret [German] I.G. Farben laboratories. This time, however ... the unfortunate guinea pigs were more than seven thousand American soldiers."

Nazis involved in this project? Otto Ambros acted as a consultant. Ambros, a chemist, was a convicted Nazi war criminal who was released from prison by U.S. authorities and given a visa to come to the U.S., after a new policy was instituted here called National Interest — another term for the ubiquitous National Security. The CIA's Frank Wisner was instrumental in implementing this new National Interest policy with respect to obtaining visas and passing the background checks on Nazis.

The horrible Edgewood Arsenal experiments were, technically, U.S. Army-run. But it was clear that CIA people were quite active in the project. By this time, the 1950s, as Colonel Fletcher Prouty describes in his *The Secret Team*, the CIA was fielding men who wore military uniforms but worked undercover for the CIA. Edgewood was definitely the CIA's cup of tea.

Another important Nazi who came to Edgewood (late 1940s) was Friedrich Hoffmann. As Linda Hunt describes,

Hoffmann, placed on CIA contract, "was a chemist who synthesized poison gases and toxins for the [German] University of Wuerzburg's Chemical Warfare Laboratories ..." Hoffmann's "job ... was to test the poison gases that had been invented by the Nazis during the war ... Soldiers at the [Edgewood] base were used as guinea pigs in Tabun [nerve gas] and mustard gas experiments ... In a scene horribly reminiscent of the Nazi death camps, [U.S. soldier] Don Bowen remembered what it was like to sit in the large chamber and breathe the toxic fumes... 'My immediate response was not to breathe. And when I finally did take a deep breath, the gas burned my nose, my lips and throat.'"

"Some of the soldiers," Hunt writes, "were seriously injured in the mustard tests."

In 1949, the Edgewood emphasis suddenly shifted to LSD. Both CIA and military intelligence thought they had their hands on a truth drug. "One source of CIA information about 'truth drugs' was Karl Tauboeck, I.G. Farben's leading wartime expert on sterilization drugs," Hunt writes. "... The link between Edgewood and the CIA was close. Many scientists who worked at Edgewood or under Edgewood contracts were on the CIA's payroll. Paperclip chemist [Nazi] Friedrich Hoffmann was a CIA consultant on psychochemicals." Hoffmann also was a chief researcher for the Edgewood projects, looking for new chemicals all over the world. "He traveled to foreign universities and visited marine labs and attended conferences in Switzerland, Czechoslovakia, Germany, England, Australia, Japan, and other countries. Toad venoms and poisonous fish ... a conch shell that produced a highly active venom ... Hoffmann often used the University of Delaware as a cover at international symposiums to hide his connection to Edgewood and the CIA."

The CIA Project Bluebird "made full use of Hoffmann's discoveries with psychochemicals ... [at Edgewood] at least a thousand soldiers ... were given up to twenty doses of LSD to test the drug as a possible interrogation weapon — even though Edgewood scientists already knew it could cause serious physical reactions in humans."

What sorts of reactions? Well, a soldier "fought his way

out of a locked box in stark terror ... One man suffered a grand mal seizure; another went into an acute state of paranoia and had to be hospitalized for a week. Three others developed a history of epileptic seizures." And so on.

A CIA-Nazi link? Of course.

There are other names and other experiments, and Hunt describes them. No one can claim that that the CIA was not tightly linked to Nazis in the arena of mind-control and so-called medical experiments.

QED. The CIA is not simply an intelligence agency. It is a secret society, acting far beyond anyone's legal concept of its original 1947 mission to gather crucial information for the government outside the United States.

And now that we have more than a glimpse of that, let us make the further CIA connection to corporations, to the Trilateral/CFR/Bilderberg influence outlined in an earlier chapter, and even to what may be a sinister influence over the development of technology in the country.

A perfect cameo illustration is the Bechtel Corporation, one of the world's largest privately held construction firms. Perhaps Steve Bechtel's most trusted business partner was John McCone, who, under President Eisenhower, would become chairman of the Atomic Energy Commission (AEC) and Director of the CIA. McCone was extremely enthusiastic about all things nuclear, and his friend Steve Bechtel benefited. Eventually Connecticut Senator Abraham Ribicoff would say that the AEC had given birth to an industry "so incestuous, it is impossible to tell where the public sector begins and the private one leaves off."

McCone helped pave the way for Bechtel's participation in construction of the Dresden I nuclear plant, completed in 1959. This "showpiece," plagued immediately by accidents, nevertheless helped establish Bechtel as a leader in the nuclear field, and "billions upon billions would flow in," writes Laton McCartney, author of the lucid book about Bechtel, *Friends in High Places*.

McCone also introduced Steve Bechtel to then-President Eisenhower, who appointed him to help in "drafting a report," writes McCartney, "that would determine policy for distribution of foreign aid and development loans — many to countries which would use them to employ Bechtel."

In the Middle East, after World War II, Bechtel, which would build the Trans-Arabian pipeline, one of the world's largest oil lines, began to work with the CIA. Bechtel knew more about what was happening in that region of the world than the U.S. government.

There was an exchange of favors. In 1948, the Syrian government, "furious at U.S. support for Israel," reports McCartney, "canceled an agreement to permit the Bechtel-built Tapline pipeline to cross its borders. Had the policy stood, Bechtel would have lost millions. But in 1949, the civilian Syrian government was overthrown in a CIA-sponsored coup and replaced by a military dictatorship, friendlier to U.S. interests. Shortly thereafter, Bechtel was granted permission to build Tapline across Syria."

In 1951, Bechtel executive John Simpson became friends with Allen Dulles, who would soon become CIA director. In 1952, Dulles — as CIA chief — asked Simpson to have Bechtel do a study on Iran's plan to pipe huge quantities of oil into the Soviet Union. Was such a project really possible? With Steve Bechtel's okay, Simpson had the study carried out. The conclusion was yes, the Iranians did have the technical capability to do the job.

With that intelligence in tow, the CIA carried out a 1953 coup in Iran and put the U.S. and CIA-friendly Shah Reza Pahlevi back on the throne. That revolution involved the murder of elected president Mossadeq.

The CIA put many agents into cover at international Bechtel, to spy in far-flung areas, and the corporation welcomed the partnership.

Another favor came back to Bechtel. In 1964 and 1965, old friend and CIA Director, John McCone, briefed Bechtel on the quickly developing situation in Indonesia. President Sukarno had begun to nationalize U.S. businesses.

In October 1965, according to many observers and insiders, the CIA backed a very bloody coup that installed a new President, Suharto, who was more cooperative with America.

With yet a third CIA Director, Richard Helms, who became an "international consultant" for Bechtel in 1978, after his long tour of duty with the CIA, Bechtel became the quintessential U.S. corporation linked to intelligence interests.

But there was another step. Bechtel built oil pipelines and giant oil processing plants and nuclear facilities around the world. Would the CIA allow revolutionary new energy-technologies to make all that ancient history? I believe the CIA will do what it can to shelve new technology "detrimental" to its elite partners.

Just to keep the record straight: Holly Sklar, in her masterfully edited 1980 book, *Trilateralism*, states, as if in a tip of the hat to Bechtel: "... CIA Directors Allen Dulles, John McCone, and Richard Helms were all CFR [Council on Foreign Relations] and/or Bilderberg participants and leaders."

Indeed, in a secret briefing to CFR members in 1968, in New York at CFR headquarters, Richard Bissell, once head of clandestine operations for the CIA, confirmed by his very presence that "the influential but private Council [CFR], composed of several hundred of the country's top political, military, business, and academic leaders, [had] long been the CIA's principal 'constituency' in the American public. When the agency has needed prominent citizens to front for its proprietary companies or for other special assistance, it has often turned to Council members." This quote — a piece of analysis by Victor Marchetti — is from *The CIA and the Cult of Intelligence*, co-authored by Marchetti, former executive assistant to the deputy director of the CIA. Bissell's speech became public when paraphrased notes on it were accidentally discovered in the files of a Harvard University building taken over by protesting students in 1971.

Bissell and others at the secret 1968 meeting hinted at the possible use — for staging of CIA projects — of U.S. corporations with foreign offices. Of course, such cooperation already had a long track record.

Consider this cult, the CIA. As it administers a wide-ranging program of drugging and poisoning U.S. citizens under the rubric of MKULTRA, it is seamlessly aligning its interests with those of corporations like Bechtel —

and murdering any world leader who stands in the path of business-expansion.

The mural-art of this cult, tied in as it is with the world of corporations and their fronts (World Bank, International Monetary Fund, Trilateral Commission), relies on respectability, blandness, and at the same time patriotism and all the attendant homilies for its convincing quality.

"We are America. We are righteous. We keep good books. We wear suits and polish our shoes, just like you."

There is another level of cult-art, of Secret Society Formula, when it comes to the CIA. Col. Fletcher Prouty details it in his indispensable book, *The Secret Team*. Prouty, a former liaison officer between the Department of Defense and the CIA, points out that the CIA uses its art to provoke desired reactions from other parts of the U.S. federal government, a very necessary tactic if CIA (illegal) clandestine plans are to get off the ground in any serious way. This Cold War strategy was used many times:

> The CIA's greatest strength derives from its ability to activate various parts of the U.S. Government — usually the Defense Department, with minor inputs designed to create reaction. It finds a minor fact [such as a small outbreak of banditry among peasants in a Third World country], which it interprets and evaluates to be Communist inspired, or inspired by some other favorite enemy ... then it feeds this item into the White House and to Defense, where a response re-action takes place predictably and automatically. To carry this to the next level, the CIA, by utilizing its clandestine facilities [*e.g.*, by staging a phony "escalation" of the banditry], can stir up the action it wants for further use in turn to stir up a reaction response within the U.S. Government structure. Although such actions and re-actions usually begin on a very small scale, they escalate rapidly as in Indonesia, Tibet and Greece. (They went completely out of control in Southeast Asia.)

In the case of Indonesia, Prouty is referring to the staged

coup I have just mentioned, which had a great deal to do
with President Sukarno's threat to nationalize Bechtel operations. Prouty is sketching the process by which the CIA was
able to build up a warlike reaction within the White House,
ultimately, against Sukarno. Were there other factors at work
in Indonesia? Of course. There always are. But the conjuring
efforts of the CIA are central to the direction in which the
whole show moves.

In the early Cold War years, CIA operative General Ed
Lansdale helped bring an unknown soldier in the Philippines
to heroic status and, ultimately, to the leadership of the country as President Ramon Magsaysay. Prouty describes how,
originally, lumber and sugar companies had pushed thousands
of Philippine villagers from their ancient homes. Their reloca-
tion, inducing starvation, triggered some measure of banditry
against other villagers. The CIA explanation for all of this was
Communist-inspired rioting, not corporate crimes. After all,
all sorts of local government officials were on the take from
these lumber and sugar companies. Lansdale parlayed this
situation into a revolution and a coup. In the early stages,
he even had some of the "Communist" attacks on villages
carried out by Magsaysay supporters dressed as local Huks
(Communist rebels).

Cowboys at play in the fields of the Lord.

Prouty's analysis of Vietnam is devastating. Admitting
that all such unstable situations have a number of interested
parties seeking to gain money and position and advantage,
Prouty nevertheless points out that, one, the whole disastrous
Vietnam war, almost from the time of America's first real
involvement, was a CIA operation, all the way up until 1965
when the Marines landed. Two, the U.S. motive for being in
the war was set in concrete by the CIA as a counterinsurgency
operation against the dire Communist threat that could lead
to a domino effect in Asia. And three, behind the stated inten-
tions, the conflict in Vietnam had no payoff that was anti-
Communist or pro-American. "... those wise and wily chess
players in the Kremlin," Prouty writes, "... have been the
beneficiaries of our own [CIA-inspired] defense-oriented,
reaction-prompted, intelligence-duped Pavlovian self-

destruction. How can anyone justify the fact that the United States has lost fifty-five thousand men in Indochina and that the Russians have lost none and then call that anti-Communist ... How can anyone note that we have poured more than $200 billion into Indochina since 1945 and that the Kremlin may have put up somewhere between $3 and $5 billion as their ante to keep the game going, and then call that tragic ratio anti-Communist and pro-American?"

In his book, *Blowback*, Christopher Simpson "ties together a few loose ends" that make for a staggering account of power joining together among secret societies:

Discussing the period three years after World War II, he writes,

> ... the CIA established much deeper and broader ties with the hierarchy of the Roman Catholic Church in Rome than had previously been the case [in the CIA's short life thus far] ... [This] ... laid the foundation for the agency's relationship with Intermarium, an influential Catholic lay organization ... that operated under the protection of the Vatican. At least half a dozen senior leaders of Intermarium and its member groups can be readily identified as Nazi collaborators. Some were fugitive war criminals. However, Intermarium was later to emerge as one of the mainstays of ... scores of ... CIA-sponsored clandestine operations during the next two decades.

One of Intermarium's supporters was the notorious Nazi ideologue, Alfred Rosenberg, who had been a close friend of Hitler.

The Vatican, the CIA, the Nazis.

"Leaders of the Intermarium organization," Simpson writes, "became coordinators of much of the Nazi escape effort [after the War]." The senior Ukrainian Intermarium representative, Catholic Archbishop Ivan Buchko, "successfully intervened with Pope Pius XII himself to win freedom for a [Nazi] Ukrainian Waffen SS legion ... some 11,000 men ...

Some of them — a smaller number — had served as guards in the Nazis' death camps at Treblinka, Belsen, and Sobibor. Many of these men were destined to serve in political warfare projects underwritten by the CIA. Hundreds of them are known to live in the United States and Canada today."

94

Seventy-one years after the CIA MKULTRA Hearing, on August 3, 2048, another hearing is held in the Dirksen Senate Office Building in Washington.

The Select Committee on Intelligence is sponsoring this one-day event, entitled, "America's Program in Behavioral Freedom." Senator Michael Kennedy, chairman of the Select Committee, is presiding. I trust this transcript will more than offset the preceding record of CIA efforts to affect the future through control of minds.

Senator Kennedy:

"The President has asked me to relay his concern over the deliberations of this Committee today. Much has been written in the press, over the past twenty years, about the emerging New Citizen who has essentially graduated from the collective power grid of the planet into a status of freedom unprecedented in the history of Earth. I am not just talking about Americans, but about people from every nation on the globe. This development, coupled with the triumph of infrastructure-technology as usable by small companies, has made it possible for the most elementary of communities to own land in the secure knowledge that they can afford to maintain the infrastructure of that land in excellent condition, without reference to, or reliance upon, large corporations, power utilities, or government officials. This has made much of government obsolete. It has erased the leverage which our government formerly used on the states to ensure compliance with federal programs. That leverage was money, grants, aid to the states. With the advent of massive electric power for the use of the individual, at almost pennies — through the refinement of cold fusion and hydrogen technologies — and with the advent of low-cost infrastructure technology, no state or city or community needs the money the federal government can dangle, and therefore no state need adopt Washington's programs of education, law-enforcement, healthcare, and so on. All that is finished.

"And that is just the beginning. With the freedom made possible for each individual through the triumph of 21st-century technologies, there has come the awareness that, all along, an imaginative motive force has been pushing the human race in the direction of this freedom.

"Three years ago, we sent our second domed colony, powered by cold fusion, out into the galaxy on its journey of evolution and wonder.

"Let this stand as a symbol of our unquenchable desire for more life.

"While many of our largest Earth corporations — whose loyalties have never been given to any nation or genuine human cause — have been trying to corrupt governments and hold the upper hand in global commerce, a whole host of smaller, more mobile companies has arisen whose mission is of another kind. These companies have established a Fullerian program of supplying the Groundbase Zero of life to every citizen in every nation of the world. At the moment, that program is 18% accomplished and is going strong. Groundbase Zero, as we all know, consists of adequate clothing, food, shelter, transport, unlimited education and unlimited effective healthcare. Amazingly, this program has been executed without compromising a single sovereign government, without compromising the competitiveness of a single corporation on the planet. These "Fuller" companies have simply used available technology to produce their goods at prices affordable everywhere.

"Of course it has not been easy to achieve a buying power for twelve billion Earth citizens that would guarantee them Groundbase Zero. That is a continuing struggle, but through extended employment opportunities on a planetary basis — again, without interfering with any sovereign government — tremendous progress has been made. The 21st-century space program has helped in that regard. Space colonies, the heart of the program, have not only been the object of fantastic enthusiasm, they have employed all told, almost eight hundred million of us. And the figure is growing.

"As our technologies become cleaner and cheaper, the progress of real environmentalism has been a sight to behold. There is almost no one now who either deplores 'saving the Earth' or dares use the ecological cause to further fascist-aristocratic ambitions like the depopulation of the planet. We have seen through those manipulations and we are no longer moved by them.

"In the wake of this century's progress, many governments have been shed like old skins by their populations. Not through war, but from lack of need. Ladies and gentlemen, let us face facts. That is happening to the government of the United States as we sit here. It does no good to deny it. We have become, in large measure, expendable.

"The quality of healthcare is much greater than any of us dreamed possible twenty years ago, and that care has now been made available to a far larger percentage of Americans than any previous government program could guarantee. Likewise for housing, for education, for employment opportunities, for all the so-called Entitlements. All without reference to the government in any way.

"We have dreamed our way to this place, and we have done it without having to go to war to kill millions of so-called enemies. We have seen through the program of lies set up by various monopolies, monopolies of information, of medicine, of energy, of money. We have diversified in the face of these threats and multiplied our sources of supply. We now face the prospect of a lengthy but rewarding negotiation on the subject of weapons and global disposition. Of course I am talking about the un-possession of weapons by nations and armies as well as individuals. This will encompass the important question of the need for protection from 'potential criminals.' However, those of us who have grown up in the atmosphere of education which we call Art and Imagination have confidence that in the long run we can solve this problem. We have journeyed through the islands of fear that cluster around the key concepts of "protection" and "security" and "purity" and all the rest of the stingers that cause people to retreat from their own imaginations and sink back into solutions that ultimately call for control of people's minds.

"We don't need that. We don't need another CIA to plan our future, assassinate our leaders, sow fear and chaos as a prelude to control of human beings. No one has ever been able to dismantle the entire honeycomb of kingdoms that make up the CIA. But we have been able, as a species, to expose its crimes to a great extent, and turn the people, the politicians, the leaders away from its mad influence. The CIA and their lunatic ministers and minions of disinformation live in their caves, believe they are the messiahs, and defend a way of life that is dead.

"We will continue to root them out and put them on trial for their crimes. But we will spread a true freedom over the face of the Earth. Already, a significant percentage of our global population has some time to pursue the fruits of that freedom. As predicted, thousands of small communities — self-sufficient — have grown up across America. Across every continent. These communities have the infrastructure to make their ways of life stick — and that is exactly what they are doing. They are adopting all sorts of configurations of self-government, from free-market capitalism to Marxism and beyond. Although conflicts arise between communities, by and large a spirit of tolerance is prevailing. Fewer and fewer people seem to believe that everyone has to share their particular view of life, the world, the Supreme Being, the destiny of the human race.

"Early in the 21st century we awoke to the fact that, as a nation, we had been brainwashed into thinking that good information came to us only from several reliable sources. With that mass-revelation, everything changed. Scientists, engineers, investors, entrepreneurs began to share budding new technologies with a different spirit. They quickly learned that corporate-government complexes — which included aspects of the CIA — were trying to control the flow of this kind of information. But the new channels of communication were so prolific. And their users quickly came to rely on themselves to determine what was true. Thus were born companies with a different flavor. For example, commercial groups dedicated to employing new electromagnetic and nutritional technologies to maintain, expand, and repair individual health. The federal government fought these companies tooth and nail, but in the end the force of new ideas was too great. The government and the traditional pharmaceutical cartels suffered a crushing defeat. Exposés on the decades of monopolistic control by this medical/pharmaceutical/government complex now saw the light of day in a major way.

"Several key CIA operatives came out of the cold. They told Net reporters, in great detail, about operations mounted in self-contained intelligence cells which had been pointed at controlling and limiting the development of technology in the future. Purpose? To protect huge unwieldy corporations from quicker minds. To aid in the gradual passage of more power into fewer hands. To block the possibility of wider individual freedom. That is, to keep from happening on this planet exactly what has happened. A renaissance.

"Despite massive propaganda from the major TV networks against so-called 'conspiratorial thinking,' it was proven to the American people over and over again that collusion had been a way of life in America for several centuries. Collusion among the big boys. You could call that conspiracy if you wanted to, but in truth it was something more simple. The shared desire to own and control and dominate.

"America no longer believed that all progress was slow and conflict-ridden and that history was the inevitable average of warring parties. America finally acknowledged that on the high levels, the fix was in, had been in whenever and wherever it was possible to make it so — and could be overridden.

"We of the government must acknowledge all of this.

"Nor can we think, in a desperate bid for attention, that the scandalous goings-on of our officials will captivate our citizens. They simply don't care anymore whether a Senator is sleeping with his aide. It is a joke. It is no more important to the American people than a story about a grocery-store manager having an affair with a check-out clerk.

"The American people lost faith in us because, for decades, they could see more money and power passing into the hands of fewer people. And they realized we did not have the courage to strike out boldly and do something about it. In truth, we didn't know what to do. Our minds were limited. We didn't see a way to daylight. So the people began to work around us, as new technology arrived. They fashioned communities, and they did everything they could to make those units of social life independent from Washington. They did everything they could to make those communities independent from state governments as well. For them, pride in the power of the individual returned in a tangible way.

"Today, you can buy a cold-fusion cell for six hundred dollars and use it, for the next fifty years, to power your home and office and car. We must face the implications of facts like these. A community of a hundred people, living on three acres of land in six vertical structures, can maintain their roads and sewers plus the roads and sewers in a three-mile radius outside their land, for ten years, for a private fee of twelve thousand dollars. Total. Need I go on?

"Once we Americans spoke of a more perfect union and said 'We the People,' but the government and the large corporations, and the monster we call "our intelligence services," betrayed those sentiments and used them to try to mold us into content androids. We had to act, and I count myself among the citizenry. I tried to do everything I could, as a politician, as a Senator, to reverse the trend of more control passing into fewer hands, but within the confines of government I couldn't succeed. I know many of you felt you had come to the same place.

"A decade ago the whole news-TV-political-corporate persona of Down to Earth Realism, as it was called by several authors, was exposed for the sham it really was. This persona, employed by every high-priced news anchor in the business, tried to ensure that no one took the idea of conspiracy seriously, tried to ensure that every person who went outside the system to look for answers about what was happening to our world was called a Wacko. As this persona became more and more a joke with citizens, the major sources of news on the planet began to crumble.

"Finally, several news stars, Dan King included, tried to take on the Smith Exposé on Federal Cancer Murder. King did everything in his power to defend the army of government and corporate cancer researchers at the National Institutes of Health who were still pursuing corrosive chemotherapy 'solutions', who were also helping to prosecute health practitioners employing workable alternative cures. But King ran into a new generation of businesspeople and researchers and reporters, and his more and more fervent denials of the new non-official wave of cancer cures went down in flames — with his vaunted career.

"Eventually our nation realized that in many arenas we had been presented with realities which were just fictions dressed up to protect or enrich some powerful interest. We saw through to the theatrical artistic essence of this subterfuge, and as a nation decided to turn our minds to the creation of our own worlds. Hence, the incredible cross-fertilizing patchwork-quilt of free non-controllable communities spreading across America.

"Will we ever all come together and attain a perfect union? Is it desirable? Well, I know this. First we must attain true individual freedom from our government and its machinations, from our remaining transnational corporate princes, from the associations created by those princes to plan and implement global policies inimical to us. First we must do that. We must make sure that blinding poverty and war and disease are no longer the 'eternal facts of life' used, incidentally, to keep people in a powerless 'need' for rulers.

"When all this work has been done, we can start thinking about unity and diversity. But now we know that through our own imaginations we can create out on the horizon of infinity worlds we are only beginning to understand.

"I ask this Committee to recommend, at the close of this session, a serious study of the government — to refocus on what we can do to assist in the process already well underway on the planet.

"Would it have been a great shock to early Americans that their government was searching for a way to follow the people? I don't know. We who are sitting in this room persist in thinking of ourselves as leaders only. And we like to think of the people as incompetent, as waiting for our cues. That era existed once, but it is over. It is over because we forfeited the right to lead. Maybe it was never our true function.

"Today there is no town or village or county or city in America that cannot afford to maintain its own infrastructure. That situation is spreading across the world.

"Wars are becoming passé, not because some great centralized army representing the planet is frightening nations and groups into submission. Wars are diminishing because there is no need for them. When the minds of the people are busy building their own worlds, they will not pick up a weapon and kill a stranger.

"Let me tell you about Carolasia, a community on the edge of Detroit. On one acre of land, sixty people live in two vertical structures. A third is being built for new members. Each member has access to 1047 Netlinks to other communities, for the exchange of information on everything from self-government to vegetable sales to spring celebrations to group-booking rates for lunar shuttles.

"Carolasia has executed 27 murals in the Midwest over the last thirteen years. They have published two books on Sumerian tablet research, fielded a third-place softball team in the Greater Detroit Summer League, co-sponsored with 5 other communities a common climb of the Matterhorn, produced a 4-hour film on the organic growing of fruits, nuts, and vegetables in non-city and city spaces, headed up a weekly farmer's market on the south side of Detroit, taught wrestling, chess, and Japanese cooking classes to local groups on the Traveling Rec circuit, pioneered four city vegetable gardens in Michigan, run a small medical clinic on its premises.

"Carolasia keeps a 12-person integrated diary of self-government changes within the community. The Carolasia government has swung from no council to full voting participation by every member, to elected Monarchy, to worker-committees. They are always in flux on that front ...

"Thirteen years ago, some of you may remember, the

community was prosecuted by a federal district attorney on charges of urging the overthrow of the U.S. government. This accusation, absurd on its face, was eventually dismissed when it was made clear that the whole case really rested on a manual written by three Carolasia members which forecast the decay of the American federal government, based on its failure to meet the needs of the people.

"Carolasia, in that case, was represented by James Waters, an attorney for the Fullerian corporation, Blue Game. Blue Game and Carolasia had already established a co-project involving the rental of space on a three-month Earth-orbiting module. The vessel would house four occupants who would, in a gravityless environment, carry out a vigorous program of imagination-empowering techniques. That orbiting program is underway now.

"There is no way for us, the government of the United States, or any of the old traditional global corporations, to invoke platitudes and find millions of citizens running back into our arms. That time is gone. People have awakened. They have passed us by. We can join them, help them, or we can decay into dust."

PART EIGHT

95

I have come across an ancient philosophy from India called Samkhya.

It is difficult to place in time. One estimate is 6th century BCE. According to the 1991 edition of the *Encyclopedia Americana*, volume 14, Samkhya holds that "The two basic contrasting entities are soul (purusa) and matter (prakrti) ... Souls are infinite in number and consist of pure intelligence. Each soul is independent, indivisible, unconditioned, incapable of change, immortal. It appears, however, to be bound to matter."

In *The Gods of Eden*, author William Bramley quotes British scholar, Sir Charles Eliot, on Samkhya's version of the soul's liberation: "Suffering is the result of souls being in bondage to matter, but this bondage does not affect the nature of the soul and in one sense is not real, for when souls acquire discriminating knowledge and see that they are not matter, then the bondage ceases and they attain to eternal peace."

Bramley states that, according to Samkhya, "every soul has participated in the creation and/or perpetuation of the primary elements which constitute the material universe."

If Samkhya indeed held this to be true, it would stand quite early in the Tradition of the Imagination, then running up through Tibetan practice and Giordano Bruno, whose poetic imagery is reminiscent of Samkhya cosmology.

I am not interested in arguing a case for immortality of a soul which is you. That question is up to you to decide. But when we are talking about an ancient philosophy that stresses the far reaches of the creative imagination, and views that power as involved with the bringing into being of the universe itself, we have made another potential connection in the Tradition of the Imagination.

We are talking about the creation of reality by a human being. In the final part of this book, I want to carry out another experiment along that line.

I have finally located a long-term practitioner of Tibetan visualization, including the deity-form of exercise I described in several earlier chapters.

Jim had been an active student of this discipline for fifteen years. He had done numerous retreats in Canada, the U.S., and Europe. Then he stopped.

"I was frustrated," he said. "First of all, I found very few people who seemed to be focused on what I considered was the ultimate goal of this practice."

"What goal is that?" I asked.

"The ability to materialize matter and energy at will, in a very visible way — to actually control the physical universe, which we could call the universe of appearances."

"I want to get this very straight," I said. "You're of the opinion that it's possible to make this wall disappear and walk through the empty space."

"Absolutely," Jim said. "Create it from your mind, so to speak. Just like that. But it's real. My teacher believed that passion for the goal was important, that you didn't have to become a passive or unemotional person in any way. He also believed, in the traditional way, that not creating was the other side of the coin. If you can create an object on this table, a glass figurine, you can also not do that, you can turn it on and off like a faucet, at will."

"Have you been criticized for being so straightforward?"

"Sure. There is an interpretation of all the Asian religions in which passion and desire and impatience are looked on as flaws. What is thought of as good is neutrality, and that is a signal that you are not too attached to the world. I don't agree with that interpretation. I think it's destructive. If you look at some of the most passionate teachers in recent times, from the East — Muktananda, Yogananda, Ramakrishna, you are looking at men who desired the goal of enlightenment very, very much. They were hungry for it. They were not simply ecstatic by nature. They were aggressive for their goal."

I asked, "Have you had experiences of being able to create things with your will power, with your imagination?"

"Yes, but not predictably. Most of the time it doesn't happen, but once in awhile it does. I don't know whether I want to tell you about it, because you might think I'm nuts. ... but for example I created, for about two minutes, a gold aura around a statue that several other people could see. It was a kind of joke. These were my friends. We were standing in a park in Chicago in 1984 and I said, I feel a thing coming on, a visitation. Of course I didn't feel anything like that. I just put an aura around a statue, and my friends saw it. A woman walking by saw it for a few seconds too and she looked at us and gasped. Later we all laughed, after the woman was gone. I thought we were going to be stuck with a believer. I've done things like that."

"And you don't associate this with some kind of religious connection?"

"Let me put it this way. I think religion is, as Marx said, the opiate of the masses. I also think that under certain circumstances science is the opiate of the masses. So is romantic love, under certain circumstances. So are a lot of things. And when you find you can really do things with your mind, your energy, you undrug yourself."

"Why aren't you a Tibetan practitioner anymore?" I asked.

"I still do certain exercises, like the deity visualizations, but I don't do a regimen every day now. I'm on vacation. I'm thinking things over. I don't know whether I want to stay dedicated to a practice that may take seventy lifetimes to fully realize. Believe me, I don't know of any other techniques that really do the trick either, so it's not that I'm diving into something else ..."

We discussed an experiment I had in mind. The background is this: We all tend to solidify our lives as the years pass. The clay of our actions hardens into habits. It is then difficult to believe that we are imagining, inventing, creating our lives. So, an antidote, vaguely similar to the Tibetan practice of deity-visualization, might be helpful.

Not a strict visualization, but a dialogue, almost an interview. Jim would imagine a number of people, not just one.

We didn't want to have him in the position of making up just a single person who could become so interesting he would want to maintain him, hold on to him. So we decided to devote each session to creating a new person.

I know this sounds odd, on the surface, but think about it. It sounds odd because we are so dedicated to the ordinary, we are so dedicated to thinking that if anything fantastic is going to happen it is going to be created by someone else and it is going to come down from the sky. The bizarre thing is the assumption that nothing is going to happen. I think that's the weirdest assumption of all — and it's considered realistic and sensible. It's no more sensible than living by tranquilizers and slowly fading out.

Anyway, in each session, Jim would decide who that person was that he would imagine, create — not a friend, not anyone he knew, but someone imaginary. I would then ask all sorts of questions about this person and he would fill me in, inventing the whole thing as he went along.

The object?

Perhaps after enough sessions, the act of imagining in great detail different people and their lives — creating them — would have some effect on how Jim looked at his own life. Perhaps he would gain a new spark of inspiration. Perhaps he would see his own life in a very different way.

I had no precise short-term goal. It was an experiment.

Jim said, "You think that if I invent enough people — purely invent them without any set pattern — I might shake something loose."

"You might get a big bump from your imagination that would carry you into another level. Of creative capacity. It's like going to the gym. You work out. This is an intense workout for the imagination. Of course, for any real effect, we might be talking about a few hundred sessions. For me, this is a kind of demonstration project. I just want to see what, if anything, happens."

Jim agreed to try it.

In our first session, he decided to imagine "a lady with a limp." That was enough to get started. I told him to give her a name. He chose Sandy.

I began interviewing him about her. The session lasted an hour and a half. I'm including an excerpt here.

What is she wearing?
A dark blue suit. White blouse. Shiny black high heels.

Does she walk with a cane?
Yes.

Is she boring?
No, she has a very high IQ. She works in the admissions office of a college in Arizona.

What happened to her leg?
It was broken in several places in a car accident. There was nerve damage.

When she wakes up in the morning, does she feel the way you do when you wake up?
She is happy. I'm not.

What makes her happy?
She believes in an entity who helps her.

Where is this entity?
In her mind.

What does her mind look like?
A long football field. There are objects on it, geometric objects. Each one is a storage unit for information on different types of subjects.

Where is the entity?
Next to an object.

What does he do?
He wonders how he came into existence.

And how did he?
By her neurosis.

What's a neurosis relative to the football field?
It's a cloud, a small cloud.

What does it do?
Rain. That causes the woman to become anxious.

Can the entity help her?
It can make her think it isn't raining.

... Does she have money?
No. But her father does. He's 80. He lives in Chicago. When he dies she'll inherit $600,000.

What will she do with it?
Something stupid.

Meaning what?
She'll become an alcoholic.

Why?
Because she wants to have fun.

Does she suspect that's going to happen?
No. Not yet.

Does she have a man?
Yes. He's in jail. She can visit him and spend time alone with him. He's in a minimum security facility for stock fraud.

What does she think of herself for having a man who's in jail?
She doesn't tell anybody about it.

She's secretive.
Very.

What does her nose look like?
It's short and straight.

Reddish?
No. White. But it has some slight discoloration up near her eyes.

What color discoloration?
Gray.

Does she try to cover it up?
No. Her teeth are funny too. They're a little too big in front. Very strong.

Did anybody ever make fun of her for her teeth?
Yes.

When?
When she was twelve.

Where was that?
In a small town in the Midwest.

What did the place look like where somebody made fun of her?
There were three girls. They were standing on a bridge. It was one of those delirious summer afternoons. Edith was the leader of the bad girls. She teased Sandy with a big grin on her face. She said, "Horse face. Your teeth are like a race-horse. I'd bet on you ..."

What did the sky look like?
Those faint clouds before a thunderstorm.

Did Sandy cry?
No.

Did she believe in God?
Yes.

What did she tell herself?
Nothing.

What do her fingernails look like? Now.
Short. Dirty.

The dirt comes from ...
A garden. She digs in her garden at home.

Vegetable?
Mostly flowers. She's a worker. She likes to work in the dirt ...

Does she wear rings?
A silver band on her wedding finger. A pinkie ring on her right hand. The setting is brass. Scratched. It's a fake ruby ...

In this first session, we ranged all over Sandy's life, went into great detail on the appearance of her body. I asked a number of questions about what she believed in, how she treated people, what she thought when she was alone, and so on.

There was no pressure for something major to happen.

Again — so there's no misunderstanding — Jim made up this woman. This is not someone he's known. And he made up her circumstances and the details about her. I'm not saying he didn't pick some of these details from memories, but not all of them came from memories, and in any case those that did he transposed in many ways to fit this imaginary person.

We did six more sessions on six people whom Jim made up, and they all had one quality in common. None of them was a public person.

In the seventh session that changed.

Who is it today?" I asked.
The Vice-President of the United States," Jim said.

What does he look like?
He's tall. Cadaverous.

What's his name?
Hamilton. Michael Hamilton.

Is he a figurehead?
Unwilling. He wants to go to war. He wants to destroy Syria and Lebanon and Iraq.

Why?
He's hateful.

Just that?
Yes.

He must have a reason.
There's something inside him. He thinks these people are murderers.

All people from the Middle East?
Most. Hamilton feels a sense of peace when he thinks of war.

Does he want to go himself?
No. He wants to watch. He wants to see the destruction from a distance.

Has he ever committed violence?

I don't know. He has some kind of disease. The public knows about it. It's been announced. One of those auto-immune things. Lupus.

What does it look like?

His eyes are a little buggy. Something wrong with his thyroid gland. His colon is constricted. He's a very military person. He walks upright. His hands are against his sides. He has the nails manicured and he cleans them every morning. He washes his hands with soap several times a day.

Compulsive?

Yes. He keeps taking showers. He's afraid of germs. He thinks germs are being carried into the country by people from the Southern hemisphere.

Is his mother alive?

Yes.

What do they talk about?

The farm. He grew up on a farm. He has a very diminished sense of smell, but he can smell the farm. The animals. The pigs near the troughs. The goats. He has a favorite goat in his memory. It's dead. This goat liked him. Used to lick his hands and his feet when he was a little boy.

He was a happy little boy?

Yes. Very.

What happened?

His eyes began to hurt. He got headaches. His skin turned a slightly yellow color. He retreated in his mind. He became an intellectual.

Does he wear expensive clothes?

When he's not in the White House he wears dark blue polo shirts and white polo shirts. He's an Ivy Leaguer.

So far nothing tremendous had happened in the sessions. As you can see, there was no attempt to interpret the answers Jim gave. No this-means-that. It's clear to me that the constant effort to fish for meanings stems from a complete misunderstanding about what the imagination is and what it does. The constant search for meanings is a restraining, a backpedaling of the creative impulse. It has never really been accepted by any therapy or religion that the unrestrained unanalyzed exercise of the imagination would eventually lead to liberation, to a vista of new feelings about life itself, to a blossoming of possibilities for action, to an end of what is called neurosis.

After the twelfth session Jim told me he was beginning to see something about himself, but he couldn't describe it. He reminded me of a passage I had shown him about Tibetan exercises, written by David-Neel.

> It's like her description of the becoming meditations. You sit there and become the tree. You imagine that your mind is inside the tree, and your eyes are the tree's, and your body is the trunk of the tree. And then you look out as the tree and you describe your body as a man, you describe the man sitting there next to the tree. The more you do this, the more you feel that this human being business is only one way of looking at what people are. Only one way. You see that your mind, your perception is much wider, but in order to get to that point, you have to practice a lot. We've just started here. You're interviewing me about these imaginary people that I'm making up, and I'm beginning to get the feeling that I can look at my own life in a lot of different ways. But it's slow. I need a lot of practice.

In the nineteenth session, Jim chose a person who was a witch.

"This is a witch that is part male and part female. Actually, it can be either or both."

How tall is he?
Or she.

Yes.
It's about six feet one. Large arms. Tattoos.

Comes from where?
Born in Illinois. Discovered the talent of being a witch

when she was twelve and ran away into the cities of the Midwest, and lived by doing strange things for people. Theft. Spying.

Her body?

Very wrinkled. A sea of wrinkles. Orange and gray and pink and white and gold. She thinks she's a sailor.

On the sea?

Jim stopped cold in his tracks. After a few moments he looked at me. "I did it," he said in a quiet voice.

"Did what?"

"I got inside her head. I felt what she was feeling."

"The sailor thing?"

He nodded. "Yeah. It was just a flash. It was as if I were in her head when she had a random aimless thought ... I was an inch away from it and I felt it go by. But I was imagining it all too."

He smiled slowly. "You know that Tibetan exercise? Well, this was my first real taste of being the tree, I guess. I was that witch. It was like a breath of hot air on my face. Fantastic."

When I saw Jim the next time he was different. More easygoing, grinning more, more talkative.

We did another nine sessions and he said he was feeling his life had a thousand roads he could take. "I don't mean in theory. I mean I can taste them all out there. The possibilities."

One more time the sheer power of the imagination was driven home to me.

All we were doing was imagining various people and he was describing what they were like, in detail. He was creating them. And this, over a period of weeks, was changing his moment-to-moment feeling about his life.

I said to him, "Suppose we did this about governments instead of people. You invent a government and then I ask you all sorts of questions about it. We do 50 sessions about 50 governments. And you suddenly feel that tremendous feeling, but this time it's about how the country could work, about how any country could work ..."

"Sure," he laughed. "And suppose I was the President or a Senator to begin with."

We thought about that a little.

About how it all could and would work if people saw through the basic Formula of the Secret Society to the wide open spaces.

About how if enough of us want it, nothing can stop us.

How far can this exercise of "inventing people" go? What might happen if Jim and I continue it for a year, two years? I don't know.

In Jim's 30th session, he imagined a policeman.

What's his name?
Michael.

What kind of work does he do?
Detective.

For whom?
The status quo.

What does he do?
Keeps the borders in place. Whatever it takes to keep the prisoners in.

What does he look like?
An old stag. Lots of battle scars. He's fought in all the great wars.

What color are his eyes?
Cloudy gray. He doesn't see so well anymore.

Lonely outpost?
Yes.

Where does he live?
In a room in a roominghouse. Always keeps his bags packed. Two pairs of underpants, white wool socks, toothbrush, slacks, a long lined coat for the weather. — It's happening again. I'm him. I'm Michael. I'm getting hits of how he feels. The cold air on his skin. The night. Walking alone along a wall, guarding a border. This is more than the last time. I'm getting a whole feeling about his life as if it's mine. How he lives. His dedication. His loneliness. For some reason ... it's liberating ...

The next day Jim told me he felt as if a load had been lifted from him. "I don't why," he said. "This isn't rational. I'm imagining it and suddenly it's so real ... and then I feel different. Free."

I described the sessions we were having to a writer-friend, and asked him why he thought Jim was having these experiences. "When you're writing a novel," he said, "things are built to fit in a tighter way, but you're having him invent without any strings. It's very free, and then you're doing it often and in a concentrated way. It's the freedom, I think. There are no limits on where he can go. He can imagine whoever he wants to, and then describe him in detail ... plus, most novels are imagined in such a way that they describe limited worlds, very limited situations, and the writer, after years of doing this, falls into a pattern of inventing similar kinds of limited people."

Jim said to me, "I hope people understand that the imagination functions on so many levels. People in power keep telling themselves they're living in a world, in a society that's tremendously restricted, and that they have to obey the rules and create within a very narrow range. But that's not true at all. That's just their collective fiction. That's what they're the victims of. That's their problem. They really believe that what they're imagining has some exterior proof. Do you know what I mean? They think they can't go any faster because the universe, society, whatever, is going more slowly, and they have to obey. But if enough of us stop buying that, if enough of us rip that particular phone out of the wall, it's a new ballgame. A very new ballgame."

In Jim's 36th session, he chose a woman named Sally, who was a runner:
"She does cross-country," he said.

Where?
Colorado. I see lots of hills and snow too. She runs in shorts. She has tremendous stamina.

What color is her hair?
  Black. She has it pinned up.

Lipstick?
  No. No makeup.

Does she paint her toenails?
  No. She wears yellow and black running shoes. She moves over the hills at a very brisk pace. No sign of tiring.

What is she thinking?
  She's thinking about the sun, that it's warm up that high. And about a meal she's going to order at a Chinese restaurant tonight. Cashew vegetables. Egg drop soup. She can see the steam coming up from the plates.

What color are the plates?
  Light blue. Large. Silver covers on the hot food.

How far is she running today?
  Ten miles. She's floating. She feels very excited but calm at the same time.

Where was she born?
  In Mexico. She came over here when she was nine on a truck in the middle of the night. Got over the border with her family ...

And so it went. Most of the time there were no spectacular occurrences during the sessions. But Jim began to feel more free. His sense of his own life, and the possibilities for our world expanded in his mind and in his feelings.

96

Opening up and using the imagination is the most profound form of education.

Those who think they know what human limits are have never made any substantial part of the climb. They have simply adopted a knowing attitude and used that to substitute for first-hand knowledge. None of us knows how high we can go.

Is it possible that those in the Tradition who say we have actually created this universe may be right? To answer no categorically would be to reveal one's ignorance. I am not suggesting that a person should substitute a vague belief that he is superman for the ability to earn a living, pay the rent, and enjoy life. And I am certainly not suggesting that a person should parlay a belief in the infinite possibilities of the imagination into membership in a limiting group. That would be the height of absurdity, which you can certainly see from having read this book.

But I must say that the most absurd thing I can think of is believing that we are ordinary, that life is ordinary, that no one has ever had a major agenda of controlling the human race.

I have a great deal more to say about how I think we can expand and extend our power through our creative invention. But this book is done and my points are made.

This is the first core-sample.

The reason I concentrated so heavily on the CIA and the Nazis is that those partially hidden groups seem to be able to exert large amounts of power in controlling events ... and they tie in with corporate interests which, through upward funneling, are in the process of taking over the economic and political functioning of the planet.

The ignorance of this on an historical level is profound. For example, Charles Higham, writing in his amazing and authoritative book, *Trading with the Enemy*, provides a capsule summary of the activities of ITT during World War II. Show me a school textbook that mentions this:

> After Pearl Harbor the German army, navy, and air force contracted with ITT for the manufacture of switchboards, telephones, alarm gongs, buoys, air raid warning devices, radar equipment, and thirty thousand fuses per month for artillery shells used to kill British and American troops. This was to increase to fifty thousand per month by 1944. In addition, ITT supplied ingredients for the rocket bombs that fell on London, selenium cells for dry rectifiers, high-frequency radio equipment, and fortification and field communication sets.

> Without this supply of crucial materials it would have been impossible for the German force to kill American and British troops, for the German army to fight the Allies in Africa, Italy, France, and Germany, for England to have been bombed, or for Allied ships to have been attacked at sea.

Here is a memorandum sent on February 26, 1942, from R.T. Yingling, a U.S. State Department attorney, to the Assistant Secretary of State, Breckinridge Long: "It seems that the International Telephone and Telegraph Corporation (ITT) which has been handling traffic between Latin American countries and Axis-controlled points with the encouragement or concurrence of the Department of State desires some assurance that it will not be prosecuted for such activities. It has been suggested that the matter be discussed informally with the Attorney General ..."

Higham comments, "Whether or not the [trading with enemy] license was issued, the [ITT] trading was continued with the assurance that neither the State Department nor the Department of Justice would intervene."

Using this historical platform as a jumping-off place, what is one to think, in analyzing the CIA-aided coup which overthrew President Allende of Chile in 1973, when it turns out that, known to many people, ITT and the CIA together, engineered a truckers' strike in Chile that helped paralyze the economy of the nation, destabilize the Allende administration, and set the stage for a revolution that would murder Allende and elevate the vicious fascist, pro-Nazi General Augusto Pinochet, to dictator of the country?

In September of 1973, when the coup came, there was terror in the streets, as "possible security threats" to the new regime were arrested and tortured and murdered. Among the thugs doing all this were: Chilean Secret Police (DINA) coordinating with members of the Chilean Nazi Party.

Three years later, Orlando Letelier, Allende's ambassador to the United States, would be blown up in a car outside the Chilean embassy in Washington.

The main perpetrator, the American Michael Townley, was assigned the hit by the new dictator, Pinochet, who was openly pro-Nazi. Who was Townley? Why, he was the man who had designed the electronic torture rooms at Colonia Dignidad, the 30,000-acre Nazi center in Chile, which is still operating today.

Nazis, CIA, powerful corporations.

Reminiscent of the 1954 CIA-staged coup in Guatemala, in which the elected president, Jacobo Arbenz Guzman, was overthrown. Three corporations controlled the economy of that country, the largest of which was United Fruit. UF was terrified that Guzman would nationalize it. Terrified also were the 1100 families which ran the country of four million people, the families which owned half the arable land.

Such a versatile secret society, the CIA.

In 1976, the Church Committee, representing the government of the United States, reported that the CIA, prior to 1967, had secretly published or sponsored or subsidized over a thousand books printed in the United States. Orwellian, to be sure. Who knows how many points of view which were repeated and expanded in the press and public — points of view on vital matters having to do with politics and the Cold War and technology — had originally been bought and paid for by the Agency?

The above several points about the CIA were part of a final discussion about this book with Ginger, the nurse who had participated in my "dream experiment" detailed in earlier chapters. Ginger wanted to know why I considered the role of the CIA so important in the annals of secret societies.

"No one knows how extensive their territory is," I said. "When I talk to former Agency employees, most of them are only aware of the Agency's work in their own field and one or two other provinces. I think CIA is just a word used for convenience to allow massive funds from Congress to flow to what are essentially separate kingdoms, and to give a legitimacy to activities — which, as strange as they are, are only a cover for more bizarre programs."

Ginger asked, "Do you really think the CIA has a number of areas of interest that nobody knows about?"

"Sure. But even in the areas we hear about, now and then, there is incredible ignorance. How many people know that the CIA kept secret files on American artists? Not just the FBI but the CIA. The reporter, Herbert Mitgang, researched this extensively. The Agency had files on the novelist John Cheever, on John Steinbeck, William Saroyan, Lillian Hellman. There are lots of others. This is the CIA, which isn't permitted to undertake *any* activities at all in the U.S."

The information that you just presented on ITT ... my father fought in the Second World War.

ITT was not the only U.S. corporation involved. Not by a long shot.

If my father knew that, if lots of soldiers from that time knew that ...
This would be a different country.

You say the globalization of corporate power is the modern version of the Church.

Yes, as the central office for power on the planet. More and more power is running through this structure. I present it as an evolving structure, not one that is static and has been in perfect place for centuries. These corporate men discover, as time passes, as they become more in control, how successful cooperation can be. This secret society structure coalesces over time and fits more firmly together.

When you say secret society, do you mean oaths and ceremonies and blood and all that?

I define secret society in the Introduction. It's an organized group that has a secret agenda whose purpose is to control and dominate others. When you strip the fancy stuff away, that's what you're left with.

And in the case of the corporate machine, it isn't left or right politically.

I have seen people who have the most infantile sense of politics in this country, who feel that real power passes back and forth every four years when the President is elected. These people are sure there is no conspiracy because this elected "power" changes hands. This is such a babyish point of view, it's almost charming. Get out the diapers and the crying towel. The conspiracy is an evolving upward funneling of power that passes through the corporations, three hundred of which own 25% of the world's productive capacity. At least. Now, these men don't care about left or right or Demo or Republican. Trust me. The racists in this country and the fascists and the fake Christians who really want to start a race war ... all those types exist whether the regime is Demo or Repub. So do the pharmaceutical companies which produce demonstrably poisonous compounds for general consumption. Now when the Repubs are in power maybe the pharmaceutical cartel and the money for medical research that will end up with more toxic drugs takes a slight, slight dip. Maybe, just a touch. And when the Demos are in power maybe the racist fascist activity of good old boys who are really home-grown Nazis takes a very slight dip. Maybe. But the reality is, the overwhelming course of the nation is taken regardless of who sits in the White House. I am not against government. I ran for U.S. Congress in 1994, in a very strenuous campaign, and I know lots of armchair critics of the nation and the government who can barely get up from their pie and ice cream and talk to an audience of thirty people about what is going on in this world. But the vital fact is, if Washington power is monstrously pro-corporate, regardless of political party — and with Bill Clinton we can now say with surety that that is true — then for the foreseeable future we need to use our imaginations to craft many, many worlds of living and enterprise that exist in a self-sufficient way. We need to make many real worlds of community separate from Washington. We need to do that while we try to keep the corporations from drowning the world in toxins of one kind or another. It's not an easy job. In 1996 I started something called The Great Boycott, which was an attempt to get people to stop buying the products and stock of the eight biggest pesticide companies in the world. It's also an effort to boycott working for these companies. The Boycott is still going, and I'm happy to say that other people are running it now. Again, I discovered that lots of armchair critics were unwilling to get up off their asses and help out on this or on any decent boycott, of which there are many. That's where imagination comes in — as in, are you willing to exercise yours? One of the big political barriers in this country — and I really consider it more an excuse than a barrier — is that the important decisions are made by the Demos and the Repubs and we have to choose between them as our most important job. That is sheer baloney, and of a very cheap variety. We have to go way beyond that.

You keep saying the secret society influence substitutes its own imagination for ours.

Its job, if you will, has been to submerge our own imaginations, to make us think that what we project out there, what we create, what we can invent, is meaningless, unimportant. Once that pinnacle of fascism has been reached, then whether we favor the left or the right is very minor. We're done for. We're asleep. We're in someone else's world. We're suckers who believe we have to go along with the major programs extant on Earth and pick and choose among the collection of bad programs. The best of the worst. That's the modern definition of maturity.

This is a two-sided coin. The secret society and us.

Yes. The Formula of the Secret Society, to make a world out of art and convince us that it's the best one, the only one, the one to live in, the only one to live in. And then there is the far-ranging use of our own imaginations, and what we can do with that. From now on, I hope that whenever you come across one of these armchair critics you demand that he come up with workable products of his own open imagination. You see, I know beyond a shadow of a doubt that we can each create many, many realities, and I have seen the result of that on many fronts. It's life, wild fantastic serene life. I'm basically an artist who got involved in politics and found that art was the trick of the ages. That's what they have used to ensnare us, and we have the creative power to invent our way out of that, and we need to do it. That's really the bottom line. When I concoct these various experiments, like the one you agreed to do, I'm trying to move ahead and put more muscle in the imagination, I'm trying to extend the range and the power and show at the same time that we can make our own worlds. If readers think they can do a better job by using the imagination in more fantastic experiments, I'm not in the business of building a consensus about a method. Go for it.

You don't necessarily think the same thing works for everybody.

I know it doesn't. There are people who are so tied up in being part of someone's world, or their own inhibiting world, that what they need is to shake loose from that. But the point is, we have a Tradition in history of trying to free the imagination, a largely invisible Tradition. It's there if you'll see it. At times it just says the Imagination is a wonder and it is the greatest wonder we have. At other times the Tradition goes much farther and tries to put into effect ways of liberating and extending the power of the imagination.

It's rather amazing that China is the nation that is trying to take Tibet apart.

Materialism meets imagination. Well, as Clinton shows his showbiz supporters what he is really made of by essentially ignoring the whole Tibetan tragedy, he also says, This is the age of corporations and that is the most important thing. There is no way Clinton can stand up and say we will keep corporations out of the largest market in the world simply because the Chinese government is a murderer of its neighbors. The ubiquitous *they* would kill Clinton or bring him down for that. He would be another Arbenz or an Allende all of a sudden. Gone. Blowing in the wind.

Upward funneling.

Yes. A casualty of upward funneling. As time passes, power learns. We have to understand that. We're not dealing with a static image of unchanging empire. These CEOs and their bankers and their Trilateral and Bilderberg and CFR clubs learn how to deal with their enemies and their own plans and ambitions. As the world shrinks and as they get more territory in the monopoly game, they can see the end-game come closer. This isn't conspiracy theory. It's just the way things go. It's the game they're playing.

You think that new technologies can make a big difference.

That's one reason I stressed the CIA-Bechtel connection. The secret society influence in the realm of technology exists, just from the clubbiness of it all, if from nothing else. But if you read, say, Gene Mallove's book, *Fire From Ice,* you see that cold fusion is not a hoax. Far from it. It is a door opening into a strange world that is real, that holds out the potential for bringing vast energy resources down to the level of the energy pack and the individual, and I mean any individual in the world. This is a kind of empowering I want to see, one that ignores all the baloney about what color your skin happens to be or what country you were born into or who your family is or what your connections are to the secret police or how much money you have in the bank or any of that.

When I tell people about the writing down of dreams I've been doing, they think I'm just writing down my dreams — not that I'm inventing them.

It's great that you're running into that. It shows what kind of blind spot most of us really have. People say, who cares if you have a man sitting there "inventing people" and answering all sorts of questions about them. Who cares? What good is it? And I say, who cares if you're going out there every day and every night and living a life that could be lived by a robot? Who cares if you do the same thing every day and believe that that's what life has to offer? Who cares if you have no idea how great the imagination can be? Who cares? Most people, first of all, don't realize what it means when someone like you does twenty or thirty powerful sessions in which you invent dreams. The number doesn't register. And then you keep doing it on your own for how long?

I have about 150 dreams in my book.
To really comprehend that, you have to do it.

Do you actually think we can, say, materialize objects?
We already do. I believe some of the paranormal experiments I've cited in the book indicate that. We create energy. Or if you want to be more bizarre, we use a non-energic force that moves energy and shapes it. But I believe the former is true, regardless. From that point, it's just a matter of degree. How much can you create? That's why the statements of the Tibetans about our creating the world aren't that wild at all. And when you come at it from the direction of art, from that experience, you know something about the power of imagination in your bones, in your soul. A vase that is sitting on a table where a second ago there wasn't one. But even if you find this hard to swallow, or don't believe the possibility of it at all, you should still be able to discover that through the imagination we can remake this civilization and bring it much closer to justice, beauty, the heart, and all the other virtues we pay lip service to. That is eminently possible to bring off.

And the secret society influence is to do that according to another set of values.
The values of control, domination, slavery.

You told me that as recently as 1986, there is evidence that the CIA has been at it again, secretly financing books.
Herbert Mitgang, in his book, *Dangerous Dossiers*, cites the instance. William Casey, then head of the CIA, had paid $107,430 to a Harvard professor named Nadar Safran, to "finance" a book that was called *Saudi Arabia: The Ceaseless Quest for Security*. A California Congressman at the time, Don Edwards, who was a former FBI agent, made a pretty shocking statement about this. He said,

> ... Have we forgotten that ten years ago this behavior produced a major controversy and the CIA was forced to stop publishing books? The public is entitled to know

if ... we [are] back to the bad old days when we didn't know which book was a CIA plant or if any particular professor's research was his or her own or was dictated by the Agency. How many books, magazines, and newspapers are there in the U.S. that are in reality CIA propaganda? How many professors and clergymen are on its payroll?

When does it stop?

We like to think that exposing something puts an end to it and it becomes passé. But usually research uncovers scandals from ten or twenty years earlier and everybody prefaces the public disclosure by saying, This isn't being done anymore, of course. Remember? That's the way they opened the CIA MKULTRA hearings in 1977. The truth is, when the disclosers are the government they make nice and try to placate the public by assuring one and all that "the danger" is over. We are still largely like recalcitrant Catholics wandering around inside the Sistine Chapel entranced by the Michelangelo ceiling and convinced that somehow God must have created the universe and set the tone and values for its future. But we also see the bright hues where twenty years ago the soot had gathered, before the grand restoration and cleaning, we know something about the history of Western art — and yet we feel compelled to believe, to want to live inside the art rather than appreciate it fully for what it is, a creation of the imagination. In the same way we are still to a degree inside the art of the Cold War, and we cannot view the entire art of the period and the facts of military and economic life that lay behind it with a comprehensive grasp.

You always emphasize the art of the secret society.

Yes, and the basic reason is, it is in fact art. This is so important to see. Why? Because if you just think that evil institutions and bad governments and inhuman corporations are pushing their programs on people, then the response is to say: The people must push back. And although that is true, it is only a part of the story. The truth is, the Formula of the Secret Society and ultimately organized life on this planet consists of art that is dedicated to deceiving and then controlling people. When you really see this, you begin to glimpse the fact that these artists can be outcreated by us — and if we do that, we build and evolve institutions that are not simply pushing back, they are outflanking and out-distancing and outcompelling the controllers. Then we really have done something. Then we have taken giant steps toward re-structuring the whole basis of society. Then we have built another world. Other worlds. That is called victory.

What about the power of tricks in secret society methods?

There are an endless number of them. People have written about that. The hypnotic, as a subject, itself has an array of devices. Tone of voice, soothing quality, the authoritative presence, the rolling tones of preachers. All this applies to a leader, to a person who's trying to get himself and his ideas across to influence others. There are a million tricks in that bag right away. Ways, for example, of putting people into an alpha-wave brain state in which they tend to be more recep-tive to suggestions. Then, of course, when lunatics get into force, into the sort of mind control where force is used, torture itself, duress — these things make people perform accord-ing to command. That has always been true, whether elec-tric shocks or hammers are the weapon. Students tend to focus on the details of mind control, as if that's the whole story. But it isn't. The overall context is the one I've brought out into plain view in this book. The art-universe of others draw-ing you in and helping you to forget and put aside your own creative powers, your own imagination as the fountainhead of your life, your aspirations, your future, your power.

You laid out a spectrum of creation that included an unusual array of qualities.

I hope people focus on that. I don't think this has ever been pointed out before in a cogent way. When we say create or imagine or invent, we are talking about a whole series of actions and attitudes that are not normally included together in the same fold. Theater, I think, is the best place to start with this. In the theater you create by entering into a different state. You merge with a persona, you become it, you display the persona's voice and the hills and valleys it takes, you project ideas and images. And much more. These are all ways of creating, of imagining and putting into effect various states and realities. There are other ways. You can conjure, you can evoke, you can manufacture a thought, you can worship, you can dance. The more ways you find that are really creation and imagination, the more new ones you come across. Let's call this whole thing a spectrum. It's not that organized, but it gives some idea of what's possible. We move with fluidity through these different ways of creation. That's our style naturally. That's what we do. It's the Formula of the Secret Society to try to slow this down, freeze this process, solidify the person.

If I can make the molecules of water on a glass plate shift around ever so slightly with my mind ...

Then the physicists, whether they like it or not, have to rethink the whole idea of the physical universe. Your imagination at work in bringing about some sort of reality in which those molecules move — that event has caused an instant revolution in the human assessment of the cosmos. The universe can no longer be considered ultimately as a closed system that runs like a clock. Or like a river or a series of wells or oceans or whatever. No description of the universe as an ultimate thing or process always apart from us is going to work. This is what I mean. All so-called materialists and realists like to imagine that the universe has its own laws that are in some way superior to us. We can learn how the universe works. We can learn the pattern and polish our learning of it and praise ourselves for studying the pattern and all of that, but we are basically the students of this fantastic thing or process called the Universe. That's how these people think. And they are quite satisfied with that. And they try to say that any of us who claims to affect the universe directly with his mind is far off the mark, because nothing in the physical study of the physical mechanism of the brain or the body would suggest that we possess that kind of power ... and they, the eminent scientists of the age, are certainly not going to abandon or subvert their own method of studying things from a purely physical point of view. That would be treason. That would bring forward a sea of chaos in the world of science. That's how they think. And meanwhile, the amazing and the fantastic and the unbelievable has already happened. The literature of fifty years and more on the subjects of paranormal research has shown that we are able to affect the universe and change it with our minds. This has been happening. The statistics show this as clearly as statistics imply the conclusions of any universally accepted scientific studies in any field. What I am describing here is a battleground that touches on the central issue. Your imagination in its evolving power as opposed to those artists who have taken on the mission of the Secret Society: to flood and obscure and ultimately bury your imagination. That is what is going on.

Then the philosophy of materialism has a lot to do with this.

There is no such philosophy. It's a bigger sham than any snake-oil salesman you can find. A philosophy is coherent. All of our experience tells us that we are not dead electrons and photons. The premise that we are subatomic particles has no basis. Absolutely none. I hope people understand this, or come to understand it. Once you say the word I, once you think of human beings and we and they and all the rest, the question comes racing at you like a train: How can you say I am nothing more than electrons? Under what guise can you say that? You can only say you are looking with certain instruments that give you a certain field of objects, and those objects at the lowest level are electrons and quarks. That doesn't mean I am a collection of quarks, it just means that wherever you observe and look with the instruments of physics you find those particles — or the assumed effects of them. That's all. And the materialists walk around posing as if they know something, as if what they have found out somehow automatically applies to the I. That transference factor is not real, it is fake, it is just an assumption with no more merit than the assumption that a dragon is carrying the universe on his back. But a person who claims to be a materialist can walk around affecting an attitude of earnestness and knowing and swagger and world-weariness and all the rest of what passes for authority. He can do that. But it doesn't mean he knows anything. A tremendous amount of delusion has to be assumed to come up with the idea that you are electrons. On the other hand, that doesn't mean at all that God exists and we have to read the Bible and Jesus was His son and all the rest of that mythology. Religion doesn't have to be imported to make anything make sense. Let me put it to you this way. Think of yourself getting up on a podium and arguing to a vast collection of educated men and women that you personally are a bunch of electrons which is studying other electrons and this is what all research is. Yes. You are a bunch of electrons which somehow is imbued with the idea — whatever that is — that you are alive, and starting from that delusion you are examining other electrons. Think of this. How can you be a materialist unless you believe that all electrons are fundamentally the same? There are not alive electrons and dead electrons, because alive is a term that only has meaning if you starkly assert another dimension of existence altogether — and then you are departed from the level called materialism. So you have to say that electrons are just matter and they have somehow been prompted to study other electrons, much like a rock would wake up one day when it has no quality that would permit it to do so. And having awakened, it would then proceed to investigate other rocks while remaining itself a rock. That is an absurdity on the face of it, and it is also absurd given the usual definitions of electron and matter and rocks and so on. So materialism, which is a kind of souped up propaganda, is used as yet another way to minimize the imagination — since imagination gives birth to all sorts of ideas and feelings which take us into a dimension far from rocks and electrons and dead matter.

If art hasn't taken us through into the next evolutionary level, how can we believe that certain kinds of exercises to extend the imagination are going to do it?

Art did take us through to new levels. And art isn't finished. As you've seen, inventing dreams is a very powerful experience when you do it long enough. And so is the invention of other people or beings. But of course it looks weird because we have such a gigantic blind spot in our view of history, in our opinion of what our potential is, in our opinion of what we are. So to just take the issue on with frank frontal exercises seems odd. The imagination is in disuse? All right, stretch it, and keep using it and do it freely without any prior limiting assumptions or constraints or mythologies that must be obeyed. That's the injunction, that's the plan. Let me tell you where I stand on this. I am in the process of devising different methods for increasing the power and scope of the imagination. Which increase can be applied to any field, to any area of life. And I believe there are no outer limits on that power or scope. That is where I am. That is the project I have jumped into. There is nothing secret about it, and I intend to share whatever I find out. But if you think you have better, faster, more powerful ways of going about the same thing, by all means do it. A debate about what works is the last thing I'm interested in. This is not doctrinal. This is about the future. This is open. This is work for anyone. The great platform for the human race is imagination. And I believe that when we understand all this better, we will see with our own eyes and minds that what has been called, through the ages, enlightenment, salvation, ascension, cosmic consciousness, self-realization, bliss, unconditional love, universal compassion are all attempts to describe what happens when the imagination becomes prime and goes far beyond the present barriers we assume are its boundaries.

Epilogue

Jack True, the late hypnotist I interviewed in an earlier chapter, had spoken with me at some length about secret societies and his work with ex-members.

"I don't like to be called a deprogrammer," he said, "because that implies in people's minds a lot of kidnapping and shoving people into cars and speeding away from the front doors of cult headquarters. People just came to me and I worked with them, mainly because I wanted to see what was holding them back from simply putting a former life behind them."

Jack True was a fascinating person. He had an informal collection of people who toiled in large corporations who passed him exceedingly interesting information ...

The following is an excerpt from a conversation we had about people from secret societies. And other related matters.

Jon Rappoport: You told me you tried to hypnotize several artists.

Jack True: Yes. These were definitely not New Age types. The sessions went absolutely nowhere.

Why not?

Because they were way ahead of me. They had an intuitive grasp of the fact that I was acting as a source of inspiration, so to speak, and they already knew all about that. They didn't need more sources of inspiration.

Are there anti-creativity forces in the society at large?

Yes. You find it wherever there is a group that tries to take power from individuals and use it for the common good. The common good means control of society in that case. It means "national security." It means all that, whenever somebody says the power an individual holds must be stolen from him and transferred to the world or the nation.

There are key events in history that are used to put down the creativity of the individual, that are used to reduce the power of all individuals. It's done by the raising of a certain sentiment that we are all bad; we all have to be hogtied in some way to keep us from exercising our bent for destruction. There's no distinction made between the people who did evil and those who didn't. It's a particular kind of propaganda that follows horrible events like the Nazi holocaust, like the dropping of the atomic bomb on Hiroshima, like the announcement of global warming. Somehow, on an almost subliminal level, the inference is taken that we are all responsible for those things in a way that should prohibit us from using our creativity — that is, power — when creativity is exactly what can provide us with new solutions that can take this world far beyond what we've managed to enact as a race so far.

I've hypnotized people who illustrate what you're talking about. When I fish around in their landscapes, their inner spaces, I find interesting things. They have areas of passivity, and you can actually visit these and carry on a discussion with them talking to you from those places.

From the passivity.

Yes. They'll talk to you from those spaces, as if they've just driven there in their cars and parked, and now the fog is settling in and the radio is on in the car and they're waiting for nothing in particular and they're talking.

Is it possible you're inducing them to imagine these places when they don't otherwise exist?

Sure. At times. But remember, I'm not talking here about faithful records of events that happened to them when they were six, I'm talking about what people will give you below the surface, and the answer is they'll give you the most fantastic stories. People will tell you about cloudy borders, for example, where there is a great deal of sleep going on, where there is a kind of psychic texture, as it were, a thin cloudy or foggy matter that is very passive and very relaxed and very much without opinion about anything. Passive. And the more you elicit comments from them when they are in these places, the more you feel that they are reporting to you honestly — with imagery — about parts of their lives, about states of mind that are quite familiar to them. They sense their own passivity. They wallow in it. I've had people who could hardly get the words out of their mouths because their jaws were so relaxed. They'll talk about rivers, very slow warm rivers of bathwater and they are lying in boats or on rafts and the temperature is getting warmer and they are floating and watching television sets at low volume. At first you think they're back in the womb, but it isn't that. It's more pervasive than that. You get beds and restaurants and food and the easy restful states, and the more you explore the more of this kind of thing you find. It takes up a lot of psychic inner space.

The creativity is shut down?
   To a great degree.

You find this with a lot of people?
   Yes. I take it to mean that the sum of the effect of the culture we live in brings this about.

It brings it about as long as people do not wake up to the fact that they can create widely on their own.
   That's right. I once hypnotized a man who had dropped out of medical school and he gave me that experience as if it had been a secret society. Do you understand what I'm saying?

I'm not sure.
   When under hypnosis I get the recounting of experiences out of the heart of a cult or a secret society, I usually get, right off the bat, a flatness in the report, in the memory. Everything has a sameness to it, as if it itself had originally taken place under a state of hypnosis.

No emotion.
   Much less than you would expect. Much less of everything.

Why?
   Because the person had been overloaded.

With what?
   With reality. He had been fed from a source, the prime

source of that group.

You mean information?

Basically, yes. But also rules, ways of behaving, customs, and so on.

A universe was made for him that had so many details he didn't have time to make his own.

This man told me about endless classes and rounds in a hospital and sleepless nights and all the questions he was asked and all the memorization he had to do. He had no time to ask his own questions and have a healthy attitude of skepticism toward the system he was being indoctrinated into. So he fell into a kind of hypnotic state, and that's what came out when I put him under. The passivity appeared front and center. The man had a really rich fantasy life that had to do with vacation spots and places away from civilization and magical drugs and water and sleep, and all this came out in very vivid detail.

Could you talk to this man as if he were in Hawaii or wherever it was?

Yes. And the whole thing felt quite real, as if he were reporting on a vacation he had taken or was taking now.

What was the therapeutic effect of this?

It seemed terrific at first, but the effect wore off rather quickly.

Because?

Because he was missing a link in the whole process. This could be a very long discussion, but I'll try to capsulize it. The hypnotic state is quite real, and it doesn't need an operator like me to induce it. It's a real state of consciousness. What I do is hurry the process along, I get the person there faster and I get him there as if he'd taken a ride on a train and that was the station. Do you see? When a person creates, he moves in and out of that state — which is actually a huge number of different states. Because there isn't just one level called The Hypnotic. When a person creates, he moves through a tremendous number of different perceptions and states. You can't catalogue them all and arrange them neatly. The creative process isn't a single process and it doesn't have a rulebook

— although there are lots of eager beavers out there in the social sciences who want to organize it. They'll make their own absurd beachhead and call it creativity or whatever, and it'll turn out just to be another office building with rooms and rules and little certificates and grant monies will be thrown in that direction. But when you hypnotize a person you reduce the complexity of the process he himself might go through to arrive at the place you took him to, and you also give some importance to the place you took him to, when he himself might give that place less or more importance on his own. If he is going to change in a solid way, he has to go through the whole process himself from the beginning, he has to engage in a more creative undertaking. That's what I moved into in my work. Ways of bringing people into more active states, so that they could invent their own changes and move out of their own passivities.

You could say that the medical profession is a secret society.
    Actually, that's a good label. Think about this. It's possible that by the end of the century 8 million children in America will be taking Ritalin, a form of speed, for Attention Deficit Disorder. This is making addicts. It is doing it under the guise of treating a "disorder" which is defined in the medical manuals by symptoms like "child gets out of his chair when he should be sitting down," or "shifts around in his chair." That's not an exact quote but it's surprisingly close. And this so-called disorder has never been nailed down to brain malfunction or any biological malfunction. There are only theories, no proofs. I could go on for quite awhile on this. But the point is, doctors don't have the free-floating intelligence to read their own literature and manuals and realize what an incredible and dangerous fraud is being perpetrated on the public. The truth is there for any half-wit to see, but for some reason the doctors don't see it. They can't. They've been brainwashed.

They've been trained in such a way — an illusion has been created for them in which no fraud of this magnitude could possibly exist. The same situation pertains for all the so-called neuroleptic psychiatric drugs, about twenty of them. They regularly cause motor brain damage. If you read Dr. Peter Breggin's authoritative book, Toxic Psychiatry, *you'll come away with the conviction that between 300,000 and a million cases of motor brain damage have been created in America since 1954 by the use of these drugs — which are prescribed for all sorts of "disturbed" Americans. How could this happen? Well, a very successful form of mind-control has been applied to the doctors in training. That's the bottom line. A quite clever universe of "science" and all that that implies has been built around the budding physician, and because, for example, the emergency medical wing of the profession does do much good, an unwarranted inference has been drawn about the profession in general. On a 1993* Nightline *program, during a discussion about the Clintons' proposed national health plan, it was let slip that 15 million unnecessary surgeries are performed every year in this country, and 60,000 people die from those unnecessary surgeries. Think for a moment about the cult warning bells that go off with this statistic. How can physicians who have ostensibly taken an oath to do no harm first and foremost — how can these men and women ignore this reality? Well, most of them are unaware of the statistic and would automatically deny it if it came their way. How can they be unaware of such an incredibly important fact? Again, a kind of closed universe has been painted around these high-IQ professionals. Literally, a part of their mind has been shut down to the truth. The art with which this has been done is considerable. People want to go looking for ultra-secret societies, but they can't recognize the giants of the breed when they are sitting there right in the middle of our world staring at us. We could talk about the way the doctor is kept under constant pressure during his training, about sleep-deprivation and all that — but the basic factor is far deeper than that. The imagination of the doctor is amputated, and with that clever piece of surgery the rest of the mind-control flows naturally.*

When I hypnotized this med-school dropout he reacted in the way I would expect from a cult member. The usual disorientation, the difficulty in dealing with the world around him, as if he had been kept separate from it for a long time. A confusion stemming from his compartmentalized mind.

Compartmentalized?

Yes. I'm not talking about the development of a toughness in the face of horrible physical tragedies. I'm talking about a room in the mind where all the education is held in sterile cabinets, away from any "contaminating influence." How was this accomplished? In part by the creation of a theatrical holy quest for true science against the enemies with their flags of superstition.

I have never met a doctor who had the slightest idea of the extent of research fraud in his own profession. As a reporter I researched it for several years. But the doctors were ignorant of it, of the rampant fraud afflicting the center of their profession. They weren't aware of the deaths and hospitalizations from Non-Steroidal-Anti-Inflammatory drugs — seven to eight thousand deaths a year in one study — they weren't aware of the accusations of conflict of interest and fraud concerning studies on the drug Xanax, they weren't aware of expert opinion from within their own ranks on the widespread uselessness of chemotherapy in the majority of cancers — even though the drugs are approved for use on the public like clockwork. And on it goes.

The young man I hypnotized, the med-school dropout, revealed a kind of naiveté about the real world. He was a hothouse flower who was just waking up to the condition of his professional birth. At moments, his state of mind reminded me of Brave New World. The veneer is kindness and concern, but underneath that, the pawns suffer from acute ignorance of the facts of life.

Classic secret society attitudes.

Among the membership rank and file.

What other kinds of cult members asked you for help?

A good cross-section. I had a 33rd-degree Mason who was part of a Lodge that had specialized in conspiracy theory. I mean, anybody can call himself a Mason and start a Lodge, so I don't know what precise group this man belonged to. But he saw everything as a plot in progress. There was no such thing as casual conversation with him.

Did you put him under?

Yes. I got material about him trying to perform telepathy, only the setup for it was inside the Lodge. In other words, they had a ritual by which a person could attain to this capacity. It involved a globe of the world and staring at it and a light or series of lights in the ceiling, and some mumbo-jumbo from the Bible read out loud. There were costumes and references to historical texts of the esoteric variety. But these books were just further variations on ceremonies and rituals.

He was participating in all this?

He was trying to shake it off. But he wasn't a very bright man in some ways. He had accepted the "Masons" as his only ticket out of a humdrum existence. So when he began to sense that they were conning him ...

How did this occur to him?

He felt he couldn't do telepathy or anything else like that, no matter how elaborately it was dressed up. He couldn't bring himself to fake it either. My sessions with him went pretty much nowhere. Finally I applied the shredder, as I call it. I took him on a walk around Los Angeles. We walked for five or six hours in Hollywood, and the whole time he would tell me how what he was seeing related to some conspiracy to take world power and so on. I wasn't prompting him in the slightest. A newspaper in a box on the sidewalk or an office building were sufficient to trigger a lecture. Finally, after about five hours, he began to see things as just things on the street. It took him that long to get outside his box. Do you see what I mean? Then he just talked to me and I talked to him. That's all it came down to.

Sounds almost like that patient you called Dr. Death.

Yes. There were similarities. Only Doctor Death was more exciting. He was part of a cult that focused entirely on the millennium and the apocalypse and the end of the world. I think there was a sexual twist to it, but whatever it was, it wasn't giving him much pleasure. He alternated between thinking he was "Doctor Death" and thinking that the Doctor inhabited his body. I wasn't opposed to dealing with the latter idea, but it seemed to me in this case the only possession was his own lock-up. He was in the grip of something more interesting than he was. In life he was an office worker, but after hours he turned into a wild thing, and he preferred the wildness. He would go to cult meetings and sit in a circle with other members and put curses on people outside the group. He would claim that he was bringing them closer to the coming Doom. He liked it. That was my take.

Did hypnotism help?

Not much. So I applied the old psychodrama trick. Play

along. I found that when I acted like one of his potential victims ... you see, I'd sit in my office and tell him, as if he were the Doctor, that I was having problems, I was feeling less healthy, a germ was slowing down my system. Gradually he would take the initiative and tell me that maybe I was under the influence of a certain person. One thing would lead to another and finally he would say he was Doctor Death and I was his victim. At that point I would ask him if there was any way for me to shake him off. He would recommend various exercises and rituals ...

How many times did you see him?
    Forty or fifty before we were through. He just stopped being Doctor Death.

He played it out.
    Yes. It didn't interest him anymore.

Did you ever see anyone from the intelligence community?
    As a patient? Yes. A few. I saw a man I believe was a real assassin. He had retired from the service. It wouldn't have done any good to try to cut him off at the pass because he had already been violent. He had killed people.

Did he say he was just acting on orders?
    Yes. He also said he had been promised rewards. Several-year vacations in the South Pacific, beautiful women, that kind of thing. They hadn't paid him off well. He felt they had treated him badly. I put him under and he regressed to South America in the '60s. He was apparently part of a program to teach police forces down there how to do torture. Federally funded. He recalled torture sessions. A man died. After quite a long time of working with him I saw no change. He didn't go anywhere in the regressions. He would go over the material and sometimes he would cry, but it didn't really move him. Finally the whole thing began to come apart.

What came apart?
    He was very hateful toward his former employers. He felt they had dragged him into the job from the beginning because he had a certain profile. No emotion. But that was a lie. He did have feelings. They had taken him from military

barracks and made him a killer. The orientation was very cult-like. Loyalty to the group was first. It was a kind of brother-hood of killers, at least in his unit. They didn't light candles and do incantations, but it came close to that. Anyway, as he regressed into early times in the brotherhood, he got very angry at his bosses. He got down on the floor in one session and screamed. I wasn't always sure who he was screaming at. A lot of the time I couldn't tell what was going on, what he was regressing into. There were women he was having sex with. They seemed to be supplied to him as part of his pay. He never saw any of them more than a few times. He went through strange training that had to do with perfor-mance drugs, or possibly electromagnetic radiation. A lot of the confusion, but not all of it, stemmed from the fact that he felt compelled to hide things from me. The performance drugs or machines allowed him to stay up for long periods of time and go on training in the field in harsh conditions. He would feel very up during those times. He could stay awake for thirty-six hours and feel tremendous.

Did he ever come all the way out of his association with the team of people he was loyal to?

No. He quit seeing me after about a year. I never saw him again. I think he decided the murders he had committed had cut him off from human society. He also thought that these crimes were a way of trapping him in the group, a conscious way his bosses had used. There was the good and the bad. They would give him women, and also some sort of "enhance-ment" that could keep him at peak field endurance in winter conditions for weeks at a time. That was the good. And then there was the killing — the bad. He felt that both the good and the bad had been given to him to tie him to the group. This good and bad all connected with weird fragments that came out during his sessions. Little pieces of oaths and some sort of assurances of immortality and gaining a place in a high echelon after death. I put it together like this: He was "permitted to explore good and evil" so that he could be a true warrior, and this would elevate him to a place after death that few people could wish for, let alone be installed in. It really was a piece of gruesome theater that he was fed, and he had taken it in. Or possibly he wasn't fed it, but under hypnosis he filled in blanks in this way. But at least some of it sounded real to me, as if in his particular unit, at least, there was a metaphysic about immortality and warriorship as a prelude to that.

Do you think he was in the CIA?

I don't know. I've had people come see me from all sorts of groups. Every time the slavery aspect is there. They're trying to shake it off.

Do they usually succeed?

We've discussed this before. I came to the conclusion that shaking things off is only a partial answer. It doesn't pull you all the way out of the water.

If you don't see that there was a kind of art used to hook you in the first place, and if you don't see that you have the capacity for greater art ...

Yes. If you don't see that, you're still lacking.

Reminds me of modern life in general.

That's why I stopped doing hypnosis on most people. The modern idea that surrounds our society is that by being nice, by being very nice you will fit into the system around you and everyone else will be happy with you. The only thing is, "everything around you" is hypnotic. I mainly find myself doing reverse-hypnosis these days. I do things to wake people up.

When young people are deprogrammed out of a difficult situation, especially when the deprogramming is handled by coercion, they always seem to opt for a standard version of reality and they try to fit in with the values they didn't like in the first place, the values that led them to rebel and join the cult or whatever it was.

Yes: That doesn't give them much confidence for the long haul. For the long haul, they need their own creative potential turned on to the highest degree possible. But now you're talking about everything that is anti-hypnotic. That's why I couldn't hypnotize those artists.

Getting back to the cult members ...

I had one in particular who fit the bill you're talking about. They all did, but this was so obvious. He had belonged to a

Rosicrucian society of some kind in Europe for four or five years. He was a businessman. Again, I'm sure this Lodge was just using whatever mystical premises they wanted to and called them Rosicrucian. I don't put any stock in the names of groups.

It's all art. They paint them a mural and they say it's ten thousand years old and then they weave their stories.

Yes. This man had met, he felt, a being who was without a physical body, during a ceremony in a small room in a house. The being, he said, had come to him and promised him that if he remained part of the group and worked very hard to learn his lessons, he would be rewarded.

What kind of rewards?

It was Faust-like. Wealth, power, youth. The usual. But apparently this being was very convincing.

And the man who was promised all this?

He didn't know what to do. He was scared. By the time I saw him, almost a year had passed. He was still in the group, because he felt the attraction of this being and the possibility that he would be raised out of an ordinary life into something magnificent. That was the key. He didn't have a clue about his own power. It never occurred to him that he could get what he wanted by creating it himself.

But the pull of this being ...

That was what was trapping him. I decided not to fool around with convincing him that this being was an apparition or that he, the victim, had been given drugs and hypnotized or whatever. I just took his report at face value. I just assumed that a being who was outside a body had visited him and showed him a taste of what he could get if he stayed in the group. There seemed to be visions of some kind that this being showed him.

Almost like the Church and its cathedrals.

Very much like that. Give them the big stuff and they go down on their knees. This being showed my man visions of what he could be, how life could feel, what it could look like. There were pools and gardens and the air was lovely and my man felt young again. It was very compelling.

Smellovision.

Tasteovision, smellovision, surround sound, the works.

Convincing art.

And my man had no inking that ...

That he was an artist too. That's what I'm talking about. Everybody wants to feel that the real clue, the real payoff is on the outside, is somewhere else, is going to be supplied from a distance by the people who really know what's happening and so on. They are in the dark about their own powers and their own potential and their own creativity. So what happened?

It was futile to hypnotize this man, because he was already in the grip of much better hypnosis than I could provide.

It reminds me of the Assassins, the old Middle East cult.

Yes. When they would drug the young aspirants with plenty of hashish and carry them, passed out, out of the desert into a beautiful oasis with pools. Very much like that. Beautiful women at their beck and call as soon as they woke up. They were told this was heaven and they believed it, because the desert was all they knew.

And then they would be told that they would come back here after they went out into battle and fought like crazy and died. They would be rewarded by being transported out of that hot desert into the palace and the gardens of heaven ...

And my man believed something like that from his "guide," his being who had shown him the visions. I talked to him about creativity a little, just enough to see that he didn't have a clue about his own. He didn't see that what had been done to him was what's done to soap opera audiences and movie audiences. You get a hit of another world you think is better, but you can't get there on your own — that's what you think — so you keep reaching out and yearning for the world of the soap opera, the world of the vision supplied by other people, and you're hooked. You feel that when you come back from that glimpse of the art, as you say, that it is better than what you have, and so you feel sad and unsettled ... just enough to know that the only way to assuage it is to get another hit. Tomorrow. Same time, same station.

You couldn't make your man see that he had any kind of power that could stretch him out of this bind he was in.

No. That was my problem. And it's the problem that's all around us. I'm not just talking about cults and secret societies. Anyway, what I did was take the role of the being. The demon. Whatever you want to call him. We began a dialogue, I and my man, with me playing the being.

Did your man go for it?

I was afraid he wouldn't but he was okay.

What did this being look like, the one he described.

Vague. There was a glow, there was a lithe rippling very strong body, there were eyes, there was a pacing around and intent voice. So that's who I was. We talked for a long time, over a series of weeks, every day. My man was only in the country for a short time and he was disturbed. He wanted to resolve this issue. I played the part of "the being" and I began to explain in detail how he had to be at my beck and call if he wanted me to grant him the goodies. I could make him younger, yes, but he had to do everything I said. This applied to business decisions, to his marriage, and so on. Nothing was his own, nothing was out of bounds for me.

How did he respond?

It took awhile for the whole thing to get off the ground, for him to believe just a little that we had a conversation going in this theatrical way, but eventually he came around. It was a miracle, really, the transformation that took place. It turned out that my man could play himself very well, he could provide a level of intensity and emotion that was completely missing from his own life. He loved it. He really did. Then we switched roles. Again it was very difficult at first, but finally he began to do a passable imitation of a very powerful being from another dimension. He was able to put a little wallop into it. He began ordering me around and telling me all about how my life could change if I came over to his side completely and the rest of it. He even began adopting stock mannerisms of a sort of oppressive demon. Arched eyebrows, expressions of disdain, hard stares, smooth but tough voice. His body became more graceful as he moved. When I thought he had gone to the top of that for the time being, he and I had a down-to-earth conversation. Only then. Before that it would have been futile.

Was he honest now?

He was, and I enjoyed it. He told me that a lot of the pressure was off. He no longer felt so trapped in the experience of feeling that being's presence. He felt stronger. Better equipped to deal with his life. You see, some people would say this was therapy, but they miss the whole point.

This is theater. Invention.

Well, yes. It's a very integrated art form when you do role-playing at this level, when you home in on an experience that is key to the person's life. Many times it doesn't work, it's too soon, or the person won't summon up the energy and the imagination to actually play the parts. He's determined to stay exactly in the life he's got. But in this case, my man scored a victory. He really did. He didn't say the whole visitation of the being had been his own fantasy to begin with. He didn't disavow everything that had happened to him. Not at all. But he wasn't frightened.

After he left the country and went home ...

I sent him to a woman I know in Paris. She does the kind of work I do. He saw her for a few months and he came out of his shell even more. He didn't quit his Lodge, which I thought was a very brave thing. He stuck with it for another year or so.

Because he wanted to find out about this being.

Exactly. You see, among the members there was a bit of discussion about this other-worldly wizard or whatever they called him. It wasn't bandied about, but at the higher levels of initiation the "guide" was mentioned as a kind of living legend. The whole group seemed to get its push from that. But they kept it very close to the vest. They talked about "acting on orders" from this being — who would, of course, according to their mythology, bring them closer and closer to personal realization and enlightenment and all the rest of it. The perfect Faust story.

The perfect secret society story. Religion story. Science story.
     What do you mean?

Any story that has a punchline about your power being ultimately supplied from forces that come from somewhere else, that act on their own without reference to what you decide. It's all geared to an unspoken ideology in which you finally aspire to be the perfect pawn.
     Well, my man was no longer a pawn. He wasn't a complete Hercules, but he had come a long way.

Did he ever see the being again?
     No. After a year he got tired of the Lodge and quit. That's as long as he could wait. He told me he felt that the being, if he was real, wouldn't want to approach him because his weakness had gone away and therefore he was now a risk. He might not behave well. He might become argumentative. He might spread dissension in the group.

But what about the beautiful paradise he had been shown? The better life? The return to youth? All that?
     Yes. He admitted he was still nostalgic for it. But now he was seeking it for himself, as he put it. He was aware, he said, that the promise of an extremely pleasurable world had to do with a manipulation of forces within him.

Meaning what?
     Meaning he felt that electromagnetically, if we can imagine that level, he was aware that changes in his fields, the fields that interpenetrated his body, could stimulate feelings of pleasure and ecstasy. And not just sexually. I mean on the levels of how you feel when you walk down the street and look out at the world ... a nice day can become a great day. A magnificent day. He felt he had somehow been manipulated in that way to gain a glimpse of a different level of existence.

That's pretty vague.
     After I worked with that professional assassin I did some research. Remember, he had talked about undergoing treatments which allowed him to have tremendous endurance

in field exercises that lasted thirty-six hours. No sleep at all. Harsh conditions. He also talked about a feeling of exhilaration the whole time. At first I thought this was just drugs. Speed. Something like that. But I found a reference in a military-conference summary to possible experiments with devices. Machines. Equipment. From what I could gather there was electromagnetic manipulation, and it was done for the purpose of beefing up the endurance of small groups of soldiers on the battlefield.

And this has been done?

I believe so, but I can't swear to it. At the time it was still in the experimental phase.

All right. But my point is, whatever had happened to your man in his moments with that "demon" or whatever he was, it was an experience. It came and went. It wasn't a capacity being exercised, the way I can exercise the magic of music, for example, if I can actually play the piano very well. Your man may have felt elevated, but he just found himself in a beautiful place for a few moments, he didn't do anything to get there. Therefore, he was at the mercy of some unknown factor.

Sure. And I never tried to decide whether this demon was real.

Do you think he was?

I know there are lots of reports, historically. So I don't discount it, if you strip away the religious imagery and baggage. But my approach was to bypass that question and just do whatever I could to beef up the strength of my patient. And it worked. We played roles and it worked.

We've talked about this before. The role-playing is theater. That's the primary debt of people like Fritz Perls and J.L. Moreno. Doing theater with this man brought him out of his trouble.

Art wins again.

Art wins again. Get your man to take an active part in the extension of his problem by making him an artist, making him improvise, making him be an actor, making him take part in very compressed theater.

That's right. After all that is done, then we can take up the interesting question about whether a being without a physical body can appear and severely influence a human being. Afterwards. But first let's do the right thing. Let's raise the capacity of the person, the so-called victim, to deal with such curios, such experiences, such visitations, if you want to call them that. Let's not jump into hysteria and start playing a metaphysical game that puts us in exactly the wrong ballpark. Let's not succumb to tiresome Earth-mythology that's trying to make us grovel a little. Let's strengthen our position considerably. That's what I did.

This has a direct tie-in to Tibet. These groundbreaking therapists like Fritz Perls and J.L. Moreno, with Gestalt and Psychodrama, are in that direct line to Tibet. Especially the exercises of becoming. Sitting next to a tree and becoming the tree so well that you can look out from the trunk and see your body. You no longer feel that you are only the person you are with the name you have and the identity you have taken on. You no longer feel that extreme limitation.

Perls and Moreno saw that the main problem people have is their limitation to a given identity. To put it another way, people have problems when they can't get into the theater of a situation, when they can't reach through in that way, when they feel pinched by delusory limits on how much they are.

And their way to solve that was through the imagination, through art, through theater.

Perls would have people talking to imaginary people they knew very well but weren't present. "All right, your sister is sitting in that chair, talk to her." Or be your sister in that chair and talk to you. Moreno's patients would have extended dialogues with family members which were acted out on a stage. You don't only play yourself, you play your father and your mother. Of course, Perls told his patients that they WERE all the people and things and qualities in their dreams. That was the magic. They were the whole dream, all the pieces. It's a shame that the traditions of Gestalt and Psychodrama haven't been explored to the maximum. There was a famous socio-drama, as Moreno called it, that was staged in the Minneapolis area some forty years ago, during a housing crisis that involved race relations. White people wouldn't rent to black people. So before a fairly large audience, a drama was staged in which a black man and white man played landlord and prospective tenant during a "rental interview."

Eventually both men played both roles, and the emotions ran very high at moments. The white man playing the prospective black tenant was screaming that he would burn down the apartment building if he couldn't rent an apartment there. From accounts, there were people in the audience who got the message on a very electric emotional level. Of course this was just one sane moment in a social and political sea of trouble, you might say. But it pointed the way to many moments like this, to a renewal of society through very strong art. To a kind of graduation.

I used to know a family that would have periodic days when they would make one person the perpetrator of everything people in the family always complained about. For a day the whole shmear would be Jimmy's fault and everybody could blame him and accuse him and jump down his throat. Jimmy could deal with it as a play. It was theater, pure and simple, and it functioned like Greek tragedy. It allowed a kind of catharsis. I think people make a serious mistake when they overlook this in assessing world religions and governments and armies and corporations, the really big ones. These leaders are not only artists, they are living out a form of theater which interests people more than their own humdrum lives. Before we go all mystical about the secret power of this and that, let's truly explore the art, the theater of powerful organizations. And let's exceed it. Let's be better than they are.

I've worked with a number of husbands and wives over the years, people who've had the full spectrum of problems and complaints and miseries, and to me the central invisible problem has always been their inability to treat their relationships as a kind of conscious drama, with all the attendant magic and fun and character changes. The rest of what they consider their problems is hogwash, pure nonsense. Let me suggest a play that could be taken as a form of drama to be acted out by people who want to enlarge their lives. You can't get everybody to role-play, but the people you can will come out fantastically well. You take the main person, and you have him discuss his own creativity, what he feels it potentially involves, how big it could theoretically be, and so on, and then you have him talk about possible inner sabotage. Does it feel like there is some inner governor on the velocity or the power or the scope or the artistry of his own creativity?

Finally, when he fleshes that out a little, you get him to invent a few characters that represent the sabotage and the limiter-aspect. And then you have a few people as surrogates act out these creation-limiting characters, and the main person engages in a dialogue with them on stage, an improvised play, and this goes on for some time. The topic is creativity, of course, and eventually, the people all switch roles, and they push it to the hilt.

It is getting down to the real core of what a person is. And for those who try to minimize creativity, who want to say that what we can create doesn't begin to match up with the power of the universe itself or the strange esoteric forces and beings who move in other realms, and so on, I would say, save your conclusions until after you've really worked on extending your own creativity in a major, major way. None of us knows the half of it.

Even a robot is an actor.

Playing the part of a robot.

You wanted to talk about survivors of abuse?

Yes. In so far as they appear to be ex-members of secret societies or cults or their victims.

From my perspective as a hypnotist, I found several things. First of all, it's ludicrous to accept all the reports of abuse as true. Ludicrous. Unless you just want something to believe in. Let's take the totality of the reports about UFO abduction and satanic ritual abuse and government mind-control abuse. Take those categories. Shall we automatically believe every one of them?

How do you decide what's real?

On a case-by-case basis.

What distinguishes a real case from a fake case?

It isn't just one deciding factor. First of all, there are therapists who consciously or unconsciously guide very suggestible people down roads where these patients end up fabricating stories and memories of abuse. No one knows what the percentages are. But on the other hand, it is incredibly irresponsible and unscientific to say, in a blanket way, that all such stories out of therapists' offices are pipedreams and induced by the therapists themselves. There is no single principle of psychology which automatically validates the premise that all memories of abuse which are uncovered and recovered in therapy, after being buried, are fake, made up, false. The large group called the False Memory Syndrome Foundation, out of Philadelphia, appears to be dedicated to such a non-existent principle of psychology. The fact that, among other people, Martin Orne and Louis West have sat on the board of that organization, speaks volumes. These two men have had active careers in CIA-and-military-intelligence mind-control research. So the whole field of deciding what stories of abuse are real and what are fake is very muddy. I know several excellent reporters who have left this field for that reason. It was almost impossible, in most cases, to figure out whether the stories they were being told were real or not. Let me give you, though, an example from my work. One person. One story. Remember, this story is not meant to summarize the whole field of research on this subject. You'll see as I go along why I'm choosing it.

This is a person you hypnotized?
Yes. A woman of about thirty.

She said she had been abused?
Yes. She said it happened ten years or so earlier.

Where?
A place in the country, in the Midwest, about thirty miles from the headquarters of a major American corporation. There were a number of people there.

Did she believe this when she first came to you?
No. She said she thought she had been raped, but the memory was hard to get to. And there was no doctor to go to or police report to read. I put her under and regressed her and she came up with clouds. That was the first image. She went to a road in the summer and trees and meadow and all the right sort of thing for a very relaxing scene. I got the feeling that she had been through this before.

The recounting? The remembering?
Yes. But then she seemed to sink lower and she fell into a

new space that was dark. She heard voices. She was being carried to a vehicle, a car or a truck. She was bound at the ankles. She was loaded into the back of the vehicle and driven in the evening of what seemed like a summer day to a house in the woods. It was a large house with hardwood floors. She was taken by two men to a chair by a fireplace and she sat down and was given a drink of water. While she was sitting there she remembered she had been driving her car. There was missing time. Perhaps several hours. She had been driving her car back home from work — she lived alone — and the next thing she knew there was the feeling or the sense of clouds and then the darkness and the binding around her ankles and so on. She felt the sharp end of one period of time and the beginning of the next. As she was sitting there by the fire she looked out the windows and there were lights on. The patio was lit up and several people were out there talking. She felt they wanted her to see them. Two men were dressed in suits and there was another being who was wearing very tightly fitted metallic clothes. It was one piece. He was standing near a lamp and she could see his face. It was humanoid but very sculpted, she said. More crisp, more clear than an ordinary man's, somehow. His ears were small. She took him to be an alien ... We ended the session soon after that. Between sessions I contacted several people I knew from different fields, shall we say, and asked them what they thought about UFO abductions. A reporter told me there was no doubt in his mind that the people who were telling these stories were either crazy or interested in getting attention. Two UFO researchers told me they were quite sure at least some of these stories were real. However, they were divided about the motives of the ETs. One man said that despite horrible stories of abuse by victims, in truth the ET contacts were all on the side of education and ultimate good, with the intent of raising the level of our consciousness for a leap into a quite different future. He said that people who told horror stories were putting an unconscious spin on a very strong contact with beings who could relate on many levels beyond our five senses, and to fill the void and the fear, these abductees would insert accounts of torture which, in fact, never took place.

Not in one single abduction. The other pro-UFO analyst told me that among the ET races who had visited Earth, at least two were definitely in the business of control and tyranny, and they had no qualms about treating their captives quite badly, just as, say, Nazis did in the concentration camps. Departing sharply from all of this, a researcher-friend said that UFO tales were floated out there by intelligence agencies, and the abductions themselves could be carried out by military-ops people in alien costumes as a cover. The whole abduction scam, he said, was there to bring the citizenry up to a pitch of expectation and hysteria about the UFO phenomenon, as a prelude to a fake apocalyptic event that would necessitate the abrogation of civil liberties and the bringing on, at least temporarily, of martial law. A group of Christian UFO researchers said the UFO phenomenon was a fake, engineered to make people think that God was a relative entity among many other entities in the vast universe. A ritual abuse expert told me that bloody cults used the alien abduction scenario as a cover for their ceremonies, which included rape and murder. Yet another ritual abuse researcher said that cults were often the property of very powerful "demons," beings who existed without bodies who made careers out of manipulating humans for sport and out of a devotion to evil. Each researcher had a collection of reports that purportedly backed up his view, and the reports went back in time, in some cases to antiquity. To a degree, each one of these people felt he had a stake in every analysis of abduction reports. There was reluctance to allow a report that did not fit his picture. I found all this very interesting. Perhaps each one of these people was looking at the same elephant from a different angle, and felt sure that if his version of events did not get exposure, the whole elephant would disappear into oblivion and never be understood. But then again, it was just supposition on my part to assume that all these researchers were looking at one elephant. That was not necessarily true at all. I was reminded of storytellers around a fire. What story would be told and what story would be heard and what would be accepted? A very real human impulse underlay these conflicting researchers. A strong desire to be believed — but something else too, something harder to put my finger on.

What you're describing is true of many major events that have mysteries attached to them, that have no easy answer. When I was writing a book about the origins of AIDS, I used to say it was a Jerusalem of tales. Every person who had a theory rode his mule into Jerusalem to announce the coming revelation.

That's right ... In my next session with this woman, she regressed back to the living room in the house and this time the three men outside came into the room. The two business executives told her she was their guest for a short time, and she would be examined by the third man — the alien. He was there and he looked at her and she felt he was very harsh, that he was there for a single purpose and that was all. There was no slack, no room for kindness. At this point in the session many images came through to her that she couldn't explain. She saw the buildings of a corporation without a name. It seemed to be a defense contractor. There were several landing strips and planes on runways and hangars. There was a connection between the company and the alien. The two other men in the room were executives of this company and the alien was their ally, their companion, their partner. She saw craft sitting in buildings, strange-shaped flying vessels, and she felt that they were being developed from designs supplied by the alien. She was asked to stand up in the room by the fireplace, and one of the executives bent down and unlocked the chain around her ankles. She smelled alcohol on his breath. The alien told her to follow him and she half-walked, half-floated down a corridor in the house. She could hear voices from rooms they passed. She thought there was sexual activity going on in the rooms. She came to a brightly lit area with an examining table in the center and she lay down on it. She realized she was naked. She couldn't move. Beams of light from the ceiling seemed to be holding her in place. The alien stood over her and took instruments from a tray and did a variety of things with them. Tissue samples were taken, painfully, from her skin. Her vagina was probed. She was injected several times in the arms. A dark shield was put over her eyes and an orange light swept across her body, as if it was doing a scan. A voice told her that this was necessary. Our second session ended soon after that. The whole event just faded away.

Was it hard to bring her back to waking state, after the hypnosis?

It took about a half hour. I wanted to make sure she was oriented.

She believed what she was seeing and experiencing in the session.

Yes.

No doubts.

Maybe a few, but all in all she took it to be real. I gave her ten or twelve more sessions, during which we covered basically the same event, the same material. She added details, including a telepathic conversation with the alien that involved him telling her he was here "to learn more." This felt chilling because she got the idea that we were just animals in a zoo. During this period of sessions nothing really changed for her, in her life. She had come to me in the first place because she was having trouble sleeping, she was feeling quite nervous on the weekends away from her job, and her friendships with people seemed to be more difficult, in part because she was focused completely on her problems. She had never had physical difficulties before in her life. But then something happened in our work. I can't really describe the turning point, but I could see it in her face. She was beginning to look happier. The venues of the ET event changed in session. She was now in locales in cities, underground, she was up in ships, she was no longer simply tied to the table by beams ... the stories changed, and at the end of the sessions she had a kind of smirk on her face. She wouldn't let on what was happening, but I could see it was good. In one session she fought for control of the instruments with the ET. She lost, but she was satisfied she was fighting.

It sounds as if you were graduating out of the area of hypnosis.

I began to realize that. She was dropping into the scenes of the ET contact more easily, and I could feel that the trance was not as deep. She was there all right, but the context was shifting. As I began to get an inkling of what was going on, it was thrilling to experience. She was taking over the reins of the sessions. She was changing the whole sense of what we were doing.

She was challenging reality?

Yes. Somehow she had decided on that course of action. I had nothing to do with it. The first thing that hit me was that most people want to accept what they consider their experience as a given, whether it's boring or exciting or bizarre — once they decide it's real, then it goes into that bag. That's the end of all discussion. That's what most people do. And we're taught, more and more, to be passive in the face of reality on a certain important psychic level.

You see that, for example, with very strong people who fold up after they're given a terminal medical diagnosis.

Yes, exactly. It's that kind of thing. And then I have to tell you a fascinating aspect. I went back to most of the researchers I had spoken to earlier — the ones who had all sorts of ironclad ideas on what "the ET experience" really meant — and I told them I had a patient who was having quite a rejuvenation, that as her accounts of the experience changed wildly — and on purpose, it seemed — she was coming out of her difficulties. Her nervousness was decreasing. She was getting stronger. None of these researchers was happy with my report. None. It didn't fit their hard-edged ideas of what UFOs were all about. It was too weird. It was unacceptable ultimately. Even though it was just one case, they felt disoriented and threatened by it. Anyway, my perception of what she was doing in our sessions got stronger. She was not being hypnotized anymore. She was refusing the vibration. She was taking the opportunity to try out various scenarios. I don't know where she got the idea from, but she was doing it. It was amazing to me. We didn't speak about it, but she was now, in the sessions, having tremendous battles with the ET in the examining area. She was picking up instruments and slashing him and it was going back and forth.

Are you saying she was gradually coming to a better understanding of what actually happened in the ET encounter?

I'm not saying that at all.

I didn't think so. You're saying she began to invent alternate accounts.

Out of nowhere. That was completely the abandoned sense of the thing. I tried to explain this, omitting details and her name of course, to an editor of a New Age magazine, and the editor was a little disturbed that the woman was, in session, going into violent reactions to the ET and that pitched battles were breaking out. This, I was told, was anger, and anger was a bad idea for healing. To allow this would "strengthen the negative forces," and possibly even ruin what was a positive abduction experience. I thought I was in a cartoon about New Age stereotypes, and I got quite an insight into the insidious tenets of that quasi-philosophy at its worst.

All the storytellers sitting around the fire, and vying to get their story heard and woven into the fabric of the cosmos.

The woman began running in the hills near her home. Three miles a day. Lots of sweat. The sessions were turning into art-events. Remember the so-called Happenings of the 50s? This was like that. Performance art. I just threw in a suggestion, finally, because I couldn't keep my mouth shut, about dialoguing, role-playing, talking as the characters in her scenes. I tip my hat to that old rogue Fritz Perls, and to Moreno. This woman took off with that and she was a sight to behold. She needed absolutely no direction. She played every part and talked AS the business executives and the ET and other people who hadn't even been there, government agents who were working for the corporation and so on. It was a party, let me tell you, sometimes carried on at very high volume.

How long did it go on?

I saw her for a total of about six months, and I would say this part lasted for two months. She brought me a report from her doctor. Her blood pressure, which had dropped, was now normalized. Her immune indicators were improved.

Did you ever talk with her about what she was doing in the sessions, how she had decided to take over the whole show?

I debated that and decided not to. It was her game and the best thing I could do was let her play it. She never gave me that information and, from an artistic point of view, it was better.

So you don't know whether she finally decided that the ET event was real or not real or whatever.

No, I don't. And I don't really care. I mean part of me was curious, sure, but so what? At the end there, she was going through a lot of emotion in the sessions. It was hard to say where it was coming from. She would be pounding on this ET's head and crying at the same time. The releases were sometimes huge. Once she said to me that it was like running marathons, going through this, and it was training her "inner reflexes." That's an interesting phrase.

Did any other therapist or researcher come to see how fantastic this whole thing was?

No one I talked to. No one was interested in her soul as it presented itself. Instead it was all about doctrine and hypothesis and what's supposed to be real and what isn't. The "truth" about demons and UFOs and Jesus and delusion and neurosis and all that was far more important to these people than the thrill of what was happening to this woman.

So they missed the boat.

They don't see a world opening up in a situation like this. They see a mystery that doesn't fit their picture. They see this woman as a strange individual case. But really, if they followed the thread, the implications of what she did, they would be very surprised. They have world-views and they think in large terms. Well, this woman's case implies a world-view too and that view is endless. It is infinite. It shows what the creative mind can do, what it can overcome, how elastic it is, how marvelous. In one of her last sessions, she put on a monumental conversation between herself and the alien. As I said, she took to the idea of dialogue like a duck to water. This was one of a number of exchanges between her and the alien, and it was the most exciting to me.

She gave you both sides out loud the whole time?

Yes. She approached this man, this being, as an adversary who had sorely missed the boat on the whole human adventure. He said he wasn't human, but she wouldn't accept that. She said his emotions had been re-fashioned to fit an agenda that was unacceptable. He said that was a decision she wasn't part of. She took issue with that, too, and said he was doomed to fail if he didn't learn from us, learn that power was more than just domination. She kept hammering away at this last point until he relented and asked her what she meant. She said that on Earth, as he must know, we had people who were only interested in control of large numbers of people. All sorts of excuses were given for this — that humans couldn't arrange their own affairs, that we were all too weak and too stupid to survive for very long without direction from above. You know, all the old reasons. She said that these self-styled "leaders" were like him. They had reshaped their emotions to fit a program, and they were on the tracks like a train going to one place. Total domination of the human species. She said this would fail because, in the long run, there would be a discovery, a discovery of what was inside us. Not only our refusal to surrender, but our unconquerable itch for adventure. We would not be dominated. He said he didn't believe this. She said he just refused to see the truth because his mission was too narrow. He said he was here to find out more about us, take over certain key people, and establish the beginning of an alien empire here. She said he was a pathetic specimen of life. She said he didn't have a real idea what it was about, and she was amazed that on so slender an understanding his race had gotten so far. This had bothered her, in fact. Bothered and puzzled her. Then she realized that beings could learn a great deal about how things worked without ever examining themselves, as long as they instituted a tight tyranny over themselves, to avoid breakouts and revolutions. They could develop an elite sector within their own empire which would do research and production of new technology, and they could make terrible weapons and other instruments that would help them control large numbers of people, and still they could be stupid and backward. She said that when she looked at him and heard him speak, she sensed centuries of deadness, which had been cultivated to cover over a huge ignorance about himself and his own race. He said the people of Earth were no concern to him because they were specimens, small animals, crude. She said that was another lie he was perpetrating, and that from recent battles and conversations he had been having with her, he had, in fact, realized that humans were far more than he originally had supposed. She said he was a chronic liar, and that most of his lies were laid over this huge black hole of ignorance about himself and his own race. She attacked him on this point, saying he had been lying for some time, that he was just repeating slogans to justify his mission, and that in fact he had no idea what Earth was. As in former sessions, his replies began to come back with less assurance after awhile. She got stronger. She told him there was only one legitimate reason for coming to Earth, and that was to find out what we knew, what we had glimpsed that they had lost. She said he should be down on his knees weeping at what his people had lost long ago. She said his deadness of manner told the whole story. It was the key to his soul. He said that without control there would be chaos. It had been demonstrated throughout the galaxy many times. She said there was a deeper truth which had been missed. In freedom, in adventure, in the midst of the unknown, humans — and all beings — could show their true colors, sooner or later. Their real quality would come through. Then what they were would be revealed. The alien said he wanted to see that. She said the elites of the Earth wanted to see that too, even as they were busy trying to bring the planet closer to running like a machine. In fact, the more controlled Earth became, the more hunger there was for that untapped factor in humans. That, she said, was why he was here, and no matter how arrogantly he behaved, no matter how much power he wielded among major movers and shakers, he was discovering the true reason he had come. To save himself, to save his people. To start a real revolution based on a spark of life he had glimpsed. Eventually, he came around, as never before in any of her sessions. He began to speak about what he felt as he toured the planet and saw our world. He stopped talking about technology and he started revealing his reactions to the people, to what he saw behind their masks.

Finally she got down on her knees and a weeping started, and it was impossible for me to say whether he was weeping or she was or both of them, but in her soul a peace treaty was signed, without seals or official representations or lies. She came to a whole place, which could stir a confidence of tremendous proportions ...

Acknowledgements

Many thanks to David Sielaff for synchronous research and manuscript preparation; to Stace Aspey for tracking down hard-to-find materials; and to Daphne Bellflower for word processing and typesetting.

I want to make special mention of Peter Levenda's book, *Unholy Alliance*, which uncovers and synthesizes so much vital information on Nazism as a true cult. I relied heavily on this work. I found its grasp of Nazism brilliant.

Likewise, when it came to the subject of paranormal research, I was very happy to find Dean Radin's book, *The Conscious Universe*. It is a masterful presentation of the inferences that can validly be drawn from the huge historical body of laboratory experiments on the paranormal.

Thanks also for favors and backup: Eric, Gary S, Loren, VR, the mysterious westland searchers, and NCARX. And of course, thanks to Jack True.

Bibliography

Atwood, Mary Anne. *Hermetic Philosophy and Alchemy*. Julian Press, 1960, New York.

Barnet, Richard J., and Cavanaugh, John. *Global Dreams*. Simon and Schuster, 1994, New York.

Bergson, Henri. *Creative Evolution*. Modern Library, 1944, New York.

Bernhart, Joseph. *The Vatican as a World Power*. Longmans, Green and Co., 1939, London.

Beyer, Stephan. *Magic and Ritual in Tibet*. Motilal Banarsidass, 1988, Delhi.

Billington, James. *Fire in the Minds of Men*. Basic Books, 1980, New York.

Black, Jeremy. *Gods, Demons, and Symbols of Ancient Mesopotamia*. University of Texas Press, 1992, Austin.

Blake, William. *The Complete Poetry and Selected Prose of John Donne* and *The Complete Poetry of William Blake*. Modern Library, 1941, New York.

Blofeld, John. *The Tantric Mysticism of Tibet*. E.P. Dutton, 1970, New York.

Boyd, Doug. *Rolling Thunder*. Random House, 1974, New York.

Bramley, William. *The Gods of Eden*. Avon Books, 1989, New York.

Chevalier, Jean. *A Dictionary of Symbols*. Blackwell, 1994, Oxford.

Cohen, Daniel. *Magicians, Wizards, and Sorcerers*. J.B. Lippincott, 1973, Philadelphia.

Craven, Thomas. *The Pocket Book of Greek Art*. Pocket Books, 1950, New York.

David-Neel, Alexandra. *Magic and Mystery in Tibet*. Crown Publishers, 1932, New York.

Fenollosa, Ernest. *Instigations of Ezra Pound*. Books for Libraries Press, 1967, Freeport, New York.

Flowers, Stephen E. *Fire and Ice*. Llewellyn Publications, 1994, St. Paul.

Fuller, R. Buckminster. *Utopia or Oblivion*. Overlook Press, 1969, New York.

Goodrick-Clarke, Nicholas. *The Occult Roots of Nazism*. Aquarian Press, 1985, Wellingsborough, U.K.

Hall, Manley P. *Masonic, Hermetic, Qabbalistic and Rosicrucian Symbolical Philosophy*. Philosophical Research Society, 1972, Los Angeles.

Higham, Charles. *American Swastika*. Doubleday and Co., 1985, New York.

_____ *Trading with the Enemy*. Barnes and Noble, 1995, New York.

Huang, Al. *Embrace Tiger, Return to Mountain: the essence of tai chi*. Real People Press, 1973, Moab, Utah.

Hunt, Linda. *Secret Agenda*. St. Martin's Press, 1991, New York.

Jahn, Robert and Dunne, Brenda. *Margins of Reality*. Harcourt Brace, 1987, New York.

Jobes, Gertrude. *Dictionary of Mythology, Folklore, and Symbols*. Scarecrow Press, 1962, New York.

Jung, Carl. *Collected Works*. Pantheon, 1953, New York.

Kemp, Martin (ed.). *Leonardo on Painting*. Yale University Press, 1989, New Haven.

Larson, Martin A. *The Essene-Christian Faith*. The Noontide Press, 1989, Costa Mesa.

Lasby, Clarence. *Project Paperclip*. Atheneum, 1975, New York.

Leedom, Tim C. (ed.). *The Book Your Church Doesn't Want You to Read*. Kendall/Hunt Publishing Company, 1993, Dubuque.

Levenda, Peter. *Unholy Alliance*. Avon Books, 1995, New York.

Mallove, Eugene. *Fire from Ice*. John Wiley and Sons, Inc., 1991, New York.

McCartney, Laton. *Friends in High Places: The Bechtel Story*. Simon and Schuster, 1988, New York.

Marks, John. *The Search for the "Manchurian Candidate."* Times Books, 1979, New York.

Marchetti, Victor, and Marks, John. *The CIA and the Cult of Intelligence*. Alfred A Knopf, 1974, New York.

Marrs, Jim. *Alien Agenda*. Harper Collins, 1997, New York.

Martin, Malachi. *The Jesuits*. Simon and Schuster, 1987, New York.

Mitgang, Herbert. *Dangerous Dossiers*. Donald I. Fine, Inc., 1988, New York.

Neill, A. S. *Summerhill*. Hart Publishing Company, 1960, New York.

Paine, Thomas. *Age of Reason*. Citadel Press, 1974, Secaucus, New Jersey.

Perls, Fritz. *Gestalt Therapy Verbatim*. Real People Press, 1969, Lafayette.

Prouty, L. Fletcher. *The Secret Team*. Institute for Historical Review, 1973, Costa Mesa.

Radin, Dean. *The Conscious Universe*. Harper Edge, 1997, San Francisco.

Rampa, T. Lobsang. *The Third Eye*. Ballantine Books, 1956, New York.

Read, John. *Through Alchemy to Chemistry*. G. Bell and Sons, Ltd., 1957, London.

Reich, Wilhelm. *The Function of the Orgasm*. World Publishing, 1970, New York.

Roberts, Jane. *The Nature of the Psyche*. Bantam Books, 1979, New York.

Robinson, John J. *Born in Blood*. M. Evans and Company, 1989, New York.

Samuel, Geoffrey. *Civilized Shamans*. Smithsonian Institution Press, 1993, Washington and London.

Sargent, William. *The Mind Possessed*. Lippincott, 1974, Philadelphia.

Sklar, Dusty. *Gods and Beasts*. Thomas Y. Crowell, 1977, New York.

Sklar, Holly (ed.). *Trilateralism*. South End Press, 1980, Boston.

Simpson, Christopher. *Blowback*. Weidenfeld and Nicholson, 1988, New York.

Singer, Dorothea Waley. *Giordano Bruno: His Life and Thought*. Henry Schuman, 1950, New York.

Smith, Morton. *Jesus the Magician*. Harper and Row, 1978, New York.

Speer, Albert. *Inside the Third Reich*. Macmillan, 1970, New York.

Time, "Colony of the Damned," May 16, 1988, p.58.

Vermes, Geza. *The Dead Sea Scrolls in English*. Penguin Books, 1995, London.

Webber, F.R. *Church Symbolism*. J.H. Hansen, 1927, Cleveland.

Wilkins, William Joseph. *Paganism in the Papal Church*. Sonnenschein, 1901, London.

End Notes

Chapters 1-15

For more on the spontaneity of healing, see Al Huang's *Embrace Tiger, Return to Mountain*. Also Perls.

Richard Jenkins' comments on Edward Terry Clark are confirmed in Charles Higham's excellent *Trading with the Enemy*.

Those interested in the work of Wilhelm Reich might start with *The Function of the Orgasm*.

Chapter 16

The details about pre-war Nazi Germany set out here are basically backed up by Peter Levenda's fine book, *Unholy Alliance*. Also see Goodricke-Clarke and Speer. All quotes within my quotes about Nazism in this letter are from Levenda.

The mention of the Illuminati's notion of abolishing all private property, and the passing of that notion down to Soviet Communism, comes from Billington, where the whole subject is explored from several different angles. Billington is also the source for the description of revival-Pythagorean, Illuminist, Rosicrucian, and Masonic use of "mystical" shapes to enhance the messages of those secret societies.

Chapters 17-20

Age of Reason is a Newtonian portrait of the universe that nevertheless leaves room for undetermined humans who have free choice. The book is pilloried, in part, because it leaves that remarkable space. *Age of Reason* should make the reader suspect that human freedom, clear of any anatomy,

397

has become a foe of "modern thought." Modern thought is concerned with pattern.

Chapter 21

Concerning Allen's comments about Nazis coming to America after World War II, see Simpson, and Higham's *American Swastika*. Also, for background, *Trading with the Enemy*.

Chapters 22–23

For information about Hitler's arrest of occult practitioners, and the kidnapping and rescue of Mussolini, see Levenda. Carol Schuman's statements about the SS can be found in Levenda and Dusty Sklar.

Chapters 24–26

Quotes from the Dead Sea Scrolls and general background come from Vermes. In these quotes only, brackets [ ] enclose suppositional insertions by modern scholars.

Chapters 27–28

All quotes on the paranormal are from Jahn and Dunne.

Chapter 29

All quotes on the paranormal are from Dean Radin.

Chapter 30

All quotes from Giordano Bruno are from Singer's book of commentary and original-text selections.

Chapter 31

The Kargyupa sect of Tibetan Buddhism was, according to Carol Schuman, the sect the Tibetan mentor of her father's teachers belonged to. There seems to be at least one alternative spelling of this sect.

Chapters 32–36

Quotes about messiahs, including those from Kersey Graves, and my summary statements about particular messiah tales, are derived from Leedom (ed.), *The Book Your Church Doesn't Want You to Read*. Exception: Quotes and summary statements about Osiris and Zoroastrianism are from Larson. Leedom's book is a major collection of pieces on the false façades of religion.

Chapters 37–39

All quotations from Blake are from Blake, Donne. See Samuel and also Beyer for background on the origins of Tibetan mysticism.

Chapters 40–43

See David-Neel for her extraordinary depictions of Tibetan practices.

Chapters 44–45

For history of early Masonry, see John J. Robinson. Various Brotherhood of Saturn rituals are covered in Flowers' *Fire and Ice*. For references to the Seal of Solomon, see Chevalier, Hall, Jobes, among others. For a legitimate description of the mythical Girtablullu, see Black.

Chapter 46

There are many sources for Nazi-American connections before, during, and after World War II. See Higham, for example, and Simpson. Colonia Dignidad descriptions are confirmed in Levenda. Also see *Time*, May 16, 1988, p. 58. Aside from the many magazine and newspaper articles on Carlos Lehder Rivas, Levenda establishes the Rivas "brand" of Nazism. Albert Speer's telling quote is from his *Inside the Third Reich*.

Chapter 47

The quote re a priest giving orders to God, and its companion quote from Father O'Brien, are both found in John J. Robinson. As is ample description of the Church's dedication to, and methods of, torture. The Ignatius prayer is given in Martin, who also presents the Church's hierarchical structure.

Chapters 48–49

The references to Church symbolism, and the quotes about these symbols, come from the exceedingly precise F.R. Webber.

Chapter 50

The public testimony mentioned here given on March 15, 1995, and the backup material submitted to the Committee by Valerie Wolf, are available in bound form from 213-969-1320. I put out this material, with an introduction, several years ago.

Chapters 51–52

Morton Smith provides the alternative basis for reinterpreting Jesus.

Chapters 53–54

See Jane Roberts for a wide-ranging discussion of dreams.

Chapter 55

Read Fenollosa, the section on Chinese pictographs.

Chapter 56

Beyer's book on Tibetan ritual is illuminating.

Chapters 57–59

Read *Utopia or Oblivion* by Fuller.

Chapters 60–62

The dream of war, of course, has parallels to the Gulf War of 1990–91. For information on the possible causes of Gulf War Illness, contact Joyce Riley and the American Gulf War Veterans' Association at 800-231-7631.

Chapters 63–65

The quote about the sculptors of Greece comes from Thomas Craven. His writing is fresh fifty years after publication of *The Pocket Book of Greek Art*.

Chapters 66–70

A.S. Neill's *Summerhill* is one of the most important books on the planet.

Chapter 71

The Holly Sklar (ed.) book is the most factual and detailed depiction I know on the march to power of global corporations as Trilateralism.

Chapter 72

The San Francisco economist, Douglas Dowd, has made this statement, citing *Global Dreams* (Barnet).

Chapter 73

Source on these names is Jim Marrs' *Alien Agenda*.

Chapter 74

All quotes and background are from a 1997 Special Report by *Executive Intelligence Review* (EIR) writers: "The Coming

Fall of the House of Windsor." The EIR is based in Washington D.C. The EIR is said to have a pronounced anti-Windsor bias. This may or may not be true. I have not verified the EIR's extraordinary and detailed Special Report. Hence I call this chapter a speculative sketch.

Chapters 75–79

Again, see Fuller's *Utopia or Oblivion.*

Chapter 80

See Boyd, *Rolling Thunder.*

Chapters 81–82

See *Conservation,* the newsletter of the Getty Conservation Institute. Los Angeles. 1. Winter 1993 issue. 2. Volume 2, number 3, 1996. 3. Volume IX, number 1.

Chapters 83–92

The Szent-Gyorgyi quote can be found in *Consciousness: The Missing Link.* International Society for Krishna Consciousness, 1980, Los Angeles. For the Leonardo quote, see Martin Kemp (ed.), *Leonardo on Painting.*

Chapters 93–96

The Hearing document which is the source here of CIA-MKULTRA is officially available from the U.S. Government Printing Office. I have been told by one person that that is easier said than done.

Linda Hunt has done an admirable job finding hidden connections re Edgewood Arsenal, the CIA, and Nazi scientists. This is one of those places where "the exigencies of the Cold War," as an excuse for subhuman activities, reveals itself as a cover for monsters running the store.

The information on CIA dossiers on artists, Safran's book, and Don Edwards' reaction all come from Mitgang.

The mentions of ITT activities in Chile are from Levenda. The ITT-WW2 material, including the State Department memo, comes from Higham, *Trading with the Enemy*.

The CIA-CFR connection comes from Marchetti and Marks. Their book is the first "the U.S. Government ever went to court to censor before publication," as the cover flap-copy indicates. Every deletion made by the Agency before publication is shown in the text. There are many.

Epilogue

The idea that modern medicine is a kind of secret society can be inferred from many sources. It is a perfect example of a cult that does good in one area while causing huge harm in other areas — as a result of dispensing, as gospel, misleading, false, and profitable information. In this regard, see my *AIDS INC.*, and Ulrich Abel's disturbingly orthodox *Chemotherapy of Advanced Epithelial Cancer*, an English translation of which is available from People Against Cancer, PO Box 10, Otho, Iowa, 50569. In a quite conservative assessment, Abel shows that the vast majority of cancers are unaffected by chemotherapy, despite its quite liberal use as one of the terribly toxic mainstays of medicine today.

What is now called role-playing, dialoguing, or voice dialoguing is an inheritor of Perls' and Moreno's work. It is used widely in various therapists' hands. It need not be therapy, however. It is a form of profound education, particularly when used to expand the power of the imagination.

Index

About the Author

An international investigative reporter for fifteen years, **JON RAPPOPORT** is the author of *AIDS INC., Oklahoma City Bombing: The Suppressed Truth, Kill the Monster* and *Madalyn Murray O'Hair*. He has written and hosted radio programs on politics and health in Los Angeles and Las Vegas, and in 1994 he ran for a seat in the U.S. Congress from the 29th District, Los Angeles. His paintings have been shown in Los Angeles and New York galleries, and are part of the permanent collection of Santa Monica College. He is the host and writer of a new television interview-series, *The Truth About*.